The Other America

POVERTY IN THE UNITED STATES

By Michael Harrington

*With a New Introduction
by Irving Howe*

A TOUCHSTONE BOOK
Published by Simon & Schuster

TOUCHSTONE
Rockefeller Center
1230 Avenue of the Americas
New York, NY 10020

First Touchstone Edition 1997

TOUCHSTONE and colophon are registered
trademarks of Simon & Schuster Inc.

Manufactured in the United States of America

3 5 7 9 10 8 6 4

Library of Congress-in-Publication Data is available

ISBN: 0-684-82678-X

Acknowledgments

There are many people whom I should like to mention in this note, but it is possible to name only a few. It was through Dorothy Day and the Catholic Worker movement that I first came into contact with the terrible reality of involuntary poverty and the magnificent ideal of voluntary poverty. Anatole Shub, then of *Commentary* magazine, suggested the subject of poverty in the United States for an article and worked closely with me when I began to deal with the subject in a systematic way. Herman Roseman, a young economist, was helpful in technical advice and indispensable for moral support.

These are only a few of those who helped. Others are present in these pages as nameless workers in Chicago, as organizers in the fields of California, and as alcoholics from the Bowery.

And finally, I would dedicate this volume to my mother, from whom I first learned of justice; and to the memory of my father, that his gentleness will become the principle of the world.

Contents

Introduction

by Irving Howe

When Michael Harrington's *The Other America* began to win a large audience after its publication in 1962, both he and his friends were very much surprised. I remember thinking that Mike's book, fine as it was, would probably be numbered among those "worthy" publications that sell four or five thousand copies and then fade away. Such had been the fate of many serious books in earlier years, and such would be the fate of many serious books in later years. But when Mike's book took off, that seemed a modest signal that fundamental changes were starting to occur in this country. We now began to think that the years of conservative doldrums in which the Cold War had dominated political life were coming to an end.

The conservative mood—it would reappear in the 1980s—had found its first major post-war expression in the 1950s. Many Americans then began to assume that the cyclical recessions characteristic of capitalist economies had been eradicated or at least suppressed in the U.S., and that the economic crises and social inequities that had prevailed before the Second World War and which Franklin Roosevelt's reforms had by no means eliminated, were now becoming things of the past. Actually, we were living off the benefits of a post-war boom and, partly in consequence, a mood of self-congratulation

swept the country. This was especially noticeable among intellectuals, some of them ex-radicals who would soon transform themselves into "new conservatives." Attitudes of social complacency
would dominate the years of Dwight Eisenhower's presidency,
spreading even to segments of the liberal community. It now seems a
little comic to recall that leading liberal intellectuals wrote solemn
essays taking for granted that we had solved our social problems and
therefore could turn to themes of a "higher," more spiritual nature.
The intellectuals, in short, grew enamored, as they often do, of the
zeitgeist, that most treacherous of deceptions. Mary McCarthy, for
example, could write something so absurd as this: "Class barriers
disappear or tend to become porous; the factory worker is an economic aristocrat in comparison to the middle-class clerk. . . . The
America . . . of vast inequalities and dramatic contrasts is rapidly
ceasing to exist."

Only a handful of intellectuals—a few liberals, a few radicals,
some of them huddling around the newly-created magazine *Dissent*—
kept up a stringent criticism of American society. Michael
Harrington, still very young, was one of these, joining in our polemics
against the dominant trend. These polemics, I must admit, were little
heeded.

One of the things that helped change the mood of the country was
the daring of the Freedom Riders, a group of black and white young
people who traveled to the South in order to help blacks assert their
right to vote. President Kennedy's youthful earnestness and charm
promised an America more sensitive to the many problems that were
festering just beneath the surface of social life. And Mike's book
helped too.

In his autobiographical *Fragments of the Century,* Mike writes
about the sudden rise to fame and success which *The Other America*
brought him. He had published an article, "Our Fifty Million Poor," in
Commentary magazine—then quite different from the rigidly conservative *Commentary* of today—and this article, he said, caused "a
small stir." Then the Macmillan Publishing Company offered Mike a
$500 advance, not bad for a young writer in those days, so that he

could enlarge the article into a book. In its first several months after publication, *The Other America* did fairly well, earning Mike royalties of about $1,500, enough for a visit to Paris. As Mike was browsing one day in a Paris bookshop, he noticed a lengthy and absolutely first-rate essay/review by Dwight Macdonald in *The New Yorker* dealing with American poverty in general and Mike's book in particular. Macdonald had been a comrade of Mike's and mine in a small socialist group some years earlier, but had since gone his own way politically. Still, we remained friends and, unlike many other intellectuals of those days, Macdonald retained a strong capacity for moral response—which most of the time means moral indignation. He was also a brilliant journalist, lucid, witty, sharp. His essay/review, almost a small book in its own right, "made poverty a topic of conversation," wrote Mike, "in the intellectual-political world of the Northeast." And Mike continued: "Then John Kennedy, who had been deeply moved by the suffering he had seen in West Virginia during the 1960 primary, asked Walter Heller, the chairman of his Council of Economic Advisors, if there were anything to these new theories about poverty. Heller told him that there was and gave him a copy of [Mike's] book. . . . Shortly thereafter Kennedy decided to make the abolition of poverty a major domestic goal." So books can sometimes (not very often) change the course of things.

In his autobiography Mike confesses that he worried about the fact that nowhere in *The Other America* did he openly declare his socialist convictions—his belief that it would take governmental planning and social investments to deal with poverty "even in a reformist way." He need not have worried. There are social and economic problems regarding which liberals and socialists can work together in harmony, to enact reforms that decent men and women will endorse. In any case, Mike in his numerous speeches and articles was making it perfectly clear what his political opinions were. I doubt that many readers of *The Other America* didn't know.

Reading *The Other America* again after a lapse of some thirty years, I have been impressed by how well the book has stood the test of time. Of course, some of the facts are by now dated, and one of Dwight Macdonald's criticisms—that Mike should have included reference notes—is to the point. More problematic, though a matter of great importance, is the central premise out of which Mike wrote: that if only people *knew* the reality they would respond with indignation, that if only people became aware of "the invisible poor," they would act to eliminate this national scandal. Alas, we have seen in the intervening years that people can indeed know and yet remain passive, in fact that some know and can even become calloused. All of us who live in big cities share the experience of having learned to walk past the homeless as if their being on the streets were some sort of natural event. Maybe we dig up a few coins, maybe we don't, but the indignation we may have felt upon first noticing the homeless gradually wears off. I suppose Mike came to recognize this with the passage of the years, but I think that somehow he could not quite bring himself to acknowledge it. Some remnant of his earlier Christian belief, some part of the ethic he had learned from the Catholic Worker movement, led him to feel that sooner or later human beings will respond to a moral appeal. I can almost hear him saying, "They must!"

The youthful purity of feeling, the sweetness of temper, which marked Mike's words and deeds seem to me as touching, now that I turn back to his book, as they did thirty years ago. Even after becoming a socialist leader without very many followers, Mike never spoke with the dryness of soul one finds in many a professional politician, including some on the left. One felt about him that the compassion in his books came out of the very depths of his being.

The prose of *The Other America* is clean and lucid. Mike structured his book as a sequence of vignettes—poverty here, poverty there, with appended sketches of the moral and psychological costs, and just enough of a sprinkling of statistics to back up his case.

One of the first questions he had to confront is by no means as simple as it may seem: What is poverty? He defined it as an historically relative concept, clearly different in a rich country like the United States from what it would be in a stricken country like Bangladesh:

There are new definitions [in America] of what man can achieve, of what a human standard of life should be. Those who suffer levels of life well below those that are possible, even though they live better than medieval knights or Asian peasants, are poor. . . . Poverty should be defined in terms of those who are denied the minimal levels of health, housing, food and education that *our present stage of scientific knowledge specifies as necessary for life as it is now lived in the United States.* (Emphasis added)

At the time Mike wrote, the U.S. Bureau of Labor Statistics estimated that $4,000 a year for a family of four and $2,000 a year for an individual living alone constituted the dividing line between modest well-being and poverty. According to Mike's estimates, this meant that between 40 and 50 million Americans, or about one fourth of the population, were living in poverty. This came as a shock to many people. They refused to believe it, they thought Mike was exaggerating. But he was merely following official statistics, and everything that would later happen in this country suggests that he was essentially right. People had only to remember Franklin Roosevelt's famous phrase—one third of the nation ill-housed, ill-clad, ill-nourished. In the 1930s, during the depth of the Depression, we were better prepared to acknowledge such dismal facts than we were in the 1960s, a time of widespread social delusion.

One of the most interesting points in *The Other America* is Mike's insistence that poverty is not just one social attribute among others; it is an encompassing condition. Experienced for any length of time, poverty made people feel "hopeless and passive, yet prone to bursts of violence: the poor are lonely and isolated, often rigid and hostile. To be poor is not simply to be deprived of the material things of this world. It is to enter a fatal, futile universe, an America within America, with a twisted spirit." At another point in his book Mike offered a still more vivid description of the extreme states to which poverty could drive people:

The other America is becoming increasingly populated by those who do not belong to anyone or anything. They are no longer participants in an ethnic culture from the old country; they are less and less religious; they do not belong to unions or clubs. They are not seen, and because of that they themselves cannot see. Their horizon has become more and more restricted; they see one another, and that means they see little reason to hope.

I suspect that Mike may have been offering an overdrawn description, that he was claiming too tight a connection between material condition and spiritual-emotional consequences. What he wanted was to shock the country. He wanted to show that there was a vast difference between, say, the poverty of earlier immigrant generations which could hope that hard work and frugal living would enable them to improve their lot, and the poverty of the kinds of people he was describing—the blacks driven off Southern plantations, the folks rotting in Appalachia, the slum dwellers who see no escape. When poverty was a condition spread through much of the population, its effects seemed not as damaging socially and psychologically as when it became concentrated in a large minority of Americans.

By the 1960s, wrote Mike, poverty had become "invisible":

The poor are increasingly slipping out of the very experience and consciousness of the nation. If the middle class never did like ugliness and poverty, it was at least aware of them. "Across the tracks" was not a very long way to go. . . . Now the American city has been transformed. The poor still inhabit the miserable housing in the central area, but they are increasingly isolated from contact with, or sight of, anybody else.

Finally Mike's book was a *cri de coeur,* an appeal to the conscience of the country: How can you allow such a scandal to fester in this country?

I wish I knew the answer to that question, since it would tell us a great deal, not necessarily pleasant, about the moral and psychological composition of the American people. True, during the 1960s, as a result of the once-famous "War Against Poverty," there was a significant reduction in the number of poor Americans; but the trend became reversed in the 1970s and 1980s. Now, some thirty years since

Mike's book came out, there have been thousands of articles and speeches, scores of books depicting and analyzing poverty. Everyone has had a say, yet poverty remains. This is not the result of some decree of nature, as certain benighted souls maintain, nor is it a result of the "laziness" of the poor, as some cab drivers and right-wing ideologues will tell you. It is due to social neglect and cynicism. It is due to a failure of political will.

In these thirty years there have of course been changes with regard to the American poor. The total number of poor has decreased somewhat. And while I do not write as an expert on poverty, let me try very briefly to list some of the new factors.

There has been one distinct improvement, and that is in the condition of the elderly. Partly because they have become a politically potent group that has learned how to organize and exert pressure on behalf of its needs, and partly because programs like Social Security and Medicare have helped a good deal, poverty among the elderly has decreased significantly in the last thirty years. However, at the time of writing this, I would note the danger that is posed to the elderly by the increasing number of corporations and companies that are forfeiting on their promise to provide health insurance for retirees.

There have been a number of negative developments. The rise of the single-parent family has led to increased poverty among both adults and children. Indeed, one of the most terrible developments has been the large increase of poverty among children. Another factor in the increase of poverty has been the use of drugs among some of the poor, especially black youth—it is hard to say whether poverty leads to drug use or drug use to poverty; probably the two combine to make a vicious circle. Still another reason for the rise in poverty has been the decline in government assistance programs for the poor and unemployed. Perhaps the most important factor in the increase of poverty during the 1980s has been the steady decline in wage levels, so that we now have in America a group we call the working poor—people who do have jobs, who work hard, who try desperately to stay afloat as providers of families (sometimes men, sometimes women) but who earn such wretchedly low wages that they sink below the poverty line. Some of these developments Mike anticipated; others he could not have foreseen.

Let me quote from two authoritative studies about recent American poverty. The Center on Budget and Policy Priorities, headed by Robert Greenstein, reports that

in 1991 the number of poor Americans hit its highest level in more than 20 years, as 2.1 million more Americans fell into poverty . . .
The increase in poverty was particularly sharp among children. . . . Some 900,000 additional children became poor [in 1991] as the child poverty rate rose from 20.6 percent in 1990 to 21.8 percent in 1991. Some 14.3 million were poor last year. Like the overall number of poor people, the number of poor children was greater than in any other year.
A Census report issued in May 1992 showed that the proportion of full-time year-round workers who are paid wages too low to lift a family of four out of poverty has grown sharply in recent years. In 1979, some 12.1 percent of full-time year-round workers were paid wages this low. In 1990, some 18 percent were.

And the Economic Policy Institute, in a richly detailed study, *The State of Working America,* by Larry Meshel and Jared Bernstein, reports:

Despite the growing economy between 1983 and 1989, poverty rates were high by historic standards. In fact, those in poverty in 1989 were significantly poorer than the poor in 1979. For example, 8 percent more poor persons had incomes at 50 percent of the poverty line in 1989 than in 1979 . . .
The poverty rates of blacks have been at least three times that of whites since 1979, reaching 32.7 percent in 1991. The Hispanic rate has climbed from 21.9 percent in 1973 to 28.7 percent in 1991.
The reason poverty rates remained high despite the [economic] recovery has to do with wage decline and the failure of the "safety net," i.e., the government system of taxes and transfers designed to ameliorate poverty. Over the 1980s, the already low wages of low-income workers fell 15.9 percent for male and 6.9 percent for female workers in the bottom 20 percent of the earnings' distribution.

Enough of statistics. The fact is that poverty remains a major blight on the American scene. That it persists over the years only makes it worse, since many people sink more deeply into what has been called "the culture of poverty," losing all hope and sometimes giving up the search for jobs. And the scandal is heightened when you remember that in the Reagan-Bush years there was an orgy of financial speculation, often resulting in tremendous increases of wealth among the already wealthy, as well as an increasing polarization between the rich and all others in the American population.

The scandal persists, and that makes *The Other America* a book as significant now as it was on the day of its publication. I only wish Mike were still here among us, to cry out at the shame of a nation.

The Other America

One: The Invisible Land

There is a familiar America. It is celebrated in speeches and advertised on television and in the magazines. It has the highest mass standard of living the world has ever known.

In the 1950's this America worried about itself, yet even its anxieties were products of abundance. The title of a brilliant book was widely misinterpreted, and the familiar America began to call itself "the affluent society." There was introspection about Madison Avenue and tail fins; there was discussion of the emotional suffering taking place in the suburbs. In all this, there was an implicit assumption that the basic grinding economic problems had been solved in the United States. In this theory the nation's problems were no longer a matter of basic human needs, of food, shelter, and clothing. Now they were seen as qualitative, a question of learning to live decently amid luxury.

While this discussion was carried on, there existed another America. In it dwelt somewhere between 40,000,000 and 50,000,000 citizens of this land. They were poor. They still are.*

To be sure, the other America is not impoverished in the same

* The statistical basis of this statement, and a definition of poverty, are contained in the Appendix.

1

sense as those poor nations where millions cling to hunger as a defense against starvation. This country has escaped such extremes. That does not change the fact that tens of millions of Americans are, at this very moment, maimed in body and spirit, existing at levels beneath those necessary for human decency. If these people are not starving, they are hungry, and sometimes fat with hunger, for that is what cheap foods do. They are without adequate housing and education and medical care.

The Government has documented what this means to the bodies of the poor, and the figures will be cited throughout this book. But even more basic, this poverty twists and deforms the spirit. The American poor are pessimistic and defeated, and they are victimized by mental suffering to a degree unknown in Suburbia.

This book is a description of the world in which these people live; it is about the other America. Here are the unskilled workers, the migrant farm workers, the aged, the minorities, and all the others who live in the economic underworld of American life. In all this, there will be statistics, and that offers the opportunity for disagreement among honest and sincere men. I would ask the reader to respond critically to every assertion, but not to allow statistical quibbling to obscure the huge, enormous, and intolerable fact of poverty in America. For, when all is said and done, that fact is unmistakable, whatever its exact dimensions, and the truly human reaction can only be outrage. As W. H. Auden wrote:

> Hunger allows no choice
> To the citizen or the police;
> We must love one another or die.

I

The millions who are poor in the United States tend to become increasingly invisible. Here is a great mass of people, yet it takes an effort of the intellect and will even to see them.

I discovered this personally in a curious way. After I wrote my first article on poverty in America, I had all the statistics down on paper. I had proved to my satisfaction that there were around 50,000,000 poor in this country. Yet, I realized I did not believe my own figures. The poor existed in the Government reports; they were percentages and numbers in long, close columns, but they were not part of my experience. I could prove that the other America existed, but I had never been there.

My response was not accidental. It was typical of what is happening to an entire society, and it reflects profound social changes in this nation. The other America, the America of poverty, is hidden today in a way that it never was before. Its millions are socially invisible to the rest of us. No wonder that so many misinterpreted Galbraith's title and assumed that "the affluent society" meant that everyone had a decent standard of life. The misinterpretation was true as far as the actual day-to-day lives of two-thirds of the nation were concerned. Thus, one must begin a description of the other America by understanding why we do not see it.

There are perennial reasons that make the other America an invisible land.

Poverty is often off the beaten track. It always has been. The ordinary tourist never left the main highway, and today he rides interstate turnpikes. He does not go into the valleys of Pennsylvania where the towns look like movie sets of Wales in the thirties. He does not see the company houses in rows, the rutted roads (the poor always have bad roads whether they live in the city, in towns, or on farms), and everything is black and dirty. And even if he were to pass through such a place by accident, the tourist would not meet the unemployed men in the bar or the women coming home from a runaway sweatshop.

Then, too, beauty and myths are perennial masks of poverty. The traveler comes to the Appalachians in the lovely season. He sees the hills, the streams, the foliage—but not the poor. Or perhaps he looks at a run-down mountain house and, remembering Rousseau rather than seeing with his eyes, decides that "those people" are truly fortunate to be living the way they are and that they are lucky to be exempt from the strains and tensions of the middle class. The only problem is that "those people," the quaint inhabitants of those hills, are undereducated, underprivileged, lack medical care, and are in the process of being forced from the land into a life in the cities, where they are misfits.

These are normal and obvious causes of the invisibility of the poor. They operated a generation ago; they will be functioning a generation hence. It is more important to understand that the very development of American society is creating a new kind of blindness about poverty. The poor are increasingly slipping out of the very experience and consciousness of the nation.

If the middle class never did like ugliness and poverty, it was at least aware of them. "Across the tracks" was not a very long way to go. There were forays into the slums at Christmas time; there were charitable organizations that brought contact with the poor. Occasionally, almost everyone passed through the Negro ghetto or the blocks of tenements, if only to get downtown to work or to entertainment.

Now the American city has been transformed. The poor still inhabit the miserable housing in the central area, but they are increasingly isolated from contact with, or sight of, anybody else. Middle-class women coming in from Suburbia on a rare trip may catch the merest glimpse of the other America on the way to an evening at the theater, but their children are segregated in suburban schools. The business or professional man may drive along the fringes of slums in a car or bus, but it is not an important experience to him. The failures, the unskilled, the disabled, the aged, and the minorities are right there, across the tracks, where they have always been. But hardly anyone else is.

In short, the very development of the American city has removed poverty from the living, emotional experience of millions upon millions of middle-class Americans. Living out in the suburbs, it is easy to assume that ours is, indeed, an affluent society.

This new segregation of poverty is compounded by a well-meaning ignorance. A good many concerned and sympathetic Americans are aware that there is much discussion of urban renewal. Suddenly, driving through the city, they notice that a familiar slum has been torn down and that there are towering, modern buildings where once there had been tenements or hovels. There is a warm feeling of satisfaction, of pride in the way things are working out: the poor, it is obvious, are being taken care of.

The irony in this (as the chapter on housing will document) is that the truth is nearly the exact opposite to the impression. The total impact of the various housing programs in postwar America has been to squeeze more and more people into existing slums. More often than not, the modern apartment in a towering building rents at $40 a room or more. For, during the past decade and a half, there has been more subsidization of middle- and upper-income housing than there has been of housing for the poor.

Clothes make the poor invisible too: America has the best-dressed poverty the world has ever known. For a variety of reasons, the benefits of mass production have been spread much more evenly in this area than in many others. It is much easier in the United States to be decently dressed than it is to be decently housed, fed, or doctored. Even people with terribly depressed incomes can look prosperous.

This is an extremely important factor in defining our emotional and existential ignorance of poverty. In Detroit the existence of social classes became much more difficult to discern the day the companies put lockers in the plants. From that moment on, one did not see men in work clothes on the way to the factory, but citizens in slacks and white shirts. This process has been magnified with the poor throughout the country. There are tens of thousands of Americans in the big cities who are wearing shoes, perhaps even a stylishly cut suit or dress, and yet are hungry. It is not a matter of planning, though it almost seems as if the affluent society had given out costumes to the poor so that they would not offend the rest of society with the sight of rags.

Then, many of the poor are the wrong age to be seen. A good number of them (over 8,000,000) are sixty-five years of age or better; an even larger number are under eighteen. The aged members of the other America are often sick, and they cannot move. Another group of them live out their lives in loneliness and frustration: they sit in rented rooms, or else they stay close to a house in a neighborhood that has completely changed from the old days. Indeed, one of the worst aspects of poverty among the aged is that these people are out of sight and out of mind, and alone.

The young are somewhat more visible, yet they too stay close to their neighborhoods. Sometimes they advertise their poverty through a lurid tabloid story about a gang killing. But generally they do not disturb the quiet streets of the middle class.

And finally, the poor are politically invisible. It is one of the cruelest ironies of social life in advanced countries that the dispossessed at the bottom of society are unable to speak for themselves. The people of the other America do not, by far and large, belong to unions, to fraternal organizations, or to political parties. They are without lobbies of their own; they put forward no legislative program. As a group, they are atomized. They have no face; they have no voice.

Thus, there is not even a cynical political motive for caring about the poor, as in the old days. Because the slums are no longer centers of powerful political organizations, the politicians need not really care about their inhabitants. The slums are no longer visible to the middle class, so much of the idealistic urge to fight for those who need help is gone. Only the social agencies have a really direct involvement with the other America, and they are without any great political power.

To the extent that the poor have a spokesman in American life, that role is played by the labor movement. The unions have their own particular idealism, an ideology of concern. More than that, they realize that the existence of a reservoir of cheap, unorganized labor is a menace to wages and working conditions throughout the entire economy. Thus, many union legislative proposals—to extend the coverage of minimum wage and social security, to organize migrant farm laborers—articulate the needs of the poor.

That the poor are invisible is one of the most important things about them. They are not simply neglected and forgotten as in the old rhetoric of reform; what is much worse, they are not seen.

One might take a remark from George Eliot's *Felix Holt* as a basic statement of what this book is about:

. . . there is no private life which has not been determined by a wider public life, from the time when the primeval milkmaid had to wander with the wanderings of her clan, because the cow she milked was one of a herd which had made the pasture bare. Even in the conservatory existence where the fair Camellia is sighed for by the noble young Pineapple, neither of them needing to care about the frost or rain outside, there is a nether apparatus of hot-water pipes liable to cool down on a strike of the gardeners or a scarcity of coal.

And the lives we are about to look back upon do not belong to those conservatory species; they are rooted in the common earth, having to endure all the ordinary chances of past and present weather.

Forty to 50,000,000 people are becoming increasingly invisible. That is a shocking fact. But there is a second basic irony of poverty that is equally important: if one is to make the mistake of being born poor, he should choose a time when the majority of the people are miserable too.

J. K. Galbraith develops this idea in *The Affluent Society,* and in doing so defines the "newness" of the kind of poverty in contemporary America. The old poverty, Galbraith notes, was general. It was the condition of life of an entire society, or at least of that huge majority who were without special skills or the luck of birth. When the entire economy advanced, a good many of these people gained higher standards of living. Unlike the poor today, the majority poor of a generation ago were an immediate (if cynical) concern of political leaders. The old slums of the immigrants had the votes; they provided the basis for labor organizations; their very numbers could be a powerful force in political conflict. At the same time the new technology required higher skills, more education, and stimulated an upward movement for millions.

Perhaps the most dramatic case of the power of the majority poor took place in the 1930's. The Congress of Industrial Organizations literally organized millions in a matter of years. A labor movement that had been declining and confined to a thin stratum of the highly skilled suddenly embraced masses of men and women in basic industry. At the same time this acted as a pressure upon the Government, and the New Deal codified some of the social gains in laws like the Wagner Act. The result was not a basic transformation of the American system, but it did transform the lives of an entire section of the population.

In the thirties one of the reasons for these advances was that misery was general. There was no need then to write books about unemployment and poverty. That was the decisive social experience of the entire society, and the apple sellers even invaded Wall Street. There was political sympathy from middle-class reformers; there were an élan and spirit that grew out of a deep crisis.

Some of those who advanced in the thirties did so because they had unique and individual personal talents. But for the great mass, it was a question of being at the right point in the economy at the right time in history, and utilizing that position for common struggle. Some of those who failed did so because they did not have the will to take advantage of new opportunities. But for the most part the poor who were left behind had been at the wrong place in the economy at the wrong moment in history.

These were the people in the unorganizable jobs, in the South, in the minority groups, in the fly-by-night factories that were low on capital and high on labor. When some of them did break into the economic mainstream—when, for instance, the CIO opened up the way for some Negroes to find good industrial jobs—they proved to be as resourceful as anyone else. As a group, the other Americans who stayed behind were not originally composed primarily of individual failures. Rather, they were victims of an impersonal process that selected some for progress and discriminated against others.

Out of the thirties came the welfare state. Its creation had been stimulated by mass impoverishment and misery, yet it helped the poor least of all. Laws like unemployment compensation, the Wagner Act, the various farm programs, all these were designed for the middle third in the cities, for the organized workers, and for the upper third in the country, for the big market farmers. If a man works in an extremely low-paying job, he may not even be covered by social security or other welfare programs. If he receives unemployment compensation, the payment is scaled down according to his low earnings.

One of the major laws that was designed to cover everyone, rich and poor, was social security. But even here the other Americans suffered discrimination. Over the years social security payments have not even provided a subsistence level of life. The middle third have been able to supplement the Federal pension through private plans negotiated by unions, through joining medical insurance schemes like Blue Cross, and so on. The poor have not been able to do so. They lead a bitter life, and then have to pay for that fact in old age.

Indeed, the paradox that the welfare state benefits those least who need help most is but a single instance of a persistent irony in the other America. Even when the money finally trickles down, even when a school is built in a poor neighborhood, for instance, the poor are still deprived. Their entire environment, their life, their values, do not prepare them to take advantage of the new opportunity. The parents are anxious for the children to go to work; the pupils are pent up, waiting for the moment when their education has complied with the law.

Today's poor, in short, missed the political and social gains of the thirties. They are, as Galbraith rightly points out, the first minority poor in history, the first poor not to be seen, the first poor whom the politicians could leave alone.

The first step toward the new poverty was taken when millions of people proved immune to progress. When that happened, the failure was not individual and personal, but a social product. But once the historic accident takes place, it begins to become a personal fate.

The new poor of the other America saw the rest of society move ahead. They went on living in depressed areas, and often they tended to become depressed human beings. In some of the West Virginia towns, for instance, an entire community will become shabby and defeated. The young and the adventurous go to the city, leaving behind those who cannot move and those who lack the will to do so. The entire area becomes permeated with failure, and that is one more reason the big corporations shy away.

Indeed, one of the most important things about the new poverty is that it cannot be defined in simple, statistical terms. Throughout this book a crucial term is used: aspiration. If a group has internal vitality, a will—if it has aspiration—it may live in dilapidated housing, it may eat an inadequate diet, and it may suffer poverty, but it is not impoverished. So it was in those ethnic slums of the immigrants that played such a dramatic role in the unfolding of the American dream. The people found themselves in slums, but they were not slum dwellers.

But the new poverty is constructed so as to destroy aspiration; it is a system designed to be impervious to hope. The other America does not contain the adventurous seeking a new life and land. It is populated by the failures, by those driven from the land and bewildered by the city, by old people suddenly confronted with the torments of loneliness and poverty, and by minorities facing a wall of prejudice.

In the past, when poverty was general in the unskilled and semi-skilled work force, the poor were all mixed together. The bright and the dull, those who were going to escape into the great society and those who were to stay behind, all of them lived on the same street. When the middle third rose, this community was destroyed. And the entire invisible land of the other Americans became a ghetto, a modern poor farm for the rejects of society and of the economy.

It is a blow to reform and the political hopes of the poor that the middle class no longer understands that poverty exists. But, perhaps more important, the poor are losing their links with the great world. If statistics and sociology can measure a feeling as delicate as loneliness (and some of the attempts to do so will be cited later on), the other America is becoming increasingly populated by those who do not belong to anybody or anything. They are no longer participants in an ethnic culture from the old country; they are less and less religious; they do not belong to unions or clubs. They are not seen, and because of that they themselves cannot see. Their horizon has become more and more restricted; they see one another, and that means they see little reason to hope.

Galbraith was one of the first writers to begin to describe the newness of contemporary poverty, and that is to his credit. Yet because even he underestimates the problem, it is important to put his definition into perspective.

For Galbraith, there are two main components of the new poverty: case poverty and insular poverty. Case poverty is the plight of those who suffer from some physical or mental disability that is personal and individual and excludes them from the general advance. Insular poverty exists in areas like the Appalachians or the West Virginia coal fields, where an entire section of the country becomes economically obsolete.

Physical and mental disabilities are, to be sure, an important part of poverty in America. The poor are sick in body and in spirit. But this is not an isolated fact about them, an individual "case," a stroke of bad luck. Disease, alcoholism, low IQ's, these express a whole way of life. They are, in the main, the effects of an environment, not the biographies of unlucky individuals. Because of this, the new poverty is something that cannot be dealt with by first aid. If there is to be a lasting assault on the shame of the other America, it must seek to root out of this society an entire environment, and not just the relief of individuals.

But perhaps the idea of "insular" poverty is even more dangerous. To speak of "islands" of the poor (or, in the more popular term, of "pockets of poverty") is to imply that one is confronted by a serious, but relatively minor, problem. This is hardly a description of a misery that extends to 40,000,000 or 50,000,000 people in the United States. They have remained impoverished in spite of increasing productivity and the creation of a welfare state. That fact alone should suggest the dimensions of a serious and basic situation.

And yet, even given these disagreements with Galbraith, his achievement is considerable. He was one of the first to understand that there are enough poor people in the United States to constitute a subculture of misery, but not enough of them to challenge the conscience and the imagination of the nation.

Finally, one might summarize the newness of contemporary poverty by saying: These are the people who are immune to progress. But then the facts are even more cruel. The other Americans are the victims of the very inventions and machines that have provided a higher living standard for the rest of the society. They are upside-down in the economy, and for them greater productivity often means worse jobs; agricultural advance becomes hunger.

In the optimistic theory, technology is an undisguised blessing. A general increase in productivity, the argument goes, generates a higher standard of living for the whole people. And indeed, this has been true for the middle and upper thirds of American society, the people who made such striking gains in the last two decades. It tends to overstate the automatic character of the process, to omit the role of human struggle. (The CIO was organized by men in conflict, not by economic trends.) Yet it states a certain truth—for those who are lucky enough to participate in it.

But the poor, if they were given to theory, might argue the exact opposite. They might say: Progress is misery.

As the society became more technological, more skilled, those who learn to work the machines, who get the expanding education, move up. Those who miss out at the very start find themselves at a new disadvantage. A generation ago in American life, the majority of the working people did not have high-school educations. But at that time industry was organized on a lower level of skill and competence. And there was a sort of continuum in the shop: the youth who left school at sixteen could begin as a laborer, and gradually pick up skill as he went along.

Today the situation is quite different. The good jobs require much more academic preparation, much more skill from the very outset. Those who lack a high-school education tend to be condemned to the economic underworld—to low-paying service industries, to backward factories, to sweeping and janitorial duties. If the fathers and mothers of the contemporary poor were penalized a generation ago for their lack of schooling, their children will suffer all the more. The very rise in productivity that created more money and better working conditions for the rest of the society can be a menace to the poor.

But then this technological revolution might have an even more disastrous consequence: it could increase the ranks of the poor as well as intensify the disabilities of poverty. At this point it is too early to make any final judgment, yet there are obvious danger signals. There are millions of Americans who live just the other side of poverty. When a recession comes, they are pushed onto the relief rolls. (Welfare payments in New York respond almost immediately to any economic decline.) If automation continues to inflict more and more penalties on the unskilled and the semiskilled, it could have the impact of permanently increasing the population of the other America.

Even more explosive is the possibility that people who participated in the gains of the thirties and the forties will be pulled back down into poverty. Today the mass-production industries where unionization made such a difference are contracting. Jobs are being destroyed. In the process, workers who had achieved a certain level of wages, who had won working conditions in the shop, are suddenly confronted with impoverishment. This is particularly true for anyone over forty years of age and for members of minority groups. Once their job is abolished, their chances of ever getting similar work are very slim.

It is too early to say whether or not this phenomenon is temporary, or whether it represents a massive retrogression that will swell the numbers of the poor. To a large extent, the answer to this question will be determined by the political response of the United States in the sixties. If serious and massive action is not undertaken, it may be necessary for statisticians to add some old-fashioned, pre-welfare-state poverty to the misery of the other America.

Poverty in the 1960's is invisible and it is new, and both these factors make it more tenacious. It is more isolated and politically powerless than ever before. It is laced with ironies, not the least of which is that many of the poor view progress upside-down, as a menace and a threat to their lives. And if the nation does not measure up to the challenge of automation, poverty in the 1960's might be on the increase.

II

There are mighty historical and economic forces that keep the poor down; and there are human beings who help out in this grim business, many of them unwittingly. There are sociological and political reasons why poverty is not seen; and there are misconceptions and prejudices that literally blind the eyes. The latter must be understood if anyone is to make the necessary act of intellect and will so that the poor can be noticed.

Here is the most familiar version of social blindness: "The poor are that way because they are afraid of work. And anyway they all have big cars. If they were like me (or my father or my grandfather), they could pay their own way. But they prefer to live on the dole and cheat the taxpayers."

This theory, usually thought of as a virtuous and moral statement, is one of the means of making it impossible for the poor ever to pay their way. There are, one must assume, citizens of the other America who choose impoverishment out of fear of work (though, writing it down, I really do not believe it). But the real explanation of why the poor are where they are is that they made the mistake of being born to the wrong parents, in the wrong section of the country, in the wrong industry, or in the wrong racial or ethnic group. Once that mistake has been made, they could have been paragons of will and morality, but most of them would never even have had a chance to get out of the other America.

There are two important ways of saying this: The poor are caught in a vicious circle; or, The poor live in a culture of poverty.

In a sense, one might define the contemporary poor in the United States as those who, for reasons beyond their control, cannot help themselves. All the most decisive factors making for opportunity and advance are against them. They are born going downward, and most of them stay down. They are victims whose lives are endlessly blown round and round the other America.

Here is one of the most familiar forms of the vicious circle of poverty. The poor get sick more than anyone else in the society. That is because they live in slums, jammed together under unhygienic conditions; they have inadequate diets, and cannot get decent medical care. When they become sick, they are sick longer than any other group in the society. Because they are sick more often and longer than anyone else, they lose wages and work, and find it difficult to hold a steady job. And because of this, they cannot pay for good housing, for a nutritious diet, for doctors. At any given point in the circle, particularly when there is a major illness, their prospect is to move to an even lower level and to begin the cycle, round and round, toward even more suffering.

This is only one example of the vicious circle. Each group in the other America has its own particular version of the experience, and these will be detailed throughout this book. But the pattern, whatever its variations, is basic to the other America.

The individual cannot usually break out of this vicious circle. Neither can the group, for it lacks the social energy and political strength to turn its misery into a cause. Only the larger society, with its help and resources, can really make it possible for these people to help themselves. Yet those who could make the difference too often refuse to act because of their ignorant, smug moralisms. They view the effects of poverty—above all, the warping of the will and spirit that is a consequence of being poor—as choices. Understanding the vicious circle is an important step in breaking down this prejudice.

There is an even richer way of describing this same, general idea: Poverty in the United States is a culture, an institution, a way of life.

There is a famous anecdote about Ernest Hemingway and F. Scott Fitzgerald. Fitzgerald is reported to have remarked to Hemingway, "The rich are different." And Hemingway replied, "Yes, they have money." Fitzgerald had much the better of the exchange. He understood that being rich was not a simple fact, like a large bank account, but a way of looking at reality, a series of attitudes, a special type of life. If this is true of the rich, it is ten times truer of the poor. Everything about them, from the condition of their teeth to the way in which they love, is suffused and permeated by the fact of their poverty. And this is sometimes a hard idea for a Hemingway-like middle-class America to comprehend.

The family structure of the poor, for instance, is different from that of the rest of the society. There are more homes without a father, there are less marriage, more early pregnancy and, if Kinsey's statistical findings can be used, markedly different attitudes toward sex. As a result of this, to take but one consequence of the fact, hundreds of thousands, and perhaps millions, of children in the other America never know stability and "normal" affection.

Or perhaps the policeman is an even better example. For the middle class, the police protect property, give directions, and help old ladies. For the urban poor, the police are those who arrest you. In almost any slum there is a vast conspiracy against the forces of law and order. If someone approaches asking for a person, no one there will have heard of him, even if he lives next door. The outsider is "cop," bill collector, investigator (and, in the Negro ghetto, most dramatically, he is "the Man").

While writing this book, I was arrested for participation in a civil-rights demonstration. A brief experience of a night in a cell made an abstraction personal and immediate: the city jail is one of the basic institutions of the other America. Almost everyone whom I encountered in the "tank" was poor: skid-row whites, Negroes, Puerto Ricans. Their poverty was an incitement to arrest in the first place. (A policeman will be much more careful with a well-dressed, obviously educated man who might have political connections than he will with someone who is poor.) They did not have money for bail or for lawyers. And, perhaps most important, they waited their arraignment with stolidity, in a mood of passive acceptance. They expected the worst, and they probably got it.

There is, in short, a language of the poor, a psychology of the poor, a world view of the poor. To be impoverished is to be an internal alien, to grow up in a culture that is radically different from the one that dominates the society. The poor can be described statistically; they can be analyzed as a group. But they need a novelist as well as a sociologist if we are to see them. They need an American Dickens to record the smell and texture and quality of their lives. The cycles and trends, the massive forces, must be seen as affecting persons who talk and think differently.

I am not that novelist. Yet in this book I have attempted to describe the faces behind the statistics, to tell a little of the "thickness" of personal life in the other America. Of necessity, I have begun with large groups: the dispossessed workers, the minorities, the farm poor, and the aged. Then, there are three cases of less massive types of poverty, including the only single humorous component in the other America. And finally, there are the slums, and the psychology of the poor.

Throughout, I work on an assumption that cannot be proved by Government figures or even documented by impressions of the other America. It is an ethical proposition, and it can be simply stated: In a nation with a technology that could provide every citizen with a decent life, it is an outrage and a scandal that there should be such social misery. Only if one begins with this assumption is it possible to pierce through the invisibility of 40,000,000 to 50,000,000 human beings and to see the other America. We must perceive passionately, if this blindness is to be lifted from us. A fact can be rationalized and explained away; an indignity cannot.

What shall we tell the American poor, once we have seen them? Shall we say to them that they are better off than the Indian poor, the Italian poor, the Russian poor? That is one answer, but it is heartless. I should put it another way. I want to tell every well-fed and optimistic American that it is intolerable that so many millions should be maimed in body and in spirit when it is not necessary that they should be. My standard of comparison is not how much worse things used to be. It is how much better they could be if only we were stirred.

Two: The Rejects

In New York City, some of my friends call 80 Warren Street "the slave market."

It is a big building in downtown Manhattan. Its corridors have the littered, trampled air of a courthouse. They are lined with employment-agency offices. Some of these places list good-paying and highly skilled jobs. But many of them provide the work force for the economic underworld in the big city: the dishwashers and day workers, the fly-by-night jobs.

Early every morning, there is a great press of human beings in 80 Warren Street. It is made up of Puerto Ricans and Negroes, alcoholics, drifters, and disturbed people. Some of them will pay a flat fee (usually around 10 per cent) for a day's work. They pay $0.50 for a $5.00 job and they are given the address of a luncheonette. If all goes well, they will make their wage. If not, they have a legal right to come back and get their half-dollar. But many of them don't know that, for they are people that are not familiar with laws and rights.

But perhaps the most depressing time at 80 Warren Street is in the afternoon. The jobs have all been handed out, yet the people still mill around. Some of them sit on benches in the larger offices.

There is no real point to their waiting, yet they have nothing else to do. For some, it is probably a point of pride to be here, a feeling that they are somehow still looking for a job even if they know that there is no chance to get one until early in the morning.

Most of the people at 80 Warren Street were born poor. (The alcoholics are an exception.) They are incompetent as far as American society is concerned, lacking the education and the skills to get decent work. If they find steady employment, it will be in a sweatshop or a kitchen.

In a Chicago factory, another group of people are working. A year or so ago, they were in a union shop making good wages, with sick leave, pension rights, and vacations. Now they are making artificial Christmas trees at less than half the pay they had been receiving. They have no contract rights, and the foreman is absolute monarch. Permission is required if a worker wants to go to the bathroom. A few are fired every day for insubordination.

These are people who have become poor. They possess skills, and they once moved upward with the rest of the society. But now their jobs have been destroyed, and their skills have been rendered useless. In the process, they have been pushed down toward the poverty from whence they came. This particular group is Negro, and the chances of ever breaking through, of returning to the old conditions, are very slim. Yet their plight is not exclusively racial, for it is shared by all the semiskilled and unskilled workers who are the victims of technological unemployment in the mass-production industries. They are involved in an interracial misery.

These people are the rejects of the affluent society. They never had the right skills in the first place, or they lost them when the rest of the economy advanced. They are the ones who make up a huge portion of the culture of poverty in the cities of America. They are to be counted in the millions.

I

Each big city in the United States has an economic underworld. And often enough this phrase is a literal description: it refers to the kitchens and furnace rooms that are under the city; it tells of the place where tens of thousands of hidden people labor at impossible wages. Like the underworld of crime, the economic underworld is out of sight, clandestine.

The workers in the economic underworld are concentrated among the urban section of the more than 16,000,000 Americans denied coverage by the Minimum-Wage Law of 1961. They are domestic workers, hotel employees, bus boys, and dishwashers, and some of the people working in small retail stores. In the most recent Government figures, for example, hotel workers averaged $47.44 a week, laundry workers $46.45, general-merchandise employees $48.37, and workers in factories making work clothing $45.58.

This sector of the American economy has proved itself immune to progress. And one of the main reasons is that it is almost impossible to organize the workers of the economic underworld in their self-defense. They are at the mercy of unscrupulous employers (and, in the case of hospital workers, management might well be a board composed of the "best" people of the city who, in pursuing a charitable bent, participate in a conspiracy to exploit the most helpless citizens). They are cheated by crooked unions; they are used by racketeers.

In the late fifties I talked to some hospital workers in Chicago. They were walking a picket line, seeking union recognition. (They lost.) Most of them made about $30 a week and were the main support of their families. The hospital deducted several dollars a week for food that they ate on the job. But then, they had no choice in this matter. If they didn't take the food, they had to pay for it anyway.

When the union came, it found a work force at the point of desperation. A majority of them had signed up as soon as they had the chance. But, like most of the workers in the economic underworld, these women were hard to keep organized. Their dues were miniscule, and in effect they were being subsidized by the better-paid workers in the union. Their skills were so low that supervisory personnel could take over many of their functions during a strike. It required an enormous effort to reach them and to help them, and in this case it failed.

An extreme instance of this institutional poverty took place in Atlanta, Georgia, among hospital workers in mid-1960. Men who worked the dishwashing machines received $0.68 an hour; women kitchen helpers got $0.56; and the maids $0.55 an hour. If these people all put in the regular two thousand hours of work a year, they would receive just over $1,000 for their services.

The restaurants of the economic underworld are somewhat like the hospitals. The "hidden help" in the kitchen are an unstable group. They shift jobs rapidly. As a result, a union will sign up all the employees in a place, but before a union certification election can occur half of those who had joined will have moved on to other work. This means that it is extremely expensive for the labor movement to try to organize these workers: they are dispersed in small groups; they cannot pay for themselves; and they require constant servicing, checking, and rechecking to be sure that the new workers are brought into the union structure.

The fact that the economic underworld is so hard to organize makes it a perfect place for two types of racketeers to operate: labor racketeers and their constant companions the management racketeers. In the mid-fifties, some of the locals of the Hotel and Restaurant Employees Union in Chicago were under racket domination. (The crooks have since been cleaned out.) The deal was very simple. The dishonest union man would demand a payoff from the dishonest restauranteur. Sometimes it was figured as a percentage tax on the number of place settings in an establishment. In return for this money, the "unionist" would allow management to pay well below the prevailing union wage. This meant that waitresses were brought into the economic underworld along with the kitchen help.

In New York, a city that specializes in sweatshops, this crooked unionism was even more blatant. There are Puerto Ricans who are "members" of unions they never even heard of. Their rights in these labor organizations are confined to the payment of dues. The businessman, who is so essential to racketeering unionism, makes his payment to the union leader. In return he gets immunity from organization and the right to pay starvation wages. The contracts that come out of these deals are "black and white." All the standard provisions of an honest union contract providing for wage rates, fringe benefits, and the protection of working conditions in the shop are *x*'ed out. The only agreement is that the place is unionized, which is to say that it is protected from honest unionism.

Indeed, one of the paradoxical consequences of the AFL-CIO "No Raiding" agreement is that it helps to keep some of these lowest-paid workers in the grip of labor racketeers. As long as the racket local manages to keep a charter in a recognized international (and, in the late fifties, this was becoming more difficult, but not impossible), then the honest unions are stopped from going in and decertifying the crooks. Many unionists who see the positive value in the No Raiding procedure have argued for an amendment: "Raiding" will be permitted if an honest union can show that the local in a given situation is a racket outfit creating substandard conditions.

Finally, the economic underworld is made up of small shops, of handfuls of workers, but that does not mean that its total population is insignificant. When the hotels, the restaurants, the hospitals, and the sweatshops are added up, one confronts a section of the economy that employs millions and millions of workers. In retailing alone, there are 6,000,000 or 7,000,000 employees who are unorganized, and many of them are not covered by minimum wage. For instance, in 1961 the general-merchandise stores (with an average weekly wage of $48.37) counted over 1,250,000 employees. Those who made work clothes, averaging just over $45.00 a week, totaled some 300,000 citizens, most of them living in the other America of the poor.

Thus, in the society of abundance and high standards of living there is an economically backward sector which is incredibly capable of being exploited; it is unorganized, and in many cases without the protection of Federal law. It is in this area that the disabled, the retarded, and the minorities toil. In Los Angeles they might be Mexican-Americans, in the runaway shops of West Virginia or Pennsylvania, white Anglo-Saxon Protestants. All of them are poor; regardless of race, creed, or color, all of them are victims.

In the spring of 1961, American society faced up to the problem of the economic underworld. It decided that it was not worth solving. Since these workers cannot organize the help themselves, their only real hope for aid must be directed toward the intervention of the Federal Government. After the election of President Kennedy, this issue was joined in terms of a minimum-wage bill. The AFL-CIO proposed that minimum-wage coverage should be extended to about 6,500,000 new workers; the Administration proposed new coverage for a little better than 3,000,000 workers; the conservatives of the Dixiecrat-Republican coalition wanted to hold the figure down to about 1,000,000.

There was tremendous logrolling in Congress over the issue. In order to win support for the Administration approach, concessions were made. It does not take much political acumen to guess which human beings were conceded: the poor. The laundry workers (there are over 300,000 of them, and according to the most recent Bureau of Labor statistics figures they averaged $47.72 a week) and the hospital workers were dropped from the extension of coverage. The papers announced that over 3,000,000 new workers had been granted coverage—but they failed to note that a good number of them were already in well-paid industries and didn't need help.

In power politics, organized strength tells. So it was that America turned its back on the rejects in the economic underworld. As one reporter put it, "We've got the people who make $26 a day safely covered; it's the people making $26 a week who are left out." Once again, there is the irony that the welfare state benefits least those who need help most.

II

The men and women in the economic underworld were, for the most part, born poor. But there is another, and perhaps more tragic, type of industrial poverty: the experience of those who become poor.

This is what happens to them.

On a cold evening in Chicago (winter is a most bitter enemy of the poor) I talked to a group of Negro workers. Until a short time before our meeting, they had worked in the meat-packing industry and were members of the Packinghouse Workers Union. They had been making around $2.25 an hour, with fringe benefits and various guarantees for sick leave, vacation, and the like. More than that, they had found a certain dignity for themselves in that they belonged to one of the most integrated unions in the United States. (The industry had traditionally employed many Negroes; one factor was that much of the work was regarded as "dirty," that is, Negro, tasks.)

A number of these people had found jobs in a plant making artificial Christmas trees. They received $1 an hour and no fringe benefits. The shop was, of course, nonunion. Several workers were fired every day, and crowds gathered on Monday morning to compete for their places.

The $1 an hour was bad enough, but there was an even more important aspect to this impoverishment. When they worked at Armour, these employees knew a certain job security; they had rights in the shop because of the union. It was not only that their wages had been cut by more than half when the plant closed; it was also that they had been humiliated. This was particularly true of these Negroes. As members of a minority group, they had been fortunate to get such good jobs and to belong to a union that took civil rights seriously. Now that they had been thrust into the economic underworld, that racial gain was wiped out. The Christmas-tree shop hired Negroes only. That was because they were available cheap; that was because they could be "kept in their place."

One of the workers I talked to was a woman in her thirties. When she spoke, the bitterness was not so much directed against the low pay: what concerned her most was the "slavery" of her working conditions. She had to ask the supervisor permission to go to the bathroom. At any moment she could be fired for insubordination, and there was no grievance procedure or arbitration to protect her rights. She was vivacious and articulate, a born leader. So she tried to organize the shop. A majority of the workers had signed cards asking for a union election, but the National Labor Relations Board had postponed the date. The election will never take place. The Christmas-tree season is over, and these people are out on the streets again.

Yet the workers in the sweatshop considered themselves lucky. They were making $1 an hour, which was something. Two men I talked to were in a different classification: they had passed the line of human obsolescence in this industrial society. They were over forty years of age. They had been laid off at Armour in the summer of 1959. Eighteen months later, neither of them had found a steady job of any kind. "When I come to the hiring window," one of them said, "the man just looks at me; he doesn't even ask questions; he says, 'You're too old.' "

Other men talked of how racial discrimination worked against them when the plant closed. One technique is simplicity itself. A job is rated by a plant well over its actual skill level. Training and educational qualifications are specified in great detail. When the white worker applies, these criteria are waived. When the Negro worker shows up in the hiring line, the letter of the law is enforced. Technically, there has been no discrimination. The Negro was turned down for lack of skill, not because of race. But that, of course, is the most obvious and palpable evasion.

What happens to the man who goes eighteen months without a steady job? The men told me. First, the "luxuries" go: the car, the house, everything that has been purchased on installment but not yet paid for. Then comes doubling up with relatives (and one of the persistent problems in becoming poor is that marriages are often wrecked in the process). Finally—and this is particularly true of the "older" worker—there is relief, formal admission into the other America.

The Armour workers who became poor were, to a considerable extent, Negro. In attitudes toward poverty, there is a curious double standard. America more or less expects the Negro to be poor (and is convinced that things are getting better, a point to be dealt with in a later chapter). There is no emotional shock when people hear of the experience of these human beings in Chicago. The mind and the feelings, even of good-willed individuals, are so suffused with an unconscious racism that misery is overlooked.

But what happened at Armour is not primarily racial, even though the situation is compounded and intensified by the fact that Negroes are involved. The same basic process is at work in Pennsylvania and in Detroit.

In a brilliant report, Harvey Swados wrote of his first impression of Saint Michael, Pennsylvania: "It is a strange thing to come to a town and find it full of grown men. They stroll the narrow, shabby streets, chat at the corners, lean against the peeling pillars of the town saloon, the St. Michael Hotel & Restaurant, and they look more like movie actors than real human beings, because something is wrong."

That "something" happened on April 24, 1958, when Maryland Shaft Number 1 closed down. Since then some of the miners have been able to get jobs elsewhere. But for most of them, there are idleness and a profound change in the way of life. What, after all, do you do with a man who is a skilled coal miner? When the mine closes down, what industry do you put him into? He is physically strong; he has lived his life in a tight community of coal miners; and he has intense loyalties to his fellow workers and to his little town in the mountains. But he has a skill that is hardly transferable.

Some of the men from Maryland Shaft Number 1 got jobs in the steel industry, but they have already been hit by layoffs there. The automation process that destroyed the work in coal is spreading to steel: their problem is following after them. Others are working, for a fraction of their previous wage, as orderlies in hospitals and institutions, as janitors and stockmen in big stores.

But, again, the most humiliating part of this experience maims the spirit. As Swados puts it, "It is truly ironic that a substantial portion of these men, who pride themselves on their ability to live with danger, to work hard, fight hard, drink hard, love hard, are now learning housework and taking over the woman's role in the family."

For the miners have always been an almost legendary section of the work force. Their towns are as isolated as ships, and they have had the pride of métier, the élan of seamen. Their union battles were long and bloody, sometimes approaching the dimensions of civil war, as in the fabled Harlan County struggles. They had a tough life, but part of the compensation was the knowledge that they were equal to it. Now the job has been taken away, and the pride with it.

In many of these mining areas, there are small garment shops that are running away from union labor in New York and other established centers. Their pay is miserable, and they look for the wives of the unemployed. So the miners do the housework and hang around the saloon, and the wife has become the breadwinner.

In Detroit one can see still another part of this process: it is not minority poverty as with the Armour workers, nor is it depressed-area poverty as in the case of the coal miners. It is the slide backward, the becoming poor, that takes place in the midst of a huge American industrial city.

In 1956 Packard closed out a Detroit factory and destroyed some 4,000 jobs. What happened to the men and women involved has been carefully described in a special study of the Senate Committee on Unemployment Problems. The report is entitled "Too Old to Work, Too Young to Retire."

When the Packard plant closed, the world fell in on some of the men. There were those who cried. They had worked in the shop for years, and they had developed a personal identification with the car they built. Some of them were particularly bitter because they felt the company had blundered by lowering standards and turning out an inferior product. They were laid off in 1956, but many of them had still not found regular work when the recession hit in 1958 and again in 1960.

The workers in the best position were those who were both young and skilled. Their unemployment averaged "only" a little better than five and a half months. The young and semiskilled were out on the street for an average of seven and a half months, the old, skilled workers for eight and a half months. Finally, the "old" semi-skilled workers (say, machine operators over forty-five) averaged better than a year of unemployment. The old and unskilled were out for fourteen months.

For almost every one of these human beings, there was a horrible sinking experience. Of those who were able to find jobs, almost 40 per cent took a position inferior to the one they had held. Skilled workers took semiskilled or even common-laborer jobs. Most of these did not become poor. They were humiliated and downgraded, but not dragged below the subsistence level. But some of the old, the unskilled, and the Negroes entered the other America in the late fifties. They came from a well-organized and relatively high-paying industry. They ended by becoming impoverished.

So it was in Detroit, Michigan, and the story is substantially the same as in Saint Michael, Pennsylvania or Chicago, Illinois. In the fifties and early sixties, a society with an enormous technology and the ability to provide a standard of living for every citizen saw millions of people move back. Some of them retrogressed all the way, and ended where they had been before the gains of the welfare state were made. Many of them slid back but did not become impoverished.

In the next section there will be a more precise description of the dimensions of this development in American industry. At this point, however, the main data are not statistical, but personal and individual. Psychological deprivation is one of the chief components of poverty, as we noted in the opening chapter. And the terrible thing that is happening to these people is that suddenly they feel themselves to be rejects, outcasts. At that moment the affluent society ceases to be a reality or even a hope; it becomes a taunt.

III

The human rejects who have become poor are a particular, and striking, case of the invisibility of poverty in the other America.

In the thirties, as noted before, unemployment was a general problem of the society. A quarter of the work force was in the streets, and everyone was affected. Big business was hit by the stock crash; small business failed because of the general climate; white-collar workers were laid off like everyone else. From out of this experience, there came a definition of "good times": if the statistics announced that more people were working than ever before, that was prosperity; if there was a dip in employment, with 4,000,000 to 6,000,000 temporarily laid off, that was a recession.

But the definitions of the thirties blind us to a new reality. It is now possible (or rather it is the reality) to have an increase in the number of employed, an expansion of consumption, a boom in production and, at the same time, localized depressions. In the midst of general prosperity, there will be types of jobs, entire areas, and huge industries in which misery is on the increase. The familiar America of high living standards moves upward; the other America of poverty continues to move downward.

Professor John Dunlop, of Harvard, has made an illuminating distinction to describe this process. In the thirties, he notes, there was mass unemployment; in the postwar period there has been class unemployment. Special groups will be singled out by the working of the economy to suffer, while all others will experience prosperity.

When class unemployment takes place, the peculiar law that it is better to be miserable when everyone else is miserable goes into effect. It is possible for conservatives and other opponents of Federal action to point to figures showing production and total unemployment at record highs. The average citizen assumes that this means that good times are general; the class hit by depression conditions is forgotten or ignored.

In the fifties and early sixties, the people who were downgraded and even impoverished came primarily from the mass-production industries. In 1929, according to the Bureau of Labor Statistics, 59 per cent of the work force was blue collar, 41 per cent white collar. By 1957 the blue-collar percentage had declined to 47 per cent; the service industries and professions had risen to 53 per cent. These figures chart the decline of industrial jobs in a period when the economy as a whole was moving upward.

For many people this development was a sign that America was becoming a classless, economically democratic society. The nation, they argued, was becoming more and more white collar, and non-manual. Yet what this thesis misses is that at least part of this shift is downward, that when a worker moves from a unionized industrial job to a nonunionized service job he loses pay, working conditions, and pride. Here again there is a social problem of the eyes. Class becomes somewhat less obvious—there are fewer blue shirts and lunch boxes—but the disabilities of class remain and, in some cases, are intensified.

So it was that the Government announced in 1960 that during a period of high employment in the fifties, one-fifth of those out of work came from chronically depressed areas and industries. At such a time the unemployment rate for blue-collar workers was almost three times that of white-collar workers. In the depressed areas fully a quarter of the jobless had been out of work for better than half a year. A high percentage of them were family men with dependent children. And unemployment for Negroes was two and a half to three times higher than for whites.

George Meany, president of the AFL-CIO, focused on the class nature of this unemployment with a few simple figures: between 1953 and 1959, 1,500,000 blue-collar jobs, 11 per cent of the total, were eliminated from the economy; at the same time the number of clerical and professional workers increased by some 600,000.

During this period the amount of unemployment considered "normal" was constantly on the rise. After the 1949 recession, an unemployment rate of 3.1 per cent existed inside prosperity; after the 1954 recession the figure had gone up to 4.3 per cent; and after the business recovery from the downturn of 1958, 5.1 per cent of the work force was still idle. (The 1961 "recovery" began with almost 7 per cent unemployed.) In a matter of a decade, the "normal" unemployment of 1958 was equal to the recession unemployment of 1949.

But—and this is important for the culture of poverty in America —it must be emphasized that these figures contain an increase in long-term joblessness. It is bad enough for a worker to be laid off for a matter of weeks. When this becomes months, or even years, it is not simply a setback. It is a basic threat to fundamental living standards, a menace of impoverishment. Put in the dry but accurate words of the Bureau of Labor Statistics: "All of the moderate increase in the rate of total unemployment was accounted for by the proportionately much greater rise in the continuing unemployed."

Once depression hits an area, its very life seems to leave. The tax base narrows; public services decline; a sort of civic disintegration takes over. Low-paying industry may come in, but that is an exploitation of the problem, not a solution. Or else nothing happens. And then the vicious circle begins to work. Because a place is poor and dispirited, manufacturers don't want to locate there; because of this, the area becomes even poorer. To quote the Bureau of Labor Statistics again: "However, the very fact of being an area of high unemployment as against being a prosperous area, in turn, has an influence on the kinds of industries that might be attracted." More simply: no one, particularly corporations, is attracted by the smell of defeat.

In 1961 the Congress addressed itself to this problem. Its response was as inadequate for those becoming poor as it was for those who had been living in the economic underworld all along. A pathetically small amount of money was set aside for retraining individuals. The main emphasis was on loans that would help the depressed areas to bring in industry. The money appropriated was not enough, according to the analysis of the Administration that proposed the law. But more than that, there was no real provision for regional planning, for a massive assault on the institutions of pessimism and incompetence that develop in a depressed area.

As of this writing, the new rejects face a future as bleak as that of the old rejects: the Federal Government, the one force strong enough to act, has been unable to come up with an effective program. The result, if this situation continues, will be an expansion of the other America, a new recruitment of the poor.

But then, there are those who have an easy answer, who can tell a man how to avoid becoming poor. Their advice is summed up in a single word: Move! Here again, however, a familiar irony is at work. The poor generally are those who cannot help themselves. And those most hurt by class unemployment are precisely the ones who can't move.

Unemployment in the depressed area hits the married man with children. It strikes the older worker who has been a model citizen and who has saved up to buy a house. ("Owning a home is perhaps the most formidable barrier to moving out of a labor-surplus area," the statisticians note.) It involves the semiskilled and the unskilled who will not be able to find decent jobs even if they do move.

The upside-down effect is also at work: what was intended as an advantage becomes a disability. In the postwar period many people hailed the negotiation of "fringe" benefits by unions. They believed that this was providing a stability for the wage worker that would eventually bring him the security of an annual salary. And, to be sure, significant gains were made. But one of the side effects of this process comes into play when an area or an industry becomes depressed. Because of these benefits, and particularly because of the pension system, there has been a decline in the number of workers who quit their jobs. Arthur M. Ross, of the University of California, has spoken of our "industrial feudalism," a system that binds the worker to his plant.

Take the mines as a case in point. The United Mine Workers contracts provide that a man must have worked for twenty years out of the last thirty if he is to be eligible for a pension of $100 a month at the age of sixty. Seniority under this system cannot be transferred from one company to another, or even from one company mine to another, unless there happens to be a shortage of miners. (And, in the fifties, the number of miners declined by better than half: from 441,631 to 218,600.)

The mine closes. A man who needs only a year or two to complete his eligibility stays around, hoping against hope that something will happen, that he can get enough work to secure his pension. If a worker has already put in his twenty years, there is a tendency to wait it out at home until the pension comes. For both types, there is increasing penury, idleness, the grim, debilitating experience of doing nothing.

Progress in this case has, as it so often does in the other America, become upside-down. The pension plan, negotiated to give security and a decent life to the worker, becomes a fetter on his mobility. It ties him into the fate of the company, the industry, the area. It keeps him from moving—if that would do any good.

And finally, there are some simple human reasons why people don't move. Perhaps they have children in school and don't want to take them away from their friends; perhaps, like the miners, they are part of a work clan or an ethnic group and can't imagine life apart from the familiar ways. Riding through the coal and steel towns of Pennsylvania and West Virginia, it is hard for the outsider to imagine people developing affection for these gouged and scarred hills. The fact is that they do.

In short, the simple prescription of the comfortable middle-class citizen, "I can't see why those people don't just move, but I guess they're lazy," is spoken out of profound ignorance. There are many reasons why they can't move; and in many cases it wouldn't make any difference if they did. These are not people that are subject to a temporary, cyclical kind of joblessness. They are more often the ones who have had their very function in the economy obliterated.

Yet, aren't there cushions that have been built up by the welfare state and the unions to handle these problems?

The answer is Yes. These workers are better off than they were before the New Deal and the rise of mass industrial unionism. But the Yes must be qualified in the usual way: those who need protection and cushions most have them the least. It is precisely the worker who is in danger of tumbling over the abyss and into the other America who gets the least support from society.

In the industrial states where organized labor has political strength, the unemployment-compensation rates are usually higher. In the backward states, where the most grinding poverty exists, they are low. Even then, Professor Seymour Harris, of Harvard, has pointed out that unemployment compensation in the fifties was less of a percentage of the working wage than it had been in the late thirties. At any rate, there has been a real advance: the roof does not fall in all at once.

During the fifties, about half of the unemployed shared in these welfare benefits. But the other half were not covered. (Their occupations were excluded from the law; they were involved in shifting, menial jobs, and didn't work long enough over a year to qualify.) Those who had salable skills could use this money for the transition to a new job. The others had a respite before they had to face plain poverty.

The conservative image would have those facing impoverishment racing to the relief office. The fact is that they do not. Those who are becoming poor were in the middle third that struggled and accomplished in the thirties and forties. They have a pride, a spirit, and the last thing they want to do is to go to welfare. The Senate study on the Packard shutdown revealed that even the workers who had been out on the streets for over a year shied away from applying for the relief rolls. They would take low-paying jobs, they would downgrade their skills, and they would accept humiliation rather than go on the public dole.

And those who finally are forced on relief face a special degradation if they had been hard-working and virtuous in the days of their prosperity. To receive public assistance, they may be required to give the state a lien on their house and a claim on their estate when they die. The American dream of saving so as to pass on opportunities to children is shattered in the bureaucratic maze.

If this process of turning the clock back, of rejecting those who had once made advances, goes on, then the other America will grow during the 1960's.

IV

These statistics can be made personal and summary, the ironies can be gathered together, by looking at what happened when the Armour plant in Oklahoma City closed in June, 1960.

When the plant closed, there were 325 people still working. There had been progressive layoffs, so the final work force was "old" (76 per cent were over forty). Their first big problem was that they had participated in the credit boom of the fifties. That magic means of expanding consumption broke down the instant the closing was announced. The Credit Union, for instance, understood that these people would be out a long time (and in other packing-house closings other creditors got the point). Debts were subtracted from severance pay.

Almost all of the 325 workers were in debt. For 265 of them, the average liability was over $900. In good times this would have provided copy for celebrations of the strength of the economy. But not now. The unemployment-compensation system ruled that the waiting period for eligibility would be computed on the basis of the total severance pay. With the debts taken out, however, the actual payment was often less than half of this theoretical figure. (The plants with a younger and more heavily indebted work force have an even more intense problem.)

These particular workers were part of the famous "middle class" work force. Well over a hundred of them owned houses, some of them mortgage free. Many of them had made recent purchases because Armour had announced, shortly before the closing, that it was going to expand. For those with houses and debts, the problem of moving on was extremely complicated.

Still, about half of the workers were surveyed and found ready to pick up stakes and move. As it happened, no one could find guarantees of work in the industry in nearby states, since the reduction in jobs was hitting many plants. (In the three years between 1956 and 1959, the industry had permanently destroyed around 30,000 jobs.) Therefore moving was no real answer, even for those who could.

Most of these Oklahoma City people will not work regularly again. In East St. Louis in a similar situation, 50 per cent of the workers were without regular employment eight months after the closing; in Fargo, a third of the workers were still on the streets after a year; and in Chicago, less than half had found regular work after sixteen months.

These are the new rejects: penalized by pensions, penalized by credit, penalized by home-owning, penalized by steadiness and by saving, they are the rightfully proud ones who will provide some of the new recruits to the other America.

The old poor of the economic underworld, the new poor of the depressed areas and industries—these are a major component of urban poverty in the United States.

So far, these groups have proved to be immune from the welfare state. If they manage to survive, if they advance, it is not because of help from the Federal Government. And the majority have no real hope of advancing. They are, like most of the population of the other America, unable to help themselves through no fault of their own.

In the early sixties the United States carefully documented the plight of these rejects. Congressional hearings and Government statistics established and defined their misery beyond doubt. Yet, having made an official effort to see these people, having demonstrated the kind of help they need, the society turned its back upon them. It passed an inadequate minimum-wage bill that excluded some of the most desperate rejects of the economic underworld; it produced a depressed-area law that by its own standards could hardly begin to deal with the problem.

As a result, the urban poverty of the rejects was given a new lease on life. And long after this book is published, the old and obsolete workers who are over forty, the married and family men at the wrong place in the economy, the ones with no skill or the wrong skill, and the people born into the backward industry or the inferior school system will be living in the midst of the affluent society.

If something is not done, the other America may grow even larger.

Three: Pastures of Plenty

There are those in the city for whom progress is upside-down, a threat rather than a promise. But this is even more true of the rural poor.

In the postwar period American agriculture continued to transform itself in the most basic way. As a result of mechanization, a vast exodus to the city took place. And yet, even given this agricultural revolution, this complete restructuring of farm life, the poor remained behind and, incredibly enough, by about the same proportion.

The big corporate farms gained, of course. So did the urban consumers. As a result of the technological gains, Americans spend less of their income for food—an average of 20 per cent—than any other nation in the world. And the cost of food has risen less since 1949 than almost any other item in the cost-of-living index. Clearly, agriculture is one of the major successes of the affluent society.

At the same time, perhaps the harshest and most bitter poverty in the United States is to be found in the fields.

In recent years, quite a few people have become aware of the migrant workers. They are not only the most obvious victims of this triumphant agricultural technology; their plight has been created by progress. In the new structure of farming, a great number of human beings are required for a brief period to do work that is too delicate for machines and too dirty for any but the dispossessed. So the Southern Negroes, the Texas-Mexicans, the California Anglos are packed like cattle into trucks and make their pilgrimage of misery.

The migrants are not the only victims. In a nation where Fourth of July speeches about the virtue of the "family farm" are still being made, there are nearly a million such farms that are centers of poverty and backwardness. The stationary farm workers, the factory hands of the new agricultural technology, suffer along with the small owners. And, as industry comes to the South and other rural sections of the nation, the independent proprietors of low-income farms have become the human reservoir for low-paying industry.

There is, to be sure, a well-publicized farm program in Washington. Yet here, even more than in the cities, the welfare state is for the middle class and the rich. The impoverished who dwell in the pastures of plenty have simply been left out.

These are the people who have hardly received a cent of the money spent for the subsidization of agriculture. The surplus foods are scrupulously cared for and controlled; the human beings are not. So these men and women form their culture of poverty in the midst of abundance; they often go hungry while the fields produce more than ever before in man's history.

I

Beauty can be a mask for ugliness. That is what happens in the Appalachians.

Driving through this area, particularly in the spring or the fall, one perceives the loveliness, the openness, the high hills, streams, and lush growth. Indeed, the people themselves are captivated by their mountain life. They cling to their patches of land and their way of living. Many of them refuse to act "reasonably"; they stay even though misery is their lot.

It is not just the physical beauty that blinds the city man to the reality of these hills. The people are mountain folk. They are of old American stock, many of them Anglo-Saxon, and old traditions still survive among them. Seeing in them a romantic image of mountain life as independent, self-reliant, and athletic, a tourist could pass through these valleys and observe only quaintness. But not quite: for suddenly the mountain vista will reveal slashed, scarred hills and dirty little towns living under the shadow of decaying mining buildings.

The irony is deep, for everything that turns the landscape into an idyl for the urban traveler conspires to hold the people down. They suffer terribly at the hands of beauty.

Though the steep slopes and the narrow valleys are a charming sight, they are also the basis of a highly unproductive agriculture. The very geography is an anachronism in a technological society. Even if the farmers had the money, machines would not make much difference. As it is, the people literally scratch their half-livings from the difficult soil.

The seasons are vivid here. The tourist perceives this in the brilliance of spring, the bracing air of fall, the lush charm of summer. The tourist will not, of course, come here in the winter. Yet the intensity of the weather also means a short growing season. The land is resistant, and even unapproachable for great portions of the year.

But, the traveler may say, granted that there is a low level of income, isn't it still true that these folk have escaped the anxiety and the rigors of industrialism? Perhaps this myth once held a real truth. Now it is becoming more false every day. Increasingly, these are a beaten people, sunk in their poverty and deprived of hope. In this, they are like the slum dwellers of the city.

During the decade of the fifties, 1,500,000 people left the Appalachians. They were the young, the more adventurous, those who sought a new life. As a result of their exile, they made colonies of poverty in the city. One newspaper in Cincinnati talked of "our 50,000 refugees." Those who were left behind tended to be the older people, the less imaginative, the defeated. A whole area, in the words of a Maryland State study, became suffused with a "mood of apathy and despair."

This, for example, is how one reporter saw the independent yeomanry, the family farmers, and the laid-off industrial workers in the Appalachians: "Whole counties are precariously held together by a flour-and-dried-milk paste of surplus foods. The school lunch program provides many children with their only decent meals. Relief has become a way of life for a once proud and aggressively independent mountain people. The men who are no longer needed in the mines and the farmers who cannot compete with the mechanized agriculture of the Midwest have themselves become surplus commodities in the mountains."

Perhaps the most dramatic statistical statement of the plight of these men and women occurred in a study produced in Kentucky: that, as the sixties begin, 85 per cent of the youth in this area would have to leave or else accept a life of grinding poverty. And a place without the young is a place without hope, without future.

Indeed, it is difficult to find any basis for optimism in this area. And yet, the various states of the Appalachians have come up with a program to offer some basic relief for the incredible plight of these people. Still, the very candor of their analysis defeats much of their purpose. One study, for instance, estimated that the Appalachians would need slightly more than one million new jobs if the area were to begin catching up with the rest of America. As of now, the vicious circle is at work making such a development unlikely: the mountains are beautiful and quaint and economically backward; the youth are leaving; and because of this poverty modern industry hesitates to come in and agriculture becomes even more marginal.

The roads are bad. Less than half of the population has had more than one or two years of high school. There is no human backlog of ready skills. The industrial incentive is for the low-paying, manpower-exploiting sharp operator. In the Appalachians this has meant the coming of textiles and apparels plants. (This is the classic association of low-paying industry with low-paying agriculture, to be described in greater detail later on.)

Some things could be done. The roads could be improved and brought up to the standards required by modern industry—but only with Federal grants. Education and the cultural life of the area could be improved. There could be regional planning. (Significantly, the Kennedy Task Force on depressed areas recommended only one regional planning commission specifically and by name: for the Appalachians.) The whole structure of backwardness and decay, including bad public facilities, lack of water control, and the struggle with soil erosion, could be dealt with.

But such a program would be truly massive. It would require a basic commitment from the Federal Government. As the sixties began, the nation cheered a Depressed-Areas law which provided that the bulk of the funds should be spent in the South. Yet even its proponents admitted that the money for bringing in industry was minimal, and the allocation for retraining and education almost miniscule. It seems likely that the Appalachians will continue going down, that its lovely mountains and hills will house a culture of poverty and despair, and that it will become a reservation for the old, the apathetic, and the misfits.

For the city traveler driving through the mountains, the beauty will persist. So too, probably, will the myth about the sturdy, happy, and uncomplicated mountain folk. But behind all this charm, nestled on the steep hills and in the plunging valleys, lies an incredible social ugliness.

II

The Appalachians are a dramatic and obvious part of a larger process. For behind the plight of these mountain folk, and of the rural poor all over America, is the workings of a curious dialectic: how a technological revolution in agriculture created the conditions for the persistence of poverty.

One of the main groups in the rural culture of poverty has a peculiar characteristic: it is composed of the property-owning poor.

During the last three decades, mechanization has re-created the American countryside. According to the United States Department of Agriculture, the average investment per farm increased some six times between 1940 and 1959. The amount of working hours spent on food production has been in almost steady decline since the end of World War I (and right after World War II the average dropped by 700,000,000 man hours a year). As a result, there has been a decline of almost 2,000,000 units in the number of farms since 1930.

At the top of agricultural society are the minority of corporation farms and big farm owners. For them, the technological revolution has meant enormous profit and fantastic feats of production. In 1954, the year of the last comprehensive farm census, some 12 per cent of the operators controlled more than 40 per cent of the land and grossed almost 60 per cent of the farm sales. These were the dramatic beneficiaries of the advance in the fields.

At the bottom of American farming, there are over a million farms. They constitute 40 per cent of all the commercial farms in the United States, yet they account for only 7 per cent of the sales. Their plight is similar to that of the slum dweller who lacks education: as the big units become more efficient and modern, as invention mounts, the poor fall further behind.

So it is that this progress resembles nothing more than a treadmill when it is viewed from the rural culture of poverty. For example, in 1954 a farmer had to double his 1944 production in order to maintain the same purchasing power. This was easy enough, or more than easy, for the huge operators with factory-like farms. It was an insuperable task for the small independent owners. Even though tens of thousands of them were driven off the land and into the cities, their proportion within agricultural society remained the same.

The centers of this property-owning poverty are in the South, the Pacific Northwest, the Rocky Mountains, and New Mexico. It is here that one finds the people so aptly described by the Department of Agriculture as "farmers dependent on their farms as the main source of income but unable to make an adequate living from farming." The houses are often dilapidated and without running water or sinks. In the case of Southern Negro farmers, the 1950 Housing Census reported that 98 per cent of their dwellings were either run-down or lacked some plumbing facilities.

It has already been noted that the proportion of these people in American agriculture shows an amazing persistence, staying at the same rate despite the most profound transformations and an exodus from the land. Their location is a similarly obstinate fact. In the mid-fifties two agricultural sociologists, Charles P. Loomis and J. Allan Beegle, made a survey of depressed farming areas. These were, they found, exactly where they had been in the thirties. The New Deal and postwar prosperity had passed over these areas without really touching them.

For years, however, the main concentration of rural poverty has been Southern. In Virginia, West Virginia, and South Carolina, for example, over half of the farm units are in the bottom-income categories of the Department of Agriculture. Kentucky, Tennessee, Alabama, Mississippi, Arkansas, and Louisiana are not far behind in agricultural backwardness. Taken together, these states make up a belt of misery that runs from the Middle Atlantic coast to the South and to the West.

One statistic should illuminate this problem dramatically. These poor farm owners live in a society with an incredibly productive agricultural system. Yet, according to Government figures, in the mid-fifties some 56 per cent of low-income farm families were deficient in one or more basic nutrients in the diet. The rural poor who did not live on farming were even worse off: 70 per cent suffered from this deficiency. Thus, there is hunger in the midst of abundance.

Food, of course, is only one item in the rural culture of poverty. In a study of the southern Appalachians made at Tuskegee Institute, it was found that this area had higher rates of infant mortality than the rest of the nation, higher rates of rejection by Selective Service, fewer doctors per thousand people, and older doctors. Schooling is, in many cases, inferior to that of the urban slum.

Mississippi, as one might expect, is one of the extreme cases of property-owning impoverishment in the United States. In 1956 the state had 211,000 farms. Of these, 60 per cent were under 50 acres; 60 per cent had product sales of less than $1,200; 8 per cent used machines; and 81 per cent harvested cotton by hand picking. The resultant poverty, it must be emphasized, was not that of the migrants. Out of 628,000 persons working, and 200,000 farm workers, there were only about 2,000 migrants. The majority of these people were members of families who owned the farms; and a sizable minority were regular hired hands.

By saying that rural poverty is most heavily concentrated in the South, one is also indicating that it has a racial aspect.

In a state like Mississippi, the Negro poor farmer is not simply impoverished; he is terrorized as well. The Southern Negroes who have been making integration news by boycotts and sit-ins are city people. Concentrated in large numbers, forming communities, they have a cohesion and social strength that is able to stand up to the forces of racism. But the rural Negro is isolated, living in a place of backwardness and ignorance. As such, he is the perfect subject for the traditional methods of terrorism.

Two means are employed in making this Southern Negro farm poverty a special horror. The Klan or the Citizens' Council can use physical violence or intimidation. The car that approaches a shack in the middle of the night is a threat. Or the racists can call in the bills at the local store, or even eliminate sharecropping units. (Hundreds of thousands of them have disappeared in the last two decades.) In Fayette County, Tennessee, both techniques have been employed. Negroes who registered to vote suddenly discovered that they could not buy supplies, get a doctor, or any other assistance from the community. Then the recalcitrant ones who still stood up for their rights were driven off the land.

The poor farmers of Fayette County demonstrated extraordinary courage and competence. They made their plight a national symbol, and built their own "Freedom Village." But for many other Negroes of the Deep South, the terror is too overwhelming. They are poor, and part of their poverty is fright and the acceptance of their own humiliation.

I remember talking to one of the Negro leaders in Mississippi. He told me of all the tricks of intimidation that I have described. When he went with some other Negroes to register, they were surrounded by state police. They had to take a lengthy examination— they were, of course, failed by the white examiners—and he said that it was difficult to remember the Mississippi Constitution while hostile and well-armed officers of the law surrounded the group.

The details of the poor farmer's situation could be multiplied almost endlessly: the Southern states where rural poverty is concentrated are statistical simplicity incarnate, the poorest, lowest, and meanest living areas of the nation by every index one can imagine. But perhaps the most dramatic and summary statement of the problem was made in a dry statistical chart published by the Department of Agriculture. The Government economists had noted that the number of low-income farm units was declining (the inevitable result of the flight from the land). Some people were seizing upon this development to argue that all was getting better in a slow, effortless, evolutionary way. In probing this theory, the Department of Agriculture worked out a measure of "relative" low income that charted the income of these farmers in relation to the gains made by the rest of the society between 1929 and 1954. Their conclusion left the complacent theory in a shambles.

In 1929 there were almost 1,700,000 low-income farms. They constituted 35.8 per cent of the total of commercial farms. During the depression their number rose as the unemployed came back to the land. In 1939 they were 39.2 per cent of all the commercial farms. During the war the figures dropped sharply. (The agricultural population gained because of the way in which price and wage stabilization worked during the war.) But in the postwar period the old pattern reasserted itself. In 1949 these low-income farms were 30.3 per cent of the total, and in 1954, 32.2 per cent. In a period of a quarter of a century, the number of low-income farms had declined to about a million. But despite this enormous change, their percentage drop was only a little better than 3 per cent. In 1929 a third of the commercial farms in America were centers of poverty; in 1954 the same relative figure still held.

However, there is still another theory which argues that the situation is not so bad as it seems. Industry, some say, is coming to these areas. All the Government figures indicate that more and more people from low-income farms are going into factory work. Consequently, the problem will be eliminated in the long run. (The penchant for looking for an easy way out when people consider the other America of poverty is ubiquitous.)

The basic assumption of this theory is true enough: part-time farming is on the increase, if only because the bottom third cannot support the people who live there. But once again the ironic dialectic that threads its way through the culture of poverty is at work. The industry that comes to these places is not concerned with moral or social uplift. It seeks out rural poverty because it provides a docile cheap labor market. There is income supplementing as a result, but what basically happens is that people who have been living in the depressed areas of agriculture now live part-time in the depressed areas of industry. They get the worst of two worlds.

A Tennessee Valley Authority study put the situation neatly: there is developing, it said, an association between low-income farming and low-income industry. Poverty, it would seem, can be quite useful if it is properly manipulated and exploited.

III

Woodrow Wilson Guthrie wrote, in "Pastures of Plenty":

It's a mighty hard row that my pore hands have hoed,
My pore feet have traveled a hot dusty road,
Out of your dustbowl and westward we rolled,
Your deserts was hot and your mountains was cold.

I've worked in your orchards of peaches and prunes,
I've slept on the ground by the light of your moon,

At the edge of your city you will find us and then
We come with the dust and we're gone with the wind.

California and Arizona, I've worked all your crops,
Then it's North up to Oregon to gather your hops,
Dig beets from your ground, cut the grapes from your vine
To place on your table your light sparkling wine.

Green pastures of plenty from dry desert ground,
From that Grand Coulee dam where the water runs down,
Every state in this union us migrants have been
And we'll work in this fight and we'll fight 'til we win.

Oh, it's always we rambled, your river and I,
All along your green valley I'll work 'til I die,
My land I'll defend with my life need it be,
Green pastures of plenty must always be free! *

One of the most distinctive things about most American cities is that it is not easy to distinguish social class on the streets. Clothes are cheap and increasingly standardized. The old "proletarian" dress—the cloth hat, the work clothes—either disappeared or else was locked up at the shop.

But when you enter Stockton, California, a center of migrant labor, this generalization fails. The field hands are obvious. All wear broad-brimmed hats; all are tanned, sometimes to a mahogany color; and all are in levis and work clothes. The middle class, the shopkeepers, and practically everybody else, are familiar Americans from any place, city dwellers. The migrants around Stockton are heavily "Anglo" (both white and not Mexican), yet it is almost as if one were looking at two different races. The field hands wear their calling like a skin.

Stockton is a town of about 90,000 permanent residents. At high tide of the migrant invasion, there are more pickers than regular inhabitants. Almost a hundred thousand of them are in the area. They sleep where they can, some in the open. They eat where they can (and sometimes when they can).

California agriculture is the richest in the nation, and its agri-

---

* "Pastures of Plenty," words and music by Woody Guthrie TRO Copyright © 1960 and 1963 by Ludlow Music Inc., New York. Used by permission.

cultural suffering is perhaps the most spectacular. People work ten-, eleven-, and twelve-hour days in temperatures over one hundred degrees. Sometimes there is no drinking water; sometimes big common barrels of it are used. Women and children work on ladders and with hazardous machinery. (The Industrial Welfare Commission was told in 1961 that 500 children are maimed each year.) Babies are brought to the fields and are placed in "cradles" of wood boxes.

In the Stockton area about a third of the migrants are "Anglos," another third, Mexican-American. Around 15 per cent are Filipinos, and the rest are Negroes. (On the East Coast the migrants are much more heavily Negro.) And everywhere, threatening the American workers, are the Braceros, the imported Mexican laborers.

I drove past the fields with an organizer from the Agricultural Workers Organizing Committee of the AFL-CIO. He had grown up in this area and had known the fields as a child. As we passed each farm, he told me who was working there. Whenever he saw a group of Braceros, his voice became sharp.

"They are poor people," he said. "That is why they come here, and work for so little. The growers get them cheap, and they know that the union can't organize them. So that keeps the rates down for the American workers. We don't want to hurt these poor people; they are like us. But it is no way to help them to hurt us. Let the Government work out some kind of a deal with Mexico for aid, or something like that. But let the American farm workers have a decent living without having to hate other poor people."

In Stockton, as in most of the migrant centers in the area, the workers "shape up" at three o'clock in the morning. There is a milling mass of human beings down by skid row, and they are there to sell themselves in the market place. The various hiring men chant out piece-work prices or hourly rates. In some of these places in California, there is a regular exchange with a voice rasping over the public-address system, announcing the going rate for a hundred-weight or a basket of fruit.

Once the worker is taken on, he is driven to the field where he will work. The trucks are packed; safety regulations are often non-existent; and there is no pay for the time spent en route. South from Stockton, along the Riviera coast near Santa Barbara, I remember seeing a most incredible contrast: the lush line of beach, coastal mountains, and rich homes, and, passing by, a truckload of stolid-faced Mexican-Americans coming back from work.

The statistics of migrant wages are low enough—they will be described shortly—yet they conceal some of the misery of this life. The pay is often according to piece rates. The good fruit picker might even make a good sum on one of his better days. But behind him are women and children who may be toiling for $0.50 an hour or less, who receive for ten hours in the hot, broiling sun less than $5.00. In 1960 and 1961, union pressure around Stockton drove the rates up somewhat, but the gain was relative. The workers are low paid, and in competition with themselves on piece rates.

These indignities are not, of course, confined to the fields. In Stockton many of the Anglos live in cheap skid-row hotels (which is better than being out in the open, but still miserable enough). They eat at the Missions. When a flood of Braceros come in and there is a layoff, it is common for men to go without food for two or three days.

Far to the South, in the Imperial Valley of California, the living is, if anything, more terrible than in Stockton. A friend of mine wrote me of some of the people there. One family he described lives in a shack and sleeps on flattened pasteboard boxes on the floor. There is no heat, and since the man of the house has been driven out of the fields by Braceros there is often no food. The mother is breastfeeding her infant—and her four-year-old as well, since that is the only way he will eat. (In this detail there is an eerie echo of the occasion in *The Grapes of Wrath* when the young girl breastfeeds a starving Oakie man. That scene was set almost thirty years ago.)

Or there is the fruit tramp in southern California who was hired to pick tangerines. He works in a gang that includes Braceros, but the pickings were slim in his section of the grove. His job kept him on a ladder all day. He and his wife are charged $18 a week for a one-room shack, with the sink stopped up, and a community stand-in-line privy. The store from which he and the other workers buy their food is owned by the grower.

And yet, incredibly enough, one occasionally encounters a pride of métier, a spirit of loving the land, among some of the migrants. I talked to one of the Filipino workers in Stockton, and he told me of his community which had been there for some years. The Filipinos work together in crews, and have developed speed and efficiency. As a result, they make much more money than the rest of the workers. They are, to be sure, a minority group and suffer discrimination. (The Filipino field hand and I ate in a cheap Chinese restaurant in Stockton; there is a sort of alliance between the minorities.) But, as so often happens at the bottom of society, they look down upon the other workers, and think of them as careless and irresponsible.

Or there was an Anglo worker who lived the year round in Stockton. I asked him why he stayed there, and he said: "It just gets in your blood. I been quitting for twelve years now."

Still, the impression of the California migrants is not one of romance and élan. It is, rather, a sight of near medieval poverty in the midst of lush abundance.

Now the union has come to the fields of California, and that may change some of this misery. The Agricultural Workers Organizing Committee has its headquarters in the AFL Labor Temple, a dark old building. The hall is filled with the bronzed Anglo and Mexican-American organizers. They have already made some gains, but arrayed against them is the enormous economic, social, and political power of the California growers.

Yet, talking to the migrant unionists, one gets a feeling of a spirit similar to that of the rise of the CIO in the thirties. One organizer told me that he could sign up hundreds and even thousands of men just for the asking, if he could only tell them something specific that was going to be done. There have been organizing efforts in the past, carried on by some of the most dedicated men in the American labor movement, but they failed for lack of money and backing. Some of the workers are wary, but conditions are so miserable that the union can summon the whole area into action.

Here too, perhaps for the first time in years, students have joined in the organizing drive. A group of young people came from the University of California at Berkeley, and were so appalled at what they saw that they joined together to help the migrants. Some of them have come over and worked in the fields. Others have tried to develop a community project for the migrants.

If the labor movement in the fields has a thirties flavor, so do the employers. When the Agricultural Workers Organizing Committee struck during the lettuce season in the Imperial Valley, the growers used every technique of "union busting" known to American history. At the morning shape-up there were deputies and guards who were heavily armed. Strikers were beaten and thrown into jail. The "good citizens" formed committees and pitched in to help the growers harvest their crops.

The Imperial Valley lettuce strike failed of its full objectives, even if it gave a most convincing demonstration of the strength of the workers. The strategy was to pull the workers out at the beginning of the short harvesting season, and to pressure the growers with the possibility that they might lose their entire crop. But the citizens' committee and, above all, the Braceros "saved" the day. By the time the Secretary of Labor got around to certifying that there was a bona fide strike and that the Mexican nationals could not be used for union busting, a good deal of the harvest had already been completed.

And yet, with all the setbacks and struggles, the union is the greatest hope that these men and women have ever had. Attempts to win a minimum wage through law have been defeated (and these depend, in any case, on the political power of the labor movement). The union is hampered by lack of money and by jurisdictional disputes within the AFL-CIO. Still, it has raised the issue of the migrants in public; it has demonstrated that organization is possible;

and it is the one major institution in American life that has cared about these dispossessed people.

In 1961, the AFL-CIO executive voted to drop its participation in the drive—another blow for the migrants. But organizing will continue on a reduced level: the union is still the main hope.

Until the union wins, however, there will be hunger in the fields. And in lush, rich California it will be as it is in Santa Barbara at "fiesta": on one day, the Mexican-Americans are actually invited into the center of the city, for they are "quaint," a living link with the Spanish past; and the next day they are forgotten and left to their misery.

IV

The simple impression of the migrants in California is dramatic enough. Yet it is important to understand that their plight and that of the field hands are national and deeply anchored in the very structure of American agriculture. Here, then, are some of the statistics of this part of the other America.

The regular farm hands (men who hire out for more than 150 days for the same employer) are less than a tenth of the farm work force and constitute about a quarter of the hired workers. They are concentrated on the big mechanized farms, and some of them have considerable skill. In the late fifties the average annual wage for male farm workers was just over $1,000. The Negro figure, predictably, was about half of that.

The West and Northwest are the best sections of the country for the farm hands: in 1959 the workers there received more than twice as much money as those in the South, and they worked more. Even at that, their money income was pathetically low (about $1,600 in the best areas), and there were hardly any fringe benefits.

The main problem of the hired hand is unemployment. With the property-owning poor on the independent farms, this fact is concealed, since the owner is theoretically "self-employed" and cannot show up in the statistics as jobless. (He can show up in reality as unemployed, by participating in a pattern of enforced leisure, of passivity and apathy.) But the spare time of the hired hand is visible to the statistician. According to the Department of Agriculture, only about a third of the farm hands had nonfarm income. For the majority, the year is made up of hard work in bursts, long periods of idleness and low income.

The migrants pose another kind of statistical problem: no one knows exactly how many of them there are. As one observer remarked, the Government takes a census of migrant birds but not of migrant human beings.

These people who travel the fields come from the classically dispossessed groups. They are Texas Mexicans, Southern Negroes, Puerto Ricans, winos from skid row, Oakies from the thirties who stayed on in the culture of poverty. On the East Coast some 50,000 move from Florida to the North, most of them Negroes. From Texas come 75,000 who travel to the Mountain States and the Northwest. These are primarily of Mexican extraction. In the rich wheat fields from Texas to Canada, 50,000 work. On the Pacific Coast another 100,000 are on the move. The Braceros number some 400,000 a year.

Taken all in all, men, women, children, and counting the Braceros, there are around 2,000,000 human beings who live and work under these inhuman conditions. In 1959 the Secretary of Labor computed the average Bracero wage, which is a fair index of what all these people are paid: it came to $0.50 an hour. In the same period a congressional study estimated that a family of Texas migrants, with five workers in the field, would make just over $3,000 a year. That means $600 to each worker for a full year's work.

One argument used to justify this system of impoverishment is that the migrant and the hired hand are not efficient workers. Yet a special Senate study concluded that the average farm hand in 1955 was 110 per cent more efficient than he had been twenty-five years earlier. With 37 per cent fewer workers, there was 54 per cent more production. The migrants and the hands contributed profits to this development, but they did not receive benefits from it.

But perhaps the most dramatic deprivation in all this is visited upon children. They work in the fields, of course. (There are laws against it, but they are inadequately enforced, and the desperate families need every bit of labor they can get.) Among the Texas Mexicans, for instance, the upper educational limit is six years of schooling, and the chances are that it was received on the fly, that it was constantly interrupted, and that it was inferior.

All of this was made specific and unmistakable by a study of the National Educational Association: in Florida, Texas, and Illinois 75 per cent of the migrant children were retarded.

These educational statistics get at a basic problem of the rural poor, both migrants and hired hands. More and more of them are being driven from the land. The average size of farms is going up; the number of opportunities is going down. In 1950 the Department of Agriculture estimated that 40 per cent of the rural youth could be spared in the coming decade. At the decade's end, a group of rural sociologists decided that this had been an understatement. In short, the vast exodus from the land is heavily weighted in the direction of the young.

In good times this is a problematic process. Study after study has indicated that, over a fifty-year period, rural young people lag behind their city counterparts when they compete together on the urban labor market. Rural education is inferior; rural youth have less information and sophistication about jobs; rural aspiration, among males at least, is lower than in the city.

In the late fifties and early sixties these drawbacks were intensified. For young people coming to the cities in the time of high unemployment, there was a grim prospect. And then, as noted before, with automation polarizing industry and putting a higher premium on skill, the lack of education was becoming more and more of a disadvantage. So it was that the farm poor were caught in their own past, the double victims of technology: exiled from their home by advances in agricultural machinery; unfitted for life in the city because of the consequences of industrial mechanization.

v

In the opening phase of the Kennedy Administration, an important political truth became apparent: that the farm poor are, for the most part, without a real voice in the United States.

The debates on depressed-areas legislation were extremely complicated. The image of West Virginia and the plight of the coal miners was probably the most dramatic fact in the public mind. The labor movement also concentrated attention on the situation of jobless urban workers like those in Detroit. In the end, the bill contained considerable provisions for loans to Southern states (most probably because the Administration was seeking support for the minimum-wage law, and needed Dixiecrat support). These provisions were, however, most minimal.

The rural poor will receive some benefits from this activity, yet it is important to understand that this development is almost accidental. The AFL-CIO was a strong voice in the debates, not the least because it represents organized political power (and, it must be noted, the labor movement does champion the cause of the migrants and the farm poor). When it was forced to the wall by a powerful coalition of conservative and reactionary forces, it surrendered the hope of a depressed-areas law that would really help urban workers in return for gains in other directions.

In agriculture the dominant voice was that of the Farm Bureau, the representative of the wealthiest, most conservative stratum of the farmers. The Bureau came out against depressed-areas legislation. The Republicans, so often associated with rural America in voting studies, are also based on the middle and upper levels of the farm economy. The bill proposed by Senator Everett Dirksen as a substitute for Senator Paul Douglas' legislation did not even include authorization for loans to rural areas.

The law that finally emerged was the result of an endless series of compromises. The conservative forces turned it into a trial law with a time limit of four years (Douglas and others wanted to make it permanent). Even more important, as noted previously, proposals for comprehensive regional studies, for some kind of planning, were defeated. This means that the grants to areas like the Appalachians may be made on an *ad hoc* and uncoordinated basis. The funds for retraining and education were so limited that they extended only to about 50,000 workers.

Thus, in the face of a massive problem involving millions of people, the political power of conservatism was able to reduce the provisions to the barest minimum. And the rural poor had no powerful spokesman of their own to plead their case. If they benefit, it will be through no fault of the power system.

This situation is one on which the public is tremendously confused. For most middle-class Americans, aid to "farmers" is a gigantic giveaway, a technique for robbing the urban millions and giving to the countryside. Yet the poor farmers do not, for the most part, receive a cent as a result of these laws. Parity, and the other sensational provisions, are pegged to farm units with big market crops. The poor farmers are left out. (This is yet another case of "socialism for the rich and free enterprise for the poor," as described by Charles Abrams in the housing field.)

Yet the farm poor must pay a political price for this lopsided program. They are excluded from the benefits of the welfare state in the countryside, but the public does not know that. When legislation comes up, these impoverished and defenseless people must bear the onus which rightly belongs to the rich farmers alone.

So it is that those who go hungry in the pastures of plenty, those who lack education and doctors, have no one to speak for them. Their needs are enormous and continuing. As Big Agriculture continues its revolution in the fields, their plight will get worse. And those who finally flee to the cities will discover that they are almost completely unprepared for the complexity of metropolitan life. They are part of the selective service of poverty; they are sent from one culture of the poor to another.

Where, then, is hope for these people?

It is one of the terrible ironies of political life in America that there are social problems that could be dealt with, where the basic research has been done and the techniques of solution demonstrated, but where there is no political force strong enough to enforce progress. This is the case with farm poverty. It is, for example, completely obvious that these areas require comprehensive inventories, careful planning, and coordinated programs. The battle for this concept, lost in the debate over the depressed-areas law, will be one of the crucial social conflicts of the sixties.

If there is not a massive and planned program, then the conditions of misery described in this chapter will continue.

The other chief avenue of hope is the labor movement. After years of ineffective but dedicated work, a major effort is being made among the migrants of California. It is still much too early to say that the present campaign will succeed. Ultimately, migrant unionism must gain some measure of control over work in the fields, through a hiring hall, or possibly, as some unionists have proposed, through a union employment agency that could enforce decent wages and rates. The growers, however, have tremendous political power. When hearings are held, they produce works of scholarship demonstrating that a few cents more an hour would nearly bankrupt the richest agricultural system in the world. (In California a great deal of agricultural research is subsidized by, and subordinate to, the big farm owners.)

But the union's importance is not confined actually to raising the money income of those who toil in the fields. Equally important is the fact that it will enfranchise these voiceless citizens and that it will finally produce a movement in which the rural poor speak out in their own name. This could happen in California; and there are now attempts to move into the South where the new agricultural technology, by creating factories in the fields, may well create the social conditions for union organization; it could also happen throughout the nation.

When Edward R. Murrow's "Harvest of Shame" appeared on television, there was a moment of national shock. Suddenly, millions of people became aware of what one part of the other America really looked like. Any union campaign to help the migrants can count on greater support from the middle class than any labor project one can think of. In this, there is great potential.

But as of now, all this is a matter of potential and of hope. The present reality is one of misery. The image of the old America, so dear to the rhetoricians and Fourth of July orators, was of a nation based on a sturdy and independent yeomanry. That is no longer true. The old America of the fields has been replaced by the other America. What was once the nation's pride is now the nation's shame.

Four: If You're Black, Stay Back

> Then it was time for the movie and we all went in to this little movie and saw a movie about America. It show rivers an factories & farms & mountains & a workingman in a blue shirt buying socks. Flash Gordon he was sittin in front of me slash the back of the seat and all the stuffin started fallin out. An Lonesome Pine unscrewed the arm of the chair with a dime. When the lights went on we made a lot of noise and Mister Shapiro hussled us out and never noticed the damage.
> —WARREN MILLER, *The Cool World*

Every Negro ghetto in America is different.

In Atlanta on a soft evening, everyone sits out on the porches of the rooming houses and on the stoops. There is an excited, persistent hum of voices. In Los Angeles, the Negro slum sprawls like everything else. The only obvious thing about it is that the streets, like the streets of the poor everywhere, are badly paved. It takes a little while to learn that the innocent, individual houses are often as rotten inside as any tenement. In Chicago, on the South Side, there is the unmistakable feeling of the great metropolitan ghetto:

high buildings, honky tonks, and on the fringes, a sense of tension in one of the most explosive racial situations in the country.

Harlem is different. It is not the solidest or the best organized Negro community (in Chicago, Negro political representation came a full decade before that in New York). It is not the most depressed, even in the New York area. That honor belongs to Bedford-Stuyvesant. But Harlem is the Negro capital, much as New York is an unofficial American capital. It is big, teeming, and brassy. It is where Marcus Garvey established the center of his Empire in Exile, where Joe Louis was cheered after he knocked out Max Schmeling, and where Fidel Castro stayed.

Yet Harlem is essentially the same as any other Negro ghetto. It exists in the midst of a city where liberal rhetoric is required for election to practically every public office. There is no legal segregation; there are a Fair Employment Practices Law, a State Commission Against Discrimination, a municipal Open Occupancy Law. And yet the white man is still 'way ahead, and in this Harlem is like any community of Negroes in the United States.

To live in Harlem is to be a Negro; to be a Negro is to participate in a culture of poverty and fear that goes far deeper than any law for or against discrimination. In this sense Harlem could well be a warning: that after the racist statutes are all struck down, after legal equality has been achieved in the schools and in the courts, there remains the profound institutionalized and abiding wrong that white America has worked on the Negro for so long.

Harlem has a discriminatory economy, a discriminatory psychology, a discriminatory society. Like the young Negroes of *The Cool World,* it watches all the wonderful movies about America with a certain bitter cynicism.

I

If the population density in some of Harlem's worst blocks obtained in the rest of New York City, the entire population of the United States could fit into three of New York's boroughs.

—CIVIL RIGHTS COMMISSION, 1959

Negro poverty is unique in every way. It grows out of a long American history, and it expresses itself in a subculture that is built up on an interlocking base of economic and racial injustice. It is a fact imposed from without, from white America.

And yet, there is the uniqueness of Negro poverty as an impression, as a walk through the streets of the ghetto will reveal. Here one sees the faces and attitudes behind the statistics: the fear, the food, the religion, the politics of Negro poverty. Looking at this surface of Negro life first, one gains a human perspective on the grim economic figures and occupational data that lie behind it.

Still, a few statistics are necessary for even the most impressionistic description of Harlem, and these can be dealt with briefly. In the mid-fifties (the last point when figures were available), there were almost 1,000,000 Negroes in New York. In this group, 50 per cent of the families had incomes under $4,000 a year (as compared with 20 per cent of the white families). On Home Relief and Aid to Dependent Children, Negroes formed the majority—and they were 40 per cent of all the people who received public assistance. Negro unemployment in the city was somewhat more than double that of the whites, and wages were around half of what white workers got. This affected every other aspect of life: in 1959 the infant mortality rate in central Harlem was 45.3 per thousand (the white district with the lowest rate had 15.4 per thousand).

The statistics could be piled on and on, but the point is obvious: Harlem, as well as every other Negro ghetto, is a center of poverty, of manual work, of sickness, and of every typical disability which America's underdeveloped areas suffer. It is on this very real and material base that the ghetto builds its unique culture.

There is, on the very surface of Harlem life, the imminence of the Man.

The Man is white. He has many guises: as policeman, as judge, as rent collector—as authority made tangible. He is to be feared and hated, for the law is especially swift and hard upon the crimes and vices that grow within these crowded, littered streets. Ultimately, he becomes anyone with a white skin. ("Offay," the old

Negro slang term for a white, is foe in pig Latin.) Because of this, Harlem is a place that is suspicious of all outsiders from the world of white America. It is stunted and sick, and the bread of its poverty has the taste of hatred and fear.

When I was doing research for this book in Harlem, I was walking around with a notebook. I stopped on Lenox Avenue to take down some prices in the window of a barbecue joint. When I looked up, everyone was watching me. I knew what they thought, and turned to the two men nearest me and said, "I'm not a cop." When I walked over and started to tell them that I was a writer, one accepted the story. The other listened for a moment, and then said, "I still think he's from the police." Then they were gone.

Part of the reason for this attitude is that there is more obvious crime in Harlem. The numbers game remains a community pastime; streetwalking still flourishes on 125th Street; and marijuana is easy to get. These things are not, of course, "natural" to the Negro. They are the by-products of a ghetto which has little money, much unemployment, and a life to be lived in the streets. Because of them, and because the white man is so ready to believe crime in the Negro, fear is basic to the ghetto. It gives Negro poverty a quality of psychological depth and torment that is unique among all the impoverished people in the United States.

So it is that Malcolm X, Harlem's Muslim leader, can boast that he can assemble a couple of hundred followers within a few minutes after any act of racial violence (or of alleged racial violence). Harlem, for all its brashness, for all the ubiquitous rhythms of rock 'n' roll, is afraid. And for good reason. The white has been the Man, and in many cases he still is.

Another aspect of this fear is the way the Negro in Harlem is a second-class citizen in his own neighborhood. Walking down 125th Street, one of the most obvious, surface impressions is that Harlem's economy is white. Practically all the stores are presided over by white men, and this has been true for years. (The situation is not nearly so extreme in other Negro ghettos, for instance in Chicago). During the riot in the forties, the rage of the people was directed against these shops—so much so that a legendary Chinese is alleged to have put up a sign, "Me Colored Too." When the proprietor (or salesman, rent agent, or other contact) is Jewish as well as white, this has been a source of Harlem anti-Semitism. The most recent variations on this theme are played by Muslim orators who relate it to a pro-Arab, anti-Israel political line.

This aspect of the Negro ghetto is also unique. In the Puerto Rican section, which borders on Harlem, the situation is quite different. Almost as soon as the Puerto Ricans arrive, Spanish-speaking shops dot the avenue. And this was true even before the big migration of Puerto Ricans in the postwar period. Writing of Harlem in 1940, Claude McKay traced the pattern all the way back to the twenties, when the Puerto Ricans were only a fringe of Harlem.

Why is this so? The sociologist Nathan Glazer has suggested that the Negro suffers from being in, but not of, American society. There are no traditions of the "old country" that bind Harlem as a Ghetto. This is the home of America's internal aliens. The people participate in the consumption cult of the white world—the Negro is an "exaggerated American" Myrdal said, and Harlem is Hollywood carried to its logical conclusion the poet Thomas Merton wrote—yet the Negroes are poor. They do not huddle together around a language and a common memory from overseas, saving, planning, waiting for the breakthrough, isolated from the lures of easy life in the magazines and on television.

That is part of it. Another part is that Harlem is quite literally the center of a migration (as every ghetto is). In 1950 almost two-thirds of the nonwhite Americans moved (as compared to a rate of 13 per cent for the entire nation). The Negro in Harlem, as Ralph Ellison has written of him, is often "shot up from the South into the busy city like wild jacks-in-the-box broken loose from our springs—so sudden that our gait becomes like that of deep-sea divers suffering from the bends."

And then there is the problem of education. It will be dealt with analytically later on in this chapter, but for now an image of what Harlem means in human terms should suffice. A white welfare worker tells of the children when they first begin school. They show off their books; they are interested and friendly. But then, in a few years, they learn. Their schools are crowded; the instruction is inferior; and the neighborhood is omnipresent and more powerful than the classroom.

These are only some of the factors, but they all point in the same direction: Harlem is not only afraid; more than that, Harlem does not even own itself; the Negro is not master even when he has retreated into the ghetto far from white eyes. The Man is still with him.

II

Bledose, you're a shameless chitterling eater! I accuse you of relishing hog bowels!
—RALPH ELLISON, *The Invisible Man*

But then, what of the old stereotype of the laughing, dancing, and singing Negro? Where does he live in the grim Harlem of fear and the Man?

He is there. Harlem is brassy, rocking and rolling. The Negro prostitutes on 125th Street are much better looking than the white girls who come up to work the same block. At the Apollo Theater there is some of the most uninhibited stage carryings on to be found in a public place in New York. "Why, man," a friend said, "if they did that in any other part of town, the preachers would have the place closed down in a minute." In the afternoon, the bars along the big avenues are jammed.

Harlem eats, drinks, and dances differently than white America. It looks happier, and sometimes it might be happier, but, as in everything else about the ghetto, being poor has a lot to do with it.

Take the food, for instance. Each national group in America, every immigrant ghetto, had its own way of eating. Alfred Kazin has a charming memory, in *A Walker in the City,* that in Browns-ville, at the height of the depression, there was always money for soda or other extras in the Jewish community. Love was expressed through food. In a city like New York, people get to know the food of the various nations. But practically no one knows of the food of Harlem and Bedford-Stuyvesant.

In a casual walk through Harlem, you will see advertised some of these things: chitterlings, ham knuckles, hog maw, pig's feet, pig's tail, pig's ear; and fish is everywhere. This food—and some of it can be fairly costly—is the diet of the poor South, brought North in the migrations. These are the things the white man did not want.

So it is that the food becomes a problem to the educated Negro. Ellison's cry—his hero is accusing a prominent Negro of the secret vice of eating chitterlings—is heard in almost every Negro novel. In the *Amsterdam News* a columnist asks, "Has eating hog kept the Race back?" A friend tells me, "We Negroes have energy because we eat food the white folks won't touch."

On the surface, the food is an oddity, a quaintness, and the names might even charm some whites. But this food, like so many of the simple things in Harlem, has the smell of poverty about it.

And yet there is a curious advantage to having known poverty so deeply: one learns to survive. In Los Angeles a welfare worker remarks that Negroes live better on relief than the whites. The whites will spend a major portion of their budget on a roast, and then live on spaghetti, macaroni, or potatoes. The Negroes, as members of the hereditary poor, have a much more balanced diet of cheap food, even if it is fat back and greens. The result is that the whites are much more prone to the classic health problems of poverty (overweight, anemia, and cardiac) than the Negroes.

And then, Harlem is distinctive because it lives so much of its life in the streets. The statistics on Negro unemployment may be abstract and distant. An afternoon block of milling, waiting men is not.

The rooms of Harlem are, more often than not, small, dingy, and mean. Everyone wants to get out, to get away. Work is harder to get in Harlem than anywhere else in the city. So the bars are doing a good business in the early afternoon, and there are men on the streets, simply standing and talking. One might walk into a sidewalk crap game. (As soon as a white comes into sight, operations will suspend with lightening speed.) Or there will be violence. Many of the fights of Harlem, or of any slum, are the consequence of mass enforced idleness, of life in the streets.

For that matter, you can judge the social class of a street in Harlem by its stoops and gutters. Where the residents are struggling upward, the gutters are not filled with refuse, and there are signs in front of the neat brownstones, "Positively No Loitering or Sitting on Rail or Stoop." But these are the oases of a middle class. For most of Harlem, the reality is one of streets filled with litter and men.

But again, there are the consolations, many of them as revealing of Harlem as the grimmer facts.

Death, for example, plays a peculiar role in the life of this Negro ghetto. One first realizes this fact by walking the streets and gradually noticing the enormous number of funeral parlors. Undertakers are among some of the most respected members of the Negro middle class; Harlem is at least allowed to bury its own. For the Negro poor, death is often the only time when there is real luxury. Many of the Negro lodges and fraternal orders have death-benefit plans. Dying is a moment of style and status, at least in the impoverished world of the racial ghetto.

This ubiquitous industry of death relates to another of the most obvious features of Harlem life: its religion. Like the funeral, the Church can provide a moment of release, even of ecstasy, in the midst of so many troubles. This is true for a good portion of the poor, but it is doubly true for the Negro. The Church was the one really Negro institution that developed under slavery and continues to this day under Negro control in the South. And even in Harlem (though to a decreasing degree) it remains a meeting place, a moment of freedom and deep expressiveness.

Some of Harlem's churches are, like Adam Powell's Abyssinian Baptist, established institutions. But the eye is caught by the storefronts, the Islamic centers, the Holy Dove Church of Christ with its picture of God as a Negro in the window. On 125th Street, there is Daddy Grace's second-story loft, and on a warm evening the sound of the meeting spills rapturously out onto the avenue. The sign says: "As Noah Was Before the Flood So Is Daddy Grace Before the Fire."

Traditionally, middle-class Negroes have tried to disown this fervid mystic religiosity. The social status of a Negro Church, some claim, can be determined by ear: the higher the class, the less commotion. This attitude is, in itself, a profound indication of the way in which so much of Negro religion is permeated by the fact of Negro poverty. And as long as the reality of Harlem is as miserable as it is, the religious imagination will soar and the funeral parlors will continue to do good business.

But there is another manifestation of this religious impulse that has gained strength in Harlem in recent years and that jars the stereotype of the simple emotional character of Negro spiritualism. That is the growth of the Muslims. They have taken the otherwordly Utopia of traditional Negro Christianity, and turned it into a bitter this-worldly vision. In a sense, they have laid bare the frustration, the repression, the anger that the hymn singing and emotional sermons softened. They base themselves on a version of Mohammedanism, but that is mainly because it is not a "slave"—or white man's—religion. Above all, their creed is one of hatred: against the middle-class leaders of the civil-rights movement, the Jewish shop-keepers, the world of white America. They have pride and forcefulness; they are neat and often abstemious.

The Muslims are a minority in Harlem. Their street meetings never even approach the size of the mass rallies of the main-stream civil-rights movement. Yet they strike a nerve. Paradoxically, this is much more true in New York, where discrimination is veiled in egalitarian rhetoric, than in some of the more embattled Negro communities of the South.

And finally, there is that other great emotional outlet in the culture of Harlem: politics. The Negro arrived at Tammany Hall in the late thirties—at the point at which Tammany's power was on the decline and regular Democratic leadership was losing its enormous importance. Since then, there has been a considerable gain, at least in the appearance of power: Adam Powell's congressional seat, the Borough presidency of Manhattan becoming, in effect, a "Negro" office, and so on.

The intricacies of Harlem's politics would lead to an extended analysis of politics and social structure. But the personality of Harlem's dominant political figure, Adam Clayton Powell, provides a sudden illumination for an impression of life in the ghetto. Powell is a minister, the head of a Church with well over 10,000 members. He is an intransigent, a demagogue, and unquestionably one of the most popular Negro leaders one could find. In recent years he has defied the Democratic leadership in New York, bolted the national ticket to support Eisenhower in 1956, and has been the center of more scandal, legal threats, and general gossip than any ten other Negroes in the United States.

To be sure, Powell has a certain effectiveness. He is not the conservative machine politician like Congressman Dawson of Chicago. On the race issue, his very flamboyance sometimes achieves results. But he is also the political symbol of Harlem's poverty and backwardness. He is a sort of Negro James Michael Curley.

One story that Powell has been said to tell of himself reveals the poverty of Negro politics as of a piece with the poverty of Harlem generally. Some candidate had taken on the impossible, thankless task of trying to unseat Powell. He was speaking at a street meeting and, as legend has it, Powell was parked in a car on the fringe of the crowd. "Adam Powell," the speaker said, "is a congressman and a minister. But he has an apartment in New York, and a place in Washington, and he's seen in night clubs, and he travels to Europe all the time, and he's hardly ever in the Congress." From the crowd, someone yelled, "Man, that's really living!"

The story is funny enough, but at bottom it is made of the same stuff as Amos 'n' Andy: the laughing, childlike, pleasure-loving Negro who must be patronized and taken care of like a child. For all of the vigor of Powell and the enthusiasm of Harlem's politics, the incident is ultimately one more tragedy within the structure of the ghetto.

All of this is not to say that Harlem is a simple charade of misery, that every laugh and dancing step is a strangled cry. The looseness, the brashness, the rhythm of Harlem give it a life of its own. Rather, it is to say that if you take a walk in Harlem, if you look behind the charming stereotype, you will find two things involved in one way or another in every gesture and every word spoken in that ghetto: the double indignity of racial discrimination and economic oppression; that unique amalgam which is Negro poverty in the world of American poverty.

You will find, right on the surface of Harlem life, as much fear as hope, as much hate as love. You will find faces that are often happy but always, even at the moment of bursting joy, haunted. That is what racism has done.

These are impressions, and they are important. More deeply, one must understand how Harlem, and every other Negro ghetto, urban or rural, is a bastion of the culture of poverty in the other America. This misery is located deep in the very structure of American life.

III

If all the discriminatory laws in the United States were immediately repealed, race would still remain as one of the most pressing moral and political problems in the nation. Negroes and other minorities are not simply the victims of a series of iniquitous statutes. The American economy, the American society, the American unconscious are all racist. If all the laws were framed to provide equal opportunity, a majority of the Negroes would not be able to take full advantage of the change. There would still be a vast, silent, and automatic system directed against men and women of color.

To belong to a racial minority is to be poor, but poor in a special way. The fear, the lack of self-confidence, the haunting, these have been described. But they, in turn, are the expressions of the most institutionalized poverty in the United States, the most vicious of the vicious circles. In a sense, the Negro is classically the "other" American, degraded and frustrated at every turn and not just because of laws.

There are sympathetic and concerned people who do not understand how deeply America has integrated racism into its structure. Given time, they argue, the Negroes will rise in the society like the Irish, the Jews, the Italians, and all the rest. But this notion misses two decisive facts: that the Negro is colored, and no other group in the United States has ever faced such a problem, and that the Negro of today is an internal migrant who will face racism wherever he goes, who cannot leave his oppression behind as if it were a czar or a potato famine. To be equal, the Negro requires something much more profound than a way "into" the society; he needs a transformation of some of the basic institutions of the society.

The Negro is poor because he is black; that is obvious enough. But, perhaps more importantly, the Negro is black because he is poor. The laws against color can be removed, but that will leave the poverty that is the historic and institutionalized consequence of color. As long as this is the case, being born a Negro will continue to be the most profound disability that the United States imposes upon a citizen.

Perhaps the quickest way to point up the racism of the American economy is to recall a strange case of jubilation.

Late in 1960 the Department of Labor issued a study, "The Economic Situation of Negroes in the United States." It noted that in 1939, nonwhite workers earned, on the average, 41 per cent as much as whites, and that by 1958 their wages had climbed to 58 per cent of that of whites. Not a little elation greeted this announcement. Some of the editorialists cited these statistics as indicating that slow and steady progress was being made. (At this rate, the Negro would reach parity with the white some time well after the year 2000.)

To begin with, the figures were somewhat more optimistic than the reality. Part of the Negro gain reflected the shift of rural Negroes to cities and Southern Negroes to the North. In both cases, the people involved increased their incomes by going into a more prosperous section of the country. But within each area their relative position remained the same: at the bottom. Then, the statistics take a depression year (1939) as a base for comparison, and contrast it to a year of recession (1958). This tended to exaggerate the advance because Negroes in 1939 were particularly victimized.

Another important aspect of the problem was obscured by the sweeping comparisons most editorialists made between the 1939 and 1958 figures. Even the Department of Labor statistics themselves indicate that the major gain was made during World War II (the increase from 1939 to 1947 was from 41.4 per cent to 54.3 of the white wage). In the postwar period the rate of advance slowed to a walk. Moreover, most of the optimism was based upon figures for Negro men. When the women are included, and when one takes a median family income from the Current Population Reports, Negroes rose from 51 per cent of white family income in 1947 to 57 per cent in 1952—and then declined back to the 1947 level by 1959.

But even without these qualifications, the fact is stark enough: the United States found cause for celebration in the announcement that Negro workers had reached 58 per cent of the wage level of their white co-workers. This situation is deeply imbedded in the very structure of American society.

Negroes in the United States are concentrated in the worst, dirtiest, lowest-paying jobs. A third continue to live in the rural South, most of them merely subsisting within a culture of poverty and a society of open terror. A third live in Southern cities and a third in Northern cities, and these have bettered their lot compared to the sharecroppers. But they are still the last hired and the first fired, and they are particularly vulnerable to recessions.

Thus, according to the Department of Labor in 1960, 4 per cent of Negro employees were "professional, technical and kindred workers" (compared to 11.3 per cent for the whites); 2.7 per cent were "managers, officials and proprietors" (the white figure is 14.6 per cent). In short, at the top of the economic structure there were

6.7 per cent of the Negroes—and 25.9 per cent of the whites. And this, in itself, represented considerable *gains* over the past two decades.

Going down the occupational scale, Negroes are primarily grouped in the bottom jobs. In 1960, 20 per cent of the whites had high-skill industrial jobs, while the Negro share of this classification was 9 per cent. Semiskilled mass production workers and laborers constituted around 48 per cent of the Negro male population (and 25.3 per cent of the white males). Negro women are the victims of a double discrimination. According to a New York State study, Negro female income as a percentage of white actually declined between 1949 and 1954 (and, in 1960, over a third of Negro women were still employed as domestics).

In part, this miserable structure of the Negro work force is an inheritance of the past. It reflects what happens to a people who have been systematically oppressed and denied access to skill and opportunity. If this completely defined the problem, there would be a basis for optimism. One could assume that the Negro would leave behind the mess of pottage bequeathed him by white America and move into a better future. But that is not the case. For the present position of the Negro in the economy has been institutionalized. Unless something basic is done, it will reproduce itself for years to come.

Take, as an example, the problem of automation. This has caused "structural" unemployment through the American work force, that is, the permanent destruction of jobs rather than cyclical layoffs. When this happens, the blow falls disproportionately upon the Negro. As the last significant group to enter the factory, the Negroes have low seniority (if they are lucky enough to be in union occupations), and they are laid off first. As one of the least skilled groups in the work force, they will have the hardest time getting another job. The "older" Negro (over forty) may well be condemned to job instability for the rest of his life.

All of this is immediate and automatic. It is done without the intervention of a single racist, yet it is a profound part of racism in the United States.

However, more is involved than the inevitable working of an impersonal system. The Negro lives in the other America of poverty for many reasons, and one of them is conscious racism reinforcing institutional patterns of the economy. In 1960, according to the report of Herbert Hill, Labor Secretary of the National Association for the Advancement of Colored People, Negroes made up only 1.69 per cent of the total number of apprentices in the economy. The exact figure offered by Hill has been disputed; the shocking fact which he describes is agreed upon by everyone. This means that Negroes are denied access precisely to those jobs that are not low-paying and vulnerable to recession.

The main cause of this problem is the attitude of management, which fundamentally determines hiring policy. But in the case of apprenticeship programs, the labor movement and the Federal and state agencies involved also bear part of the responsibility. In the AFL-CIO, it is the politically conservative unions from the building trades who are the real stumbling block; the mass-production unions of the CIO have some bad areas, but on the whole they pioneered in bringing Negroes into the plants and integrating local organizations.

With the companies, one of the real difficulties in dealing with this structure of racism is that it is invisible. Here is a huge social fact, yet no one will accept responsibility for it. When questioned as to why there are no Negroes in sales, or in the office, the personnel man will say that he himself has nothing against Negroes. The problem, he will claim, is with subordinates who would revolt if Negroes were brought into their department, and with superiors who impose the policy. This response is standard up and down the line. The subordinates and the superiors make the same assertion.

Indeed, one of the difficulties in fighting against racist practices in the American economy is the popularity of a liberal rhetoric. Practically no one, outside of convinced white supremacists in the South, will admit to discriminatory policies. So it is that the Northern Negro has, in one sense, a more personally frustrating situation than his Southern brother. In Dixie, Jim Crow is personified, an actual living person who speaks in the accents of open racism. In the rest of the country, everybody is against discrimination for the record, and Jim Crow is a vast impersonal system that keeps the Negro down.

In the past few years, some Negro groups have been using the boycott to force companies to abandon racist hiring practices. This may well be an extraordinarily momentous development, for it is a step out of the other America, and equality will come only when the Negro is no longer poor.

But, as one goes up the occupational ladder, the resistance to hiring Negroes becomes more intense. The office, for example, is a bastion of racism in American society. To some of the people involved, white-collar work is regarded as more personal, and even social, than factory work. So the integration of work appears like the integration of the neighborhood or the home. And a wall of prejudice is erected to keep the Negroes out of advancement.

Perhaps the most shocking statistic in all this is the one that describes what happens when a Negro does acquire skill and training. North, East, South, and West the pattern is the same: the more education a Negro has, the more economic discrimination he faces. Herman Miller, one of the best-known authorities on income statistics, has computed that the white Southern college graduate receives 1.85 times the compensation of his Negro counterpart, and in the North the white edge is 1.59.

What is involved in these figures is a factor that sharply distinguishes racial minorities from the old immigrant groups. When the Irish, the Jews, or the Italians produced a doctor, it was possible for him to begin to develop a practice that would bring him into the great society. There was prejudice, but he was increasingly judged on his skill. As time went on, the professionals from the immigrant groups adapted themselves to the language and dress of the rest of America. They ceased to be visible, and there was a wide scope for their talents.

This is not true of the Negro. The doctor or the lawyer will find it extremely difficult to set up practice in a white neighborhood. By far and large, they will be confined to the ghetto, and since their fellow Negroes are poor they will not receive so much money as their white colleagues. The Negro academic often finds himself trapped in a segregated educational system in which Negro colleges are short on salaries, equipment, libraries, and so on. Their very professional advancement is truncated because of it.

For the mass in the racial ghetto the situation is even more extreme. As a result of the segregation of neighborhoods, it is possible for a city like New York to have a public policy in favor of integration, and yet to maintain a system of effective segregation. In the mid-fifties, for example, the New York public-school system took a look at itself, dividing schools into Group X, with a high concentration of Negroes or Puerto Ricans, and Group Y where Negroes and Puerto Ricans were less than 10 per cent of the student body. They found that the X schools were older and less adequate, had more probationary and substitute teachers, more classes for retarded pupils, and fewer for bright children. This situation had developed with the framework of a public, legal commitment to integrated education. (Some steps have been taken to remedy the problem, but they are only a beginning.)

In the other America each group suffers from a psychological depression as well as from simple material want. And given the long history and the tremendous institutionalized power of racism, this is particularly and terribly true of the Negro.

Some commentators have argued that Negroes have a lower level of aspiration, of ambition, than whites. In this theory, the Jim Crow economy produces a mood of resignation and acceptance. But in a study of the New York State Commission Against Discrimination an even more serious situation was described: one in which Negro children had more aspiration than whites from the same income level, but less opportunity to fulfill their ambition.

In this study, Aaron Antonovsky and Melvin Lerner described the result as a "pathological condition . . . in our society." The Negro child, coming from a family in which the father has a miserable job, is forced to reject the life of his parents, and to put forth new goals for himself. In the case of the immigrant young some generations ago, this experience of breaking with the Old Country tradition and identifying with the great society of America was a decisive moment in moving upward. But the Negro does not find society as open as the immigrant did. He has the hope and the desire, but not the possibility. The consequence is heartbreaking frustration.

Indeed, Antonovsky suggests that the image of Jackie Robinson or Ralph Bunche is a threat to the young Negro. These heroes are exceptional and talented men. Yet, in a time of ferment among Negroes, they tend to become norms and models for the young people. Once again, there is a tragic gap between the ideal and the possible. A sense of disillusion, of failure, is added to the indignity of poverty.

A more speculative description of the Negro psychology has been written by Norman Mailer. For Mailer, the concept of "coolness" is a defense reaction against a hostile world. Threatened by the Man, denied access to the society, the Negro, in Mailer's image, stays loose: he anticipates disillusion; he turns cynicism into a style.

But perhaps the final degradation the Negro must face is the image the white man has of him. White America keeps the Negro down. It forces him into a slum; it keeps him in the dirtiest and lowest-paying jobs. Having imposed this indignity, the white man theorizes about it. He does not see it as the tragic work of his own hands, as a social product. Rather, the racial ghetto reflects the "natural" character of the Negro: lazy, shiftless, irresponsible, and so on. So prejudice becomes self-justifying. It creates miserable conditions and then cites them as a rationale for inaction and complacency.

One could continue describing the psychological and spiritual consequences of discrimination almost endlessly. Yet, whatever the accurate theory may be, it is beyond dispute that one of the main components of poverty for the Negro is a maiming of personality. This is true generally for the poor; it is doubly and triply true for the race poor.

How can the Negroes escape their prison in the other America?

To begin with, this wall of prejudice will be breached only when it is understood that the problem of race is not just a matter of legal and political equality. It is important that the right to the vote be won in the South, that discriminatory legislation be struck down, and so on. But that is only the beginning. The real emancipation of the Negro waits upon a massive assault upon the entire culture of poverty in American society: upon slums, inferior education, inadequate medical care, and all the rest. These things are as much a part of being a Negro as the color of a man's skin.

Housing is perhaps the most crucial element in racial poverty. As long as Negroes and other minorities are segregated into neighborhoods, the impact of all civil-rights legislation is softened. It is possible to have a public policy for integrated schooling, but if the school districts are themselves a product of residential discrimination, the schools will continue to be Jim Crow. But, here again, America at the beginning of the sixties does not seem prepared to devote the resources to the problem that are required if it is to be solved. And because of this, the terrible indignity of the ghetto will continue.

On the job, the Negro is the prime victim of the unwillingness of the society to face the crisis brought about by automation. It is, of course, the Negro "type" of job that is being destroyed. The crisis is hitting precisely in those areas where gains in integrated work were made in the past two decades, in the semiskilled jobs of mass-production industries. The Government, as noted before, is not making adequate provisions for planning and retraining and all the rest. And given the racist character of the American economy, this is a particularly severe blow against the Negro. It amounts to rebuilding the wall of prejudice, to destroying advances which have already been made.

In a sense, this technological crisis offers America a unique opportunity. The old system is being transformed. If the nation were to attack the problem of structural unemployment, it could at the same time make great strides toward racial equality. For any serious program aimed at providing displaced workers with skill and opportunity will automatically help the Negro as a Negro, so long as it does not contain racist features. A new and integrated structure could be built; the crisis could be a starting point for enormous progress.

But in recent years Negroes were more and more asked to accept their position in society, to sacrifice their own needs to the common good. Once again, the poorest were asked to pay the way of the better off. This took the form of various sincere people calling upon the Negro movement not to "obstruct" various welfare programs by insisting that they be integrated. In other words, the Negroes were being asked to help to build a welfare state that would discriminate against them in a double sense, that would not really benefit them because they are so poor as to be beyond the reach of the new benefits, and that would continue and reinforce the racist pattern of all of American society.

It is crucial that the nation understand that there can be no progress toward destroying the other America at the price of Negro rights. This is not simply a matter of morality and ethics, important as those factors are. It is also a brute sociological fact. The poor, as I have documented in describing other parts of the culture of poverty, are generally speaking those people who are beneath the welfare state. A quarter of them are Negro. Any program aimed at really aiding the dispossessed cannot exclude the Negroes without excluding millions of others who desperately need help. A housing program with discrimination against the black man is at the same time discriminatory against the white man, for it will perpetuate the segregation of poverty and it will keep the poor generally on the margin of the society. The only kind of housing program that could break through the social isolation of the poor and that could render these millions visible and return them to our society is an integrated program. And as long as the slums remain (or even as they are replaced by "poor farm" housing projects tucked away in some corner of the city), the culture of poverty will remain.

Clearly, the Negroes cannot achieve their emancipation on their own. They are, quite literally, a minority in the society, and they do not possess the political power to win the vast and comprehensive changes in public policy that are necessary if there is to be real equality. Here, once again, the fate of the lowest, the most dispossessed, depends on what the better off, and particularly the labor movement, will do.

If, as is quite possible, America refuses to deal with the social evils that persist in the sixties, it will at the same time have turned its back on the racial minorities. There will be speeches on equality; there will be gains as the nation moves toward a constitutional definition of itself as egalitarian. The Negro will watch all this from a world of double poverty. He will continue to know himself as a member of a race-class condemned by heredity to be poor. There will be occasional celebrations—perhaps the next one will be called in twenty years or so when it is announced that Negroes have reached 70 per cent of the white wage level. But that other America which is the ghetto will still stand.

There is a bitter picket-line chant that one sometimes hears when a store is being boycotted in the North:

> If you're white, you're right,
> If you're black, stay back.

It is an accurate sociological statement of the plight of the Negro in American society.

Five: Three Poverties

Most of the poor people described in this book come from the large, established cultures of poverty. They are the classic poor.

There is another kind of poverty. It exists in the interstices of the society in some cases, or else its specific quality is new. There have not been congressional investigations into the plight of these people. There are few statistics on what it means for them to be poor. Here, one learns from novels, from psychologists, from the records of Night Court, or from a walk through the streets.

There is one subculture of poverty in the United States that at times is spirited, ebullient, enthusiastic. It is the only humorous part of the other America. Here live the poor who are intellectuals, bohemians, beats. They strive or pose; they achieve or go back to the middle class from whence they usually come. But their lives are lived in the midst of physical deprivation and, often enough, of hunger.

There is a poverty that, in some ways, is the most terrible and destructive to be found in the other America. The city dweller meets it when the drifter from skid row asks for a handout. These are the alcoholic poor. They have long been defined as a major problem in our society, but they have not been understood as a problem of poverty, and that is an important fact about them.

And there is a new poverty that is becoming more and more important, a consequence of the revolution taking place in American agriculture. In Detroit, Cincinnati, St. Louis, Oakland, and other cities of the United States, one finds the rural poor in the urban slums, the hill folks, the Oakies who failed, the war workers from the forties who never went back home.

I have known the rural poor in the city and the alcoholics. I have been both participant and spectator in the intellectual slums of Chicago and New York. These are some impressions.

I

To the newspaper reader of the late fifties, the intellectuals who are poor appeared under the rather romantic guise of the Beat Generation. Bearded and eccentric, they suddenly became good copy for *Time* magazine, and that made them a phenomenon. Their aura, as the slick magazine writers described it, was compounded of Whitmanesque search, phoniness, eroticism, and perverse ingratitude. To most people, it must have seemed that they were leading an easy, indolent life. Few realized that, in addition to all the other myths and legends about them, these people were poor. In most cases, they were willfully and even joyously impoverished; but they were poor nevertheless.

The Beats are only the newest expression of an old phenomenon. There are the graduate-student poor who cluster around the great universities. There is the older tradition of Bohemia, with its more political and conscious theory of *épater les bourgeois*. All these groups have in common the experience of a curious kind of poverty. Outside religious orders, these are the only citizens of the affluent society to have chosen to be poor.

To begin with, the Beat and the Bohemian are a slum phenomenon.

The Venice West of the Beats in Los Angeles is an old real-estate scheme that went bad. Originally, it was supposed to be a new Venice, complete with picturesque canals and bridges. The plan went awry; the bridges are cracked, and there are oil riggings all over the area. The inhabitants are low-paid workers, drifters, outcasts of one kind or another, and the rebellious young people. In New York the Bohemian scene is no longer really centered in Greenwich Village, for luxury apartments are inexorably destroying the low-rent character of the area. The intellectual poor, or most of them, have moved east, to the tenements and lofts of the Lower East Side. Paradoxically, they are threatened constantly by low-income housing projects and health and safety regulations. They do not have the qualifications or the desire to move into public housing. Their freedom depends, in part, upon the culture of poverty.

Since they live in slum areas, the intellectual poor are often involved in a town-gown conflict. The Italian-Americans of the South Village in New York are regularly disturbed by the antics of the strangers in the midst. The fact that Bohemia (or the Beats, or whatever one calls it) is interracial, and often aggressively so, is a source of deep tension. In Chicago, before urban renewal destroyed one of the most extensive university slums on the South Side, the problem came from another direction. Negroes were moving into the area, and the indigenous white community was resisting. The students, whatever their views on racial equality, were white, and that was always a possible source of trouble.

I remember the strange feeling of walking down a tense street at night in the late forties. I knew myself as completely sympathetic to the Negro attempt to break through the walls of the ghetto, and I would have welcomed an integrated neighborhood. (The whites, the city planners, the forces of law and authority effectively destroyed that possibility.) At the same time, I knew that the color of my skin could give rise to violence. It was an uncomfortable irony.

But even if the intellectual poor are aliens in the slum world (or perhaps "visitors" would be a better term), they share its physical misery. The housing of Bohemia is often simply appalling. Rooms or apartments are in the cheapest, most run-down tenements, or in industrial lofts that are illegal for living purposes. The spirit may be that of *la vie de bohème:* the bugs, rats, the littered streets and the hall bathrooms are genuinely part of the culture of poverty. It is a paradox that a child of the middle class will actively seek out a damp basement room, or what might have been the servants' quarters in an old mansion.

Sometimes there is plain hunger. I remember a friend who subsisted for a while on a surplus Government ration that had been sent to starving refugees after World War II. My own discovery, realized in a rooming house in the Chelsea section of Manhattan, was that a can of corned-beef hash would make two meals. The regular dietary tricks of the born poor, the lumpy, pasty menus that give the illusion of a satisfied stomach, are quickly learned by the middle-class rebel.

But then, even hunger can be amusing in an exceptional case or two. One friend of mine whose family had stopped sending him funds by an oversight was left with a charge account in a fancy store that specialized in cocktail delicacies. As a result, he lived for some time on nuts, rattlesnake meat, turtle soup, and other exotic foods of the rich. Eventually, he developed a near allergy to all the foods of the upper class while living on a few dollars a week.

The jobs of the intellectual poor have one main requirement: they cannot really be stable. There are forays into the working world, but not careers. Some ferret out the drifters' section of the economic underworld: the dishwashing and luncheonette work of the minorities and the alcoholics. At 80 Warren Street in Manhattan, the building in New York described in the chapter on the rejects, one can regularly see an offspring of the middle class reading a book of philosophic analysis or poetry in the midst of a crowd of crushed and beaten men waiting to make a few dollars.

Then there is unemployment compensation. It comes to those who stay on a covered job long enough to qualify (and the work patterns of the intellectual poor are sometimes ruled by the state regulations). It is a sort of state subsidy for the practice and study of the arts. Indeed, some legislators might be appalled to discover how many novels had been written on these funds.

And yet, even though the intellectual poor share the tenements, the diets, the jobs of the born poor, they do not really enter into the culture of poverty. They have chosen a way of life instead of being victimized by it. They are passing through, either moving back toward the larger society or achieving a place in literature or the arts. They do not participate in the atmosphere of defeatism and pessimism that permeates the lives of the truly poor. In the contrast, one can begin to understand the importance of the spirit, the subjectivity, of poverty in the other America.

This difference can be seen most easily in the apartments of the intellectual poor. A loft or a tenement apartment will be transformed by middle-class education and ingenuity. (One friend of mine discovered that a telephone booth is a perfectly prefabricated shower.) The walls will be scraped to reveal the original bricks. A few cheap prints of good paintings will bring color and life into the room. The bathroom in the hall will still be terribly cold in the winter, the heat may come from an open oven, and baths may be taken in tubs set in the middle of the kitchen, but the physical dilapidation and privation are not destructive.

For that matter, there is a most curious irony among the intellectual poor. They come to the slums of the other America, to the physical life of impoverishment, because they are fleeing a spiritual poverty in the Affluent Society. Allen Ginsberg wrote of the Beats in *Howl, and Other Poems,* "I saw the best minds of my generation destroyed by madness." His claim is exaggerated, yet it contains a certain truth. Though many of these people have the talent and the education to win commercial success in the great society, they choose to live in the slums because they have found simple, material well-being hollow.

The interracialism of the intellectual poor is a good index of the seriousness of their rebellion. Like most of the educated middle class in America outside the South, they share the rhetoric of equality. But, unlike most people, their life has led them to an interracial world. Here, in the strange subculture of voluntary poverty, the Negro can find a social integration unknown to the rest of the society.

And yet, the prosperity of the middle class in the past decade and a half has had its impact upon the intellectual poor. In the older Bohemias, the refusal to obey social conventions was justified in terms of political radicalism or dedication to the artistic *avant-garde*. But in the fifties there were no vast social movements to identify with apart from the civil-rights organizations, and *avant-garde* had lost much of its vitality. As a result, protest among these people became more individual and personal, and the voice of Zen was heard.

Some of these people are, to be sure, enjoying a brief pose before taking up their position in the world of middle-class America. They accept the poverty because it provides them a certain freedom. As one writer brilliantly described them, they reject the working world because it does not give them time. They spend their entire life making time, until that is all there is, and still they do not produce. At best, they return sheepishly to the conventional world from whence they came; at worse, they simply vegetate.

There are tragedies, too. The slums of the intellectual poor are at the bottom of society, and, often enough, they are neighbor to the underworld. As a result, there are biographies that end in suicide, at the mental hospital, or in the police station. There is no point in romanticizing this, yet it is another sign of the failure of the great society that drives these people to hunger for value and belief rather than for food, and sometimes pushes them beyond the limits of their control.

Perhaps the most tragic group among the intellectual poor is the small minority who become narcotics addicts. There is a "junkie poverty" that is terrible. All of the turmoil and commotion and pain becomes reduced to a desire for a fix of heroin. There is a literal disintegration of the physical surroundings, and if the addict is not reduced to crime to satisfy the craving, the most complete impoverishment results.

The poseurs and the addicts make good tabloid reading, and they are the ones most people think of when they imagine the life of these middle-class rebels. Yet, perhaps it is more significant to remember that our affluent society contains those of talent and insight who are driven to prefer poverty, to choose it, rather than to submit to the desolation of an empty abundance. It is a strange part of the other America that one finds in the intellectual slums.

II

Perhaps the bitterest, most physical and obvious poverty that can be seen in an American city exists in skid row among the alcoholics.

During 1951 and 1952, I lived on Chrystie Street, one block from the Bowery in New York. I was a member of the Catholic Worker group that had a house there. Beds were given out on a "first come, first served" basis; we had a bread line in the early morning that provided coffee and rich brown bread, and a soup line at noon; and hand-me-down clothes that readers of the newspaper sent in were distributed. Those of us who came to live at the Worker house accepted a philosophy of voluntary poverty. We had no money and received no pay. We shared the living conditions of the people whom we were helping: alcoholics and the mentally ill. We did not participate in the living hell of that area, for we were not tortured by alcoholism and we had chosen our lot. But we were close, very close, to that world. We could see its horror every day.

The Bowery today does not look as it did then. The elevated tracks of the Third Avenue El have been dismantled, and in time skid row may be driven to some other part of the city, particularly if the Third Avenue property values keep going up. Thus, some of the places I describe no longer exist. Yet that is mere detail, for the essential world of these impressions is still very much with us.

The Third Avenue El gave the Bowery a sort of surrealist character. A dirty, hulking structure, it was as derelict as the men who acted out their misery beneath it. Along both sides of the street were flophouses where a man could get a bed for a night. Each morning, someone had to go through, checking to see if anyone had died during the night. The liquor stores were there, of course, specializing in cheap wine.

The men and women of the Bowery usually drank wine, or sometimes beer or shots of cheap whisky. For those in the direst straits, obsessed by the need for alcohol, there was always canned heat. It is liquid alcohol, and it can be drunk after it is strained through a handkerchief or a stale piece of bread. It has the reputation of knocking a man out before doing serious damage to his nervous system. It is, I am told, tasteless, a method of reaching oblivion and not much else.

There were other businesses around. The secondhand stores were there so that the men could sell whatever they could scavenge or steal (sometimes from one another). They preyed on the misery of the place, and they were indispensable to it. There were a couple of restaurants where at night the derelicts fought to keep their eyes open so that they would not be thrown out; these were most depressing, garishly lighted places. And there were missions, called by some "Three Sixteens" because they so often had the scriptural quotation from John 3:16 over the door: "For God so loved the world that He sent His only begotten son . . ." In warm weather the "Sallics"—Salvation Army lassies and men—would be out on the avenue.

Over the whole place there hung the smell of urine. The men lived out of doors when they didn't have money for a flop. Sometimes, in the winter, they passed out in the snow or crawled into a doorway. In the summer the stench from some of the favorite haunts was all but overpowering.

There is an almost typical face of the Bowery, or so it seemed to me. The men are dirty, and often their faces are caked with blood after a particularly terrible drunk. They wake up without knowing how they were hurt. Their clothes are ragged, ill-fitting, incongruous. Their trousers stink of the streets and of dried urine. And the human look is usually weak and afraid of direct and full contact with somone else's eyes.

In the summer the Bowery is at its best, if one can use such a word to describe a place of incredible physical and moral desolation. The men sit together and talk, or lounge along the walk in

groups. They are capable of stripping the clothes from another alcoholic when he is passed out, yet their drinking is hardly ever
solitary. If one of them is lucky enough to panhandle his way to a
bottle, he will seek out friends and share his good fortune.

Indeed, this is primarily a male society. There are a few women
here, but the overwhelming impression is of standing, waiting,
drunken men. Some psychologists have argued that there may be
a link between homosexual tendencies and alcoholism. At the Catholic Worker, we occasionally ran into trouble in the house on this
score. Whatever the eventual conclusions from scientific research,
the Bowery has a locker-room camaraderie among some of the most
broken and hurt of the society.

Active sex hardly matters here. This is a place whose inhabitants are drunk, or on their way to being drunk, twenty-four hours
a day. As a result, there is a literal impotence that is joined to the
personality impotence of defeated and self-destructive outcasts.

Winter is a catastrophe. Life on skid row is lived out of doors,
and the cold and the snow bring with them intense suffering. The
men often get drunk enough to lie in the streets in the midst of a
storm. The first time one sees a body covered with a light blanket
of snow, stretched out on the sidewalk, the sight comes as a shock
and a dilemma. Is the man dead or just drunk? Or worse, the ha-
bitués are so obsessed and driven that stealing goes on in the dead
of winter, and a man who needs a drink will take the shoes of a
fellow alcoholic in the middle of January.

The result, of course, is disease. There is a sort of war between
the Bowery and the city hospitals. The ambulance drivers and at-
tendants become cynical and inured to the sufferings of those who
seem to seek their own hurt so desperately. The administrative
staffs must worry about someone from skid row who wants a bed
for a couple of nights and who tries to simulate delirium tremens.
The officials become angry when these men sell their blood in order
to get enough money to drink—and then turn up in the hospital and
need blood transfusions.

The end of the line for the Bowery is the hospital and potter's field. Indeed, the Emergency Room of a public hospital like Belle-vue could be a study in itself. I remember a not untypical scene when I was up there with one of the men from the Catholic Worker. There were the alcoholics, the dazed old people, a Negro woman whose lip was hanging by a thread, the little children. One cannot blame the doctors or the administrators for the sickening, depress-ing atmosphere. That responsibility belongs to the city, whose char-ity is inadequately financed, maddening in its slowness, and bureau-cratically inexplicable to the uneducated poor.

Who are the men and women of the Bowery?

They are different from almost all the other poor people, for they come from every social class, every educational background to be found in the United States. At the Catholic Worker I met newspapermen, a dentist, priests, along with factory workers and drifters from the countryside. This is the one place in the other America where the poor are actually the sum total of misfits from all of the social classes.

Yet there are some strange factors at work in producing the subculture of alcoholism. One met quite a few men of Irish-Amer-ican extraction (a clear majority, it seemed to me), some Polish-Americans, some Negroes (skid row is not ideologically integrated, but it is usually too drunk to care about race), a few Italians. In the two years that I spent on the Bowery, meeting some hundreds of men and women, I don't think I ran into a single Jew.

When they "dried out," the alcoholics from the middle class used to talk about themselves much as the amateur, college-edu-cated psychologist would speak. They understood their condition as having deep roots in their personal problems and attitudes. But the ones who came from working-class or farm backgrounds were, like the mentally disturbed poor generally, mystified by what had happened to them. If they were religious—and a good many we met at the Worker were Catholic—this meant that sobering up usually involved frantic self-accusation.

I remember talking to an elderly man whom I got to know at the Worker. He was neat, hard-working, and with a great deal of self-respect whenever he was sober. He would stay off alcohol for long periods, sometimes up to three months. During that time he would lead an orderly life marked by careful religious observances. Then, suddenly, he would go on a drinking bout for two or three weeks. Sometimes we would hear about him when he had been taken into a hospital. He would come back then, and the whole process would begin anew.

I was talking to him one evening about alcoholism. I tried to say that it was not something a man chose, that it was related to deep problems, and that it could not be banished by a mere act of the will, no matter how courageous an individual was. He was frantic in his disagreement with me. "We are this way because we want to be," he said. "We are committing a mortal sin by doing it, and we are going to Hell because of it."

Sometimes this self-hatred turned toward others. One day a man stumbled in off the street. He was a physical mess: there was caked blood on his face, his clothes stank, and he wore the semi-human, possessed look that comes at the end of a long, terrible drunk. He lurched in, and I went to help him. We got him bathed and shaved and DDT'd. (The battle against lice and bedbugs was never won at the Worker, but we tried.) In a couple of days, with sleep and regular food and some new hand-me-down clothes, he was in pretty good shape.

Two or three evenings after he came in, he was standing next to me, waiting to go in for dinner. A man came in from the street, his double of two or three days earlier. There were the same blood and clothes and obsessed face. When I went to help the newcomer, the first man said to me, "Why give a hand to that bum?" In his voice there was the passion of genuine self-hatred. When the Bowery sobers up for a day or two, it promises, it sobs, it recriminates against itself. And so it goes, on and on.

Sometimes all this repressed emotion breaks out into a fist fight on the Bowery. If they were not so tragic, they might be funny. The violence is a ballet of mistakes, of drunken, sweeping, impossible punches. The men cannot really hurt each other with any calculation. The real danger is that a man will throw himself off balance when one of his roundhouse blows miscarries. The weakness and ineffectualness of the Bowery are summed up in these fights.

But then there come periods when the endless nights and days of drinking stop for a while. The sobering up is almost as horrible as the drunkenness itself. Sometimes at the Catholic Worker a man would wake with the shakes. His whole body would be trembling uncontrollably, and his face would be crumpled as if on the verge of tears. He would plead for one shot of whisky, just one, to get over the morning. It was a random risk, completely unpredictable, to answer his plea. There was no way of knowing when that one shot would actually work to tranquilize and make a day of sobriety possible, or when it would drive him out onto the street, and send him back to the world of drunkenness he had begun to flee.

Sometimes, the drying-out process would last for a week. I remember a woman who had been drunk, more or less continuously, for about three months. When she stopped and made it across the line of trembling and shaking, she was still like a caged tiger. She could not bear to sit still for more than a moment. She roamed the house for days on end.

Once they come back to the world of sobriety, the alcoholic poor face the problem of eating. Until then, their obsession is drink, and only drink. They subsist in the period of drunkenness off anything they can scavenge, including the waste in garbage cans, on food from missions, or from the cheap fare in one of the grimy restaurants of the neighborhood. When they become sober, there is a world to face, at least until the next drunk.

For the ones from middle-class families, there is the possibility of money from relatives or even of returning to a job. One of the men at the Catholic Worker when I was there is a successful magazine writer; I have seen his by-line over the years in some of the better publications. But for most of them, their working lives have been ruined by their drinking lives. They exist as a source of cheap labor for the dirty, casual jobs in the economic underworld.

"He went to the mountains" was one of the standard refrains

on the Bowery. It meant that a man had taken a job as a dishwasher or janitor in one of the Catskill resorts. Employment agencies, quick to market human desperation, always had openings for such work. Usually, the job would last a couple of weeks, perhaps for a summer. Sometimes a man would stay off the bottle for the whole time. But he would find his way back to the Bowery with a pocketful of money and he would buy drinks for his cronies for a couple of days. And then he would be exactly where he started.

One of the most tragic of these stories was told to me by the late brilliant cameraman who filmed *On the Bowery*. One of the "stars" of that picture was a Bowery habitué who had been around the Catholic Worker when I was there. During the filming of the movie he stayed off alcohol. Finally, when it was over, he had to be paid. The people who produced the film knew what might happen when he got the money—and they also knew that a doctor had told the man that one more serious binge and he would probably die. Yet he had worked, and they had no choice but to pay him. He took the money, drank, and died.

Though all this takes place in the middle of New York City, it is hardly noticed. It is a form of poverty, of social disintegration, that does not attract sympathy. People get moral when they talk about alcoholics, and the very language is loaded against such unfortunates. (I have not used the word "bum" since I went to the Catholic Worker; it is part of the vocabulary of not caring.) And since alcoholic poverty is so immediately and deeply a matter of personality, dealing with it requires a most massive effort. One hardly knows where to begin.

But, of course, nothing is being done, really. For sheer callousness and cynicism, I have never seen anything to rival the attitudes of the tourists and the police. Just below Houston on the Bowery was a place called Sammy's Bowery Follies (I don't know if it is still there; I hope not). It has been written up in magazines, and it is designed for tourists. The gimmick is that it is an old-fashioned Bowery Bar with Nineties bartenders and laughing, painted women who are fixtures of the place. Of an evening, well-dressed tourists would arrive there, walking through a couple of rows of human misery, sometimes responding to a panhandler's plea with *noblesse oblige*. They were within a few feet of desperation and degradation, yet they seemed to find it "interesting" and "quaint." This is a small, if radical, case of the invisibility of the poor.

But even more vicious was the police pickup.

I never understood how the exact number to be arrested was computed, but there must have been some method to this social madness. The paddy wagon would arrive on the Bowery; the police would arrest the first men they came to, at random; and that was that. At night, in the drama of dereliction and indifference called Night Court in New York, the alcoholics would be lined up. Sometimes they were still drunk. The magistrate would tell them of their legal rights; they would usually plead guilty, and they would be sentenced. Some of the older men would have been through this time and time again. It was a social ritual, having no apparent effect on anything. It furnished, I suppose, statistics to prove that the authorities were doing their duty, that they were coping with the problem.

These alcoholics will probably be left to themselves for a long while. Though their spiritual torment is well known by most Americans, what is not understood is the grim, terrible, physically debilitating life of the alcoholic: the fact that these people are poor.

Let me end this description with a sad incident, for that is the proper note for an impression such as this.

About six months after I had left the Catholic Worker, I had come back one evening to see some friends and to talk. I had a job, and had begun to build up the wardrobe that had been stolen from me when I first came to Chrystie Street. (The voluntary poverty of the Worker is made real by the fact that if you stay for six months, all your property will be taken anyway.) I had on a fairly decent suit, and I was standing in the back yard with a couple of men I knew from the Bowery. One of them said to me, while the other nodded agreement: "We wondered when you would wise up, Mike. Hanging around here, helping us, that's nothing. Only nuts would do it. It's good you're wised up and going someplace." They were happy that I had left. They couldn't understand why anyone would want to care for them.

III

Part of the culture of poverty in the United States is made up of urban hillbillies.

Properly speaking, only part of this group actually comes from the Appalachian hills to the big city. The others are Arkansas cotton pickers, people from southeast Missouri ("Swamp East Missouri," they call it), Oakies on the West Coast who never recovered from the migration of the thirties. Yet they share common problems —the fact that the backwoods has completely unfitted them for urban life—a common poverty, and they often like the same "country" music.

A few of them are still in the backwoods, but near the big cities. Just outside Grafton, New York, a few miles from Albany, is a settlement that is literally in the woods. None of the townspeople had talked to them (this has resulted in some marvelous myth making), and all I could do was to drive past some of the lean-tos and glimpse a few people in the distance. The legislators at the state capital nearby are discussing various modern welfare programs; these hill folk are living as if they were in the eighteenth century.

But the really important group is not out in the woods on the fringe of the cities. They are in the slums. They came up from the Appalachians to Detroit for war jobs, and stayed on; they have drifted into Chicago, where they form a sizable community with their own churches and neighborhoods and ways of life; they work in the factories of Oakland, California, at the dirtiest and most menial jobs. They can be identified by their ninth-generation Anglo-Saxon faces, by their accents, and by the ubiquity of country music.

In Oakland, California, for instance, one can walk into a bar a few miles from the Pacific Ocean and be transported into the hills or the dustbowl of Oklahoma. The singing group has been affected by radio—the guitars are electric—but the music and the patrons are country. The atmosphere is not picturesque, however; it is tough, incipient with violence, and there are brawling and prostitution. The bouncer is a uniformed officer from a private protection agency. He wears handcuffs on his belt and carries a billy.

I met some of these people about ten years ago in St. Louis, Missouri. I was working for the Board of Education as a social worker. Attached to the Madison School, I went out and visited the homes of every student who missed school more than two or three times in a row or who had been in trouble. My job was not that of a truant officer (although that was its origin). The Pupil Welfare Department was intelligent, capable, and sincere. It rejected a theory of evil, malevolent children, and sought to deal with problems of truancy by tracing their roots in the home, the neighborhood, or the personality of the child. Time has passed since then, and perhaps the neighborhood has changed. But these are still the conditions under which the country folk live, and suffer, in the cities of the other America.

These people were, for the most part, Arkansas sharecroppers and cotton pickers. They came to St. Louis when times were bad, or during the slack season. They had an intricate web of kinfolk relationships, and there was always a relative sending word from St. Louis about work in the city or calling them back to the fields. Their lives were almost completely mercurial. An entire family would literally pack up and leave on a moment's notice. They had few possessions, no roots, no homes.

They lived in one of the worst urban slums for white people that I have ever seen. This was old St. Louis, down by the river, and some of the houses had probably been the homes of aristocrats of an earlier day. There were slim windows, archways, courtyards. But this architectural charm was vestigial. The houses had been cut into rooms, and the families were packed into them. For the most part, there were no bathrooms working inside these places. There were outhouses in the back yard, and sometimes the common pump was there, too. Then the place became a quagmire. Sometimes the way to the outhouse led through somebody's room. (That occurred,

I suppose, when what was formerly a kitchen was converted into an "apartment.") When that happened, people would be passing through all night long.

As often happens in the culture of poverty, marriage was somewhat irregular among these folk. The women were not promiscuous —they lived with one man at a time, and for considerable periods. But, after some years and a child or two, the marriage would break up. It was not uncommon to meet two or three sets of half-brothers and half-sisters living under the same roof.

The children were forced to go to school under state law, but it was a battle to keep them there. As soon as they could get a work permit, they would do so in order to pick up pin money. Their world of home was dirty and often violent, and they had no motivation to change. In the eighth grade the average age was around sixteen, and for a good percentage of the pupils that was the end of education. Predictably, the IQ's were lower than those of children in middle-class schools.

I remember at one time having to investigate a serious charge made by one student against another. The family of one girl claimed that a boy had tried to rape their daughter. I talked to all sides, and my impression was strange. There were passions and clan hatreds involved, but there was also a casualness, almost a listlessness about the whole business. In the end, it was impossible to come up with a substantial conclusion one way or the other, but no one was really pressing the matter. There was an acceptance of violence and rape; it was part of life.

The school itself had a magnificent faculty. All those who wanted an easier time could get transfers after the first year or so. Those who stayed were volunteers, and they were, for the most part, competent and dedicated people. That was what made their frustrations so difficult to bear. The school had the children nine months a year, six hours or so a day. The home and the neighborhood possessed them the rest of the time. It was an unequal battle, and it was further complicated by the fact that one never knew when a family was going to pick up and leave.

There were, for example, compulsory showers. We would check a student's hair for lice as a matter of course, for bugs can spread like an epidemic in a school. The old-fashioned steel combs that one uses to get the nits out of the hair was an ordinary part of the nurses' equipment. But it was a holding action at best to work for cleanliness and hygiene. The homes were dirty and rat-infested and bug-ridden. We could do a little for a short while, but that was not much.

And yet this grim description, like the account of a Negro ghetto, misses the quality of life. As one walked along the streets in the late summer, the air was filled with hillbilly music from a hundred radios. There was a sort of loose, defeated gaiety about the place, the casualness of a people who expected little. These were poor Southern whites. In some ways, they resembled the stereotype of the happy-go-lucky Negro, and the truth in the description is about the same for both.

But their humor and easy ways were contained in an environment of misery. I remember families who could not send their children to school because there were not enough shoes for all. One family passed the shoes from child to child, so that at least a couple of them would be in school each day. The Pupil Welfare Department made valiant efforts to fill this minimal need, but it took time, and while the search was going on nothing could really be done.

But perhaps the saddest group of all were the students in the special class. They had IQ's so low that any attempt to bring them a standard education would inevitably fail. An extremely competent and dedicated young woman tried to teach them the rudiments of living in a modern society: basic things like learning to understand traffic lights, to distinguish money, and the like. Such children can appear in any social class. The particular tragedy here was that no one really understood what was happening to them. The folk traditions about people being "touched" were about as deep as anyone got, and if they received pity it was colored by toughness and taunts. (This lack of understanding of mental illness and retardation, so basic to the culture of poverty, will be discussed in greater detail in a later chapter.)

I remember vividly one instance of such callousness. There was a child who had an extremely serious chronic condition. Though he had periods of apparent health, the doctors said he was headed toward an early death. The disease had left him "strange," and his fellow students often delighted in tormenting him. Their values, their experience, had not prepared them for sympathy or pity.

The whole neighborhood lived close enough to crime to make it a danger and a possibility. Only, even here the people were impoverished. The crime was, for the most part, violent, petty, and paltry. It could wreck lives and end in prison sentences or reform schools, but it could never really pay off. The world of the organized rackets, of modern rationalized crime, was as distant from this backwoods city slum as big business.

Indeed, one of the most frustrating things about social work in this neighborhood is that one could read the fates written on some of the children's faces. It was relatively easy to guess which boys might end in a penitentiary, which girls would become pregnant before they were out of grade school. But there was nothing legally or humanly that could be done, short of the abolition of the neighborhood and the culture it contained.

All of this might be dramatized by a report from Chicago. In that city, according to an article in *Harper's,* police and merchants were becoming even more hostile toward the country folk than they were toward Negroes. The people were so rootless, so mercurial, that this racially explosive metropolis had altered some of the values of its hatred.

These settlements will continue to grow. More and more poor farmers and agricultural laborers are being pushed off the land. In the late fifties and early sixties, they came to the city in a time of recession and automation. The cards, in short, are stacked against them as never before. And there will be more of these music-filled, miserable country neighborhoods springing up in the cities of the other America.

Six: The Golden Years

> That is no country for old men. The young
> In one another's arms, birds in the trees . . .
> —W. B. YEATS

Sometimes in the course of an official Government report, a human being will suddenly emerge from the shadows of statistics and analyses. This happened in a summary statement of the Senate Subcommittee on the Problems of the Aged and Aging in 1960. Louise W——— comes to life:

Louise W———, age 73, lives by herself in a single furnished room on the third floor of a rooming house located in a substandard section of the city. In this one room, she cooks, eats and sleeps. She shares a bathroom with other lodgers. Widowed at 64, she has few friends remaining from her younger years. Those who do remain do not live near her, and it is difficult for her to see them. She feels that the other older men and women living in the same rooming house are not good enough for her company (conversations with these persons reveal that they have the same attitude, too: their fellow inhabitants are not good enough for them, either).

And so she stays confined to her one room and the bathroom shared by nine other people. When the weather is warm enough, she ventures down the long flight of stairs about once a week for a walk to the corner and back.

Louise W——— is symbolic of a growing and intense problem in American society. The nation venerates youth, yet the proportion of the population over sixty-five years of age is increasing. For many of these older people, their declining years are without dignity. They have no function; they are sick; they are without money. Millions of them wear out the last days of their existence in small apartments, in rooming houses, in nursing homes.

This is no country for old men. The physical humiliation and the loneliness are real, but to them is added the indignity of living in a society that is obsessed by youth and tries to ignore age. These people are caught, as one witness before the Senate Committee testified, in a triple "chain of causality": they are plagued by ill health; they do not have enough money; and they are socially isolated. Some of them are new entrants to the world of the other America, drifting down from a working life of decent wages to an old age of dependency and social workers. A good many are old and poor because they were young and poor, middle-aged and poor. Taken together, they constitute a section of the culture of poverty with over 8,000,000 inhabitants.

The brochure writers and the publicists talk of the "golden years" and of "senior citizens." But these are euphemisms to ease the conscience of the callous. America tends to make its people miserable when they become old, and there are not enough phrases in the dictionary to gloss over this ugly reality.

I

An aged man is but a paltry thing,
A tattered coat upon a stick . . .

The poverty of old age in America is rooted in a biological revolution. There are more aging people today than ever before, and they are still on the increase. In 1850, 2.5 per cent of the nation was over sixty-five; in 1900 the figure had risen to 4.1 per cent. In 1960 almost 9 per cent of the American population was over that limit, and the statisticians of the Department of Health, Education, and Welfare estimate that in 1975 nearly 10 per cent of the United States will be over sixty-five. It is not so much that the upper limits of life have been extended as that a great many more people are living to become old.

The causes of this great change are fairly obvious. There have been enormous strides in medicine, and if cancer and heart disease are dealt with in the immediate future there will be still another gigantic lunge. The mortality rate has gone down. The fertility rate is lower than it was. And there are no great waves of immigrants bringing youth to America. The result is a society that is becoming older.

Yet it would be a mistake to pose the general problem of age as if it could be described in terms of life expectancy or medical problems. Even when the old are not poor, they are the victims of the very technology that has given them longer life. The very advances that have created the basis for a widespread old age have also destroyed the traditional props of the declining years. The "three generation family" uniting grandchildren, parents, and grandparents under a single roof is disappearing from the nation. Even on the farm, where the old used to have some light household chores to pass the time of day, mechanization and change have wiped out various functions.

So it is that, even without poverty, the aged are lonely and isolated. The image of a querulous, nagging, meandering old age is not a description of an eternal condition of human nature. It is, in part, the impression of what society has done to people by giving them meaningless years in which to live.

Indeed, it is an irony that leisure is a burden to the aged. (How many times does one hear the remark, "He will die if he stops working"? In 1890, 70 per cent of the males over sixty-five were still working; in 1959 the figure had fallen to 34 per cent. Today, as noted before, some industries consider a factory worker obsolete when he passes forty. Business enforces retirement. So basic is this problem that there has been discussion of including the aged under the provision of antidiscrimination laws, of treating them as a minority group like the Negroes or the Mexican-Americans.

Loneliness, isolation, and sickness are the afflictions of the aged in every economic class. But for those who are poor, there is an intensification of each of these tragedies: they are more lonely, more isolated, sicker. So it is that a Government report unwittingly stated a social paradox. It noted that only a society of abundance could produce such a high proportion of old people. We can afford them, we create them, because we are so rich. But later, in discussing the reality of life for the aged, the same report noted that these human products of abundance were denied its fruits. We tolerate them as long as they are poor.

The 1960 Senate report stated the issue clearly enough: ". . . at least one-half of the aged—approximately eight million people—cannot afford today decent housing, proper nutrition, adequate medical care, preventive or acute, or necessary recreation." The same grim picture emerged from the White House Conference on Aging in 1961. As one volume put it, "Many states report that half their citizens over 65 have incomes too low to meet their basic needs."

Here are the statistics. They are some of the most incredible figures to be found in American society:

The Bureau of the Census figures for 1958 show almost 60 per cent of the population over sixty-five with incomes under $1,000 a year. This must be measured against the Government computation that an adequate budget for a retired couple in the autumn of 1959 would range from an urban low of $2,681 in Scranton to a high of $3,304 in Chicago. In short, the top couples in the 60 per cent would have a budget 20 per cent below adequacy in the cheapest city, and almost 40 per cent below adequacy in the most expensive.

Over half of these people are covered by some kind of Federal program (social security, old-age assistance, and so on). Yet, the social security payments are, by Federal admission, completely inadequate to a decent life. In 1959, for instance, they averaged a little better than $70 a month. Or, to take another expression of the same fact, the Senate report concluded that if aged couples could live within the low-cost minimum food budget of the Department of Agriculture, a quarter of them would be spending more than half their income on food alone.

Some people try to soften these statistics by noting that old people receive money from children and relatives, that money income gives a false, overly pessimistic picture. Yet in 1961 one of the White House Conference reports estimated that the total contribution from relatives and friends was $3,000,000,000, which was only 10 per cent of the money income of these people. And the bulk of this, it can be assumed, comes from the most well-off children and goes to the better-off aged. The basic fact remains: at least 8,000,000 Americans over sixty-five are poor.

But even these statistics conceal the gravity of the situation. By one of the predictable paradoxes in the culture of poverty, it is the people with the lowest incomes among the aged who have the least resources in every sense of the term. Quite a few old people own houses, but not those at the bottom of the income pyramid. Of the people who get social security benefits, it has been estimated that 25 per cent of them have no savings at all and that over half have assets of less than $1,000.

Who are these people? How did they come to the culture of poverty?

Many of them are those who have been poor before. The misery of their old age is simply the conclusion of a life of misery. They are the ones who have grown up, lived, and will die under conditions of poverty. In New York State in the mid-fifties, for example, a legislative report found that a good number of people who were among the aged poor had been driven off the land and come to the cities. They had never made a success, and the impoverishment of their declining years was a result of their having been born in the wrong group in the first place.

Another factor making for continuous poverty is ill-health. The greatest single disability of the aged poor is chronic disease. Those who have been poor all their lives are sicker than anyone else in America. As a result, they have an almost guaranteed misery at the end of their lives.

But even if all the citizens who are young and middle-aged in the other America remain poor to the end of their days, that does not account for the enormous proportion of poverty among those over sixty-five. Fifty per cent of the elderly exist below minimum standards of decency, and this is a figure much higher than that for any other age group. So it is that a good many of these people are recruited to poverty after relatively decent working lives.

One obvious group among these new poor are the workers. There are unskilled and semiskilled workers who, with luck, can stay above the poverty line when they are young and strong. But each advancing year threatens whatever they have achieved. For them, old age comes as a permanent depression. Then there are the technologically displaced workers who are suddenly dropped out of the skilled work force. There are women who are forced back into the labor force at the lowest-paying jobs because they must have money to supplement their inadequate income when they reach sixty-five. And there are the workers whose health breaks down but who must keep on working.

Some of these recruits to poverty had known days of good wages and working conditions. Then they were caught in a technological cross fire. On the one hand, technology renders them economically superfluous, fit only for the economic underworld. On the other hand, technology gives them life. To them, progress comes to mean a bitter, desperate end to their lives.

And finally, the depressed areas are suffused and overwhelmed with poverty, and the aged are caught in them more than anyone else. Agricultural workers, for instance, are sentenced to work for starvation wages in the best of times. When they get old, they are among those in the society not covered by social security. They have never had a real chance to prepare for old age, and no one helps them when the terrible moment comes.

Here perhaps is the most shocking statistic of what happens at the bottom of the society, of how the poor are persistently penalized for the original sin of poverty. Somewhere between two-thirds and three-fourths of the aged in America are covered by social security; but the poorest of the poor, the "unrelated individuals" (those living alone, quite often aged widows) with incomes of less than $1,000, had only a 37 per cent coverage in 1957.

In the same vein there is the classic report from the State of Mississippi to the White House Conference: "Mississippi's older people are a low income people in a low income state." Indeed, the White House Conference noted that the huge band of rural poverty was an area of acute suffering for the aged. Here live people who are not covered by Federal programs, who find themselves in states and counties without adequate funds for relief.

The welfare state, in short, is upside-down in the subculture of aged poverty as it is everywhere else in the other America. The protection, the guarantees, the help all tend to go to the strong and to the organized. The weakest in the society are those who are always disposed of in some congressional logrolling session. And this simple lack of income persisting into old age becomes the basis for a structure of misery and loneliness. Once this is given, medical problems become insuperable, housing becomes impossible to find, and perhaps most importantly there is a growing feeling of being a useless, functionless human being in a land where youth is worshiped and death is rarely mentioned by name.

There is a connection between all these statistics and psychological depression. It can be made specific by considering where the aged poor live.

A high proportion of America's aged live with children, out of necessity rather than from choice. This results in tensions and difficult personal situations, but it is probably the best arrangement for living in the minimal choices the nation offers the elderly. Two-thirds of the people over sixty-five live with a spouse or a relative in a two-person household. They signify the breakdown of the old patterns of family living in the United States.

Like many of the poor, these people are particularly hurt by the transformation of the city. The young and middle-aged middle class is fleeing to the suburbs. The grandparents are often left behind. They might own a fairly decent house, but the neighborhood community of their early years has been destroyed. Now they are strangers on a street they have known for forty or fifty years. Forced to cope with the difficult problems of transitional neighborhoods, they are the least equipped to do so.

The aged widows are particularly badly off. A good percentage of them, the Senate Committee reported, live alone. In 1960 there were 6,000,000 Americans over seventy-five, most of them women, most of them on their own. Government statisticians calculate that in 1980 there will be 9,000,000 people over seventy-five years of age. If the present trend continues, they will face the most extreme conditions of loneliness and of poverty.

The lonely aged poor are, as noted before, the most impoverished single group in their subculture of poverty. A quarter of them have under $580 in money income a year. That is just above the minimum low-cost food budget of the United States Department of Agriculture, and it must provide for rent, clothing, and other things as well. For most of these people, as with Louise W———, amusement will be restricted to an occasional walk to the corner in good weather.

One consequence of this isolation is that the United States has some tendencies to produce age ghettos as well as racial ghettos. In most big cities there is a rooming-house area, often a place of decayed gentility, with a high concentration of the elderly. In St. Louis, for instance, there is a neighborhood of old houses that have been cut up into furnished rooms and tiny apartments for the poor. Scattered throughout the area are old people living in rooming houses.

Public housing is another problem for the aged. With slum clearance, the old neighborhoods are torn down. But there are no real guarantees that the elderly will find a new place. They are, as the Senate report noted, the special victims of the relocation problem, and they are the ones least able to fend for themselves in finding new accommodations. The suburbs are closed to them because they lack funds; the low-income projects have yet to take real notice of their special needs.

All of this is grim enough on the surface, but the facts and the figures do not really communicate the way in which social isolation is built into the "golden years." For the younger slum dweller there is some kind of street society, even if it takes the form of gangs. But for the old person, trapped in the decaying central area of the city and living among strangers, there is a terrifying lack of simple human contact. The whole problem might be summarized in a Government statistic that, in a way, is a measure of the loneliness of the aged poor: one-third of the aged in the United States, some 5,000,000 or more human beings, have no phone in their place of residence. They are literally cut off from the rest of America.

II

The aging woman in New York called her social worker on the telephone. She was in tears. Her check had not come from Welfare on the expected day, and she was terrified that she had been cut off, that now she would literally face starvation. Her life, like those of many in her situation, was suspended by a thread from the city's welfare system. The social worker was her symbol of hope.

The social worker: It is inevitable that this figure should emerge in a book on poverty. In every part of the other America there are social workers. Among the gangs of the city slums, it is even considered a mark of honor to have a full-time worker assigned to a particular group. It shows that the authorities are taking them seriously. In the Negro ghetto, once the social worker becomes known, he or she is the one person from the outside who can move with a certain ease down the streets.

But it is particularly fitting that the social worker appear in a chapter on the misery of age in contemporary America. For the millions of aging poor, and particularly for those who live alone, one of the main facts about life is that it becomes totally dependent.

At best, they must count on the charity and love of a family; at worst, their fate belongs to the stranger from Welfare.

Much has been written against the social worker in the United States. The argument usually runs that callousness and cynicism are the inherent products of public charity. Unquestionably, social work has created some bureaucratic, unfeeling personalities, individuals who see only statistics and the mass, who never really look into the human face of poverty. There is a sort of welfare-state Lady Bountiful who subsists on a patronizing, routinized *noblesse oblige*. As time has gone on, the "clients" of these social workers have become wise. They adopt the jargon; they give the right answers; they become bureaucratically adept.

But this acid portrait is only part of the picture. To a considerable extent social workers are as they are because the funds with which they work are completely inadequate to solve the problems that confront Welfare. The case load is usually overwhelming. Often, good, warm, and sincere people who genuinely want to help human beings are simply submerged in a routine that is not of their own making. (An irony: some years ago, a union of social workers in New York struck against the authorities by staying late on their own time and writing all of the money authorizations that were legally possible.) I remember a teacher in St. Louis who moved into the slum neighborhood of her school in order to be with the people all of the time. She is a symbol of the best in the social-work impulse.

If it is tragic that a bureaucratic impersonality is imposed on many social workers throughout the other America, that fact becomes most intolerable in relation to the aged poor. These are people whose plight is expressed in a torment of loneliness and isolation. They require, above all, individual and particular care. And no matter how passionately committed to humanity a social worker is, this requires a certain amount of money. America has not provided it.

In the fifties, a young woman social worker for aged at the Montgomery County Relief Area settled in Dayton, Ohio. What follows in the next few pages is a summation of her impressions of the reality of social work in that place.

In Ohio, relief programs are on the basis of county administration (or were in the mid-fifties, the period from which this description is taken). Standards were set for minimal payments required to give the people the basis of a subsistence existence. Then, as so often happens in the other America, each county would decide what percentage of the minimum it would provide. (Relief and welfare programs throughout the United States are completely uneven; it is much better to be poor in New York City than in Montgomery County, and better to be poor in almost any place than in Mississippi.) In Montgomery County the percentage of the minimum was 90 per cent—fairly high for the state.

The first thing that an older person would encounter when coming to the relief area was the necessity of documenting eligibility. In some cases proof of age was required, and there could be a long postponement, or even a rejection, if the proper papers were not produced. Some of the programs had a residency requirement that the individual had lived in the state for five out of the last nine years.

In this particular office, the young woman relates, the screening was carried on by people who were hostile to the applicants. They regarded most of those who came to them as "deadbeats" and "bums," and they were determined to keep freeloaders off the public rolls. As a result, they have achieved a rejection rate of 55 per cent, and they were quite proud of it and determined to keep it there.

To a person from the middle class, the fact that documents are required by a public agency seems to be obvious and rational. Yet this judgment misses a basic fact about the poor generally, and the aged poor in particular: that they are precisely the ones least equipped to deal with the bureaucracy of the welfare state. Some of the American poor have difficulty with the English language, and almost all of them are undereducated. There are those who develop their relations with welfare into a fine art, but there are many more who are literally terrified by the forms and the apparatus of a relief office.

This is doubly true for the aged. They are in failing health, and are completely and totally dependent upon the authorities. A trip to the relief office is a matter of life and death for them. And they tend to be bewildered by the routines of a world in which they did not grow up. The people described by the young social worker in Montgomery County were consciously hostile to those who came to them for help. But even those who are solicitous are forced to act in somewhat the same way. Money is limited, and in order to see that everyone gets something it is necessary to be brutal and probing.

In Montgomery County there were some who tried to steer the aged poor away from clinics. They felt that if a person went to a clinic where all kinds of complaints were treated, there would be a tendency to invent illness so as to get more out of the state. So they preferred to send them to individual doctors, and to certify treatment for a single ailment.

But within the present setup the single-doctor approach is not a simple evil. One of the standard indignities in the clinic is that the doctor is likely to change with each visit. This means that the old person has to recite symptoms anew each time. Because of such repetition, it seemed to some of the people that they were beginning treatment over and over and that nothing was really being done for them. (In New York, for instance, one old man I know goes to a clinic and an individual doctor through the Welfare Department. He feels that the doctor is really helping him, but the routine of the clinic has convinced him that nothing is being done for his condition.)

But again, all this is part of the poverty of public facilities in the affluent society. In Montgomery County, for example, there was a woman who would be confined to her bed unless she had a wheel chair. A relatively small expenditure of money would have made her life infinitely more decent and dignified. When the social worker proposed that this be done, her superiors told her that there were hundreds of others who needed wheel chairs (to translate: hundreds of others who, by receiving a simple device, could have the horizons of their life broadened). The authorities granted that this particular case was a worthy one and that the benefits would be immediate and obvious, but they were afraid that it would start a run on wheel chairs. The woman stayed in bed.

In the incident of the wheel chair, the lack of public funds prolonged and made more miserable an already existing illness. In other cases, sickness and suffering are created by the squalor of the welfare services. Mrs. H——— was seventy-five. Her husband had suffered a stroke and a bad fall, and had lost control of his bowel and bladder functions. She tried to care for him, lift him, wash his sheets and underwear, and so on. There was enough government money to "live" on, but her life was near collapse and she had already been stricken by one siege of pneumonia.

Mrs. H——— was not an isolated individual. This is how the young social worker described the living conditions of her "clients": "They live in furnished rooms, as boarders with a family, in small furnished and unfurnished apartments, in homes of their own, in trailers and rest homes. Those in the furnished rooms are probably on the whole the most pitiable. Generally they are alone—single, widowed or widower, divorced—they live in complete seclusion, terribly lonely, yet deliberately cutting themselves off from their neighbors whose gossip they fear. They do not want it known that they are 'on relief.'

"If they are fortunate, they can find one neighbor whom they can learn to trust. That neighbor will function as a companion and, equally important, as a responsible protector who will call the doctor or get the client into the hospital, or who will call the case worker if the client is too sick to do so. If this neighbor moves away they may never find another to rely on."

Another hard fact of this life comes from the bureaucratic demand that there be some *quid pro quo* for relief payments. In many areas, going on relief requires the signing of a lien on all property so that Welfare has the first claim against the estate. Usually, this

is a technicality, since these people have no money and no assets
in any case. But for those who have saved and skimped and bought
a home during their middle years, this provision is a trauma, a sort
of ultimate deprivation that puts an official stamp on society's rejection of them. And for almost all, whether there are assets or not,
it is an emotional experience in which life itself is being signed away
in a legal document. The individual is being made the property of
the state in return for three inadequate meals a day, rent money,
and some medical care.

There is a woman in New York who had been a vaudeville
head-liner in the old days. When she was making money, she spent
it foolishly, signing away rights and a fortune. Now she is on relief,
and Welfare has demanded that she sign over her estate. There is a
possibility that a movie may be made about her life. In her old age
she has finally become crafty. Because she signed too much away
when she was young, she is balking now. And perhaps she won't get
care as a result.

At the end of the road, there is the county home. The staff
people around Dayton are quite proud of this institution, the young
woman relates. They regarded it as adequate to the needs of the
people who were sent to them. But many of the aged themselves
were terrified by the idea of the county home. In the popular feeling
of America, there is something utterly degrading in the very name.
(The popular feeling is partly right; the utter inadequacy of a good
many of these places will be described shortly.)

How representative are these details of welfare administration
in Ohio? As noted before, there is great variation in these programs
from state to state, from city to city. But there are also the inescap-
able mathematics of the inadequacy of social security and other
Federal programs and of the various local systems. As it is, the aged
poor in America are condemned to deal with a bureaucratic, impersonal, frustrated setup.

III

Sometimes the statistics of poverty can be read like a detective story.

This is the case with a 1960 Government publication "Older Persons, Selected Characteristics, United States, July 1957–June 1959" and some related publications. At first glance these pamphlets are dry compilations of data. But, whether it was planned that way or not, there is a dramatic theme that builds up from table to table. The crime involved is the perpetration of human misery. The villain is poverty.

First, there is the fact that the impoverished aged poor need medical care more than any other group in the society.

The lowest-income group among the aged (and it should be kept in mind that this comprises around half of their number, that is, some millions of people) had four times the number of serious limitations of activity that the highest-income group of the same age had. When it becomes a question of "chronic limitations of mobility," the really serious cases, the same pattern reasserts itself: 26 per cent of the top-income group have no chronic conditions; but only 17 per cent of the bottom group are in the same position.

The result of this shows up in another statistic: the aged poor spend more days in bed as a result of their disabilities than any other part of their generation. So there is the classic cluster of misery that one encounters so often in the other America: those with the least money are the most confined, the most sick, the most bed-ridden.

If there were decency to old age in this land, the people who were so dramatically hurt would have the finest and best of medical care. The opposite is the case. The well-off aged, who have less need for doctors, have their wants attended to; the poor do not. And this does not take into account the fact that medical care for the poor is carried on in clinics and in nursing homes—that is, the medical care is often inferior. Thus, an elderly man of seventy-five who has an income under $2,000 a year will see the doctor on the average of 6.8 times a year, while his biological brother with an annual income of $7,000 or better will go to the doctor 9.1 times a year.

The victim of this crime suffers more the older he gets, for income becomes a more decisive determinant of medical care with advancing age. So it is that the statistics can be made flesh: there are hundreds of thousands, perhaps millions, of elderly people in the United States who live on a downward spiral. Theirs is the most extreme and obvious case of the vicious circle to be found in the other America.

And perhaps the detective-story image is a summary one. In a crime novel no one ever believes that the obvious villain committed the crime. Some writers utilize this disbelief to achieve surprise. The villain of sickness and old age has been carefully described in dozens of governmental reports, and there is really no mystery to the story. Only, the American public has not really discovered this fact yet.

This process of the downward spiral is particularly acute for the aged poor who have been impoverished all their lives. More, it is a situation that, to a considerable extent, is unnecessary. The long-term poor, as noted before, are particularly sick when they are old because they were sick when they were young. The diseases of their age are the inheritance of the slum conditions, the unhygienic tenements, the disease of their whole lives. But many of these conditions, the Government reports point out, could have been corrected earlier. If the culture of poverty were attacked at its roots, that would have the automatic effect of decreasing the misery of old age in the United States.

But physical health among the aged is only part of the story. The declining years are a time of mental distress in America today. For some, it is part of the psychological process of growing old, and it culminates in senility. Until advances are made in medicine, this suffering is unavoidable. But for others, the social conditions of being poor are a major element in their torment.

Dr. Maurice Linden of the Philadelphia Public Health Service summarized the situation a few years ago: ". . . some of the major factors that contribute to the development of emotional problems in our senior citizens are social rejection of the aged, the diminution in the circle of friendly associates, intense loneliness, reduction and loss of their feeling of self-esteem, and their own sense of self-rejection."

All these conditions are most prevalent, of course, in the other America. To deal with them, Dr. Linden notes, there is a need for individualized and personal therapy. The pessimistic, depressed, bewildered old person cannot be given a sense of dignity through some gigantic collective operation. His problem is precisely a loss in his own sense of individual worth and a lack of human relationships.

America's answer to this situation has been the "nursing home." In 1960 they had a population of 500,000 in some 25,000 units. According to the Senate report, only 58 per cent of these were considered acceptable by Government standards. And these figures understate the gravity of the problem, for they exclude unlicensed homes and units with three beds or less.

There is a licensing system for these homes in most states, and some of the outrageous conditions (such as firetrap houses for old people) have been brought under control in many areas. But that is only the regulation of the most minimal, physical conditions under which these places operate. Many of them have untrained personnel who have none of the skills required to bring dignity and warmth into the lives of the elderly. The care they provide is limited: sometimes it is merely to offer a place to await death, with three meals a day.

The Senate report was understandably bitter when it dealt with these institutions. It summarized them aptly by saying that they had a "storage bin" philosophy.

Who should take care of these people? And how should it be done?

One opinion study, cited by the Senate report, documents the American feeling that these problems of age and the aged should be taken care of by the Federal Government. Washington was listed first as the place with responsibility; state governments were second, employers third, and the family fourth.

At first glance this might seem to be callous indifference. And indeed, it does reflect an America obsessed by youth and frightened by age and death. The old, in such a land, are to be kept out of sight and mind. But that is not the only element in this judgment. It is a fact that the problems of the aged are so great that families, probably the majority of them in the nation, cannot really deal with them. The psychological torment requires skilled care; the medical difficulties run up staggering bills. There is literally no alternative but governmental intervention.

During the fifties, for example, all costs on the Consumer Price Index went up by 12 per cent. But medical costs, that terrible staple of the aged, went up by 36 per cent, hospitalization rose by 65 per cent, and group hospitalization costs (Blue Cross premiums) were up by 83 per cent. These figures have clearly priced the care of the aged out of the budget of millions of American families. The Federal legislation now being put forward will make a start toward correcting the problem, but it is woefully inadequate to the total need.

If it is clear that the Government is the only institution in the society capable of dealing with the problems of the aged, the question of exactly how it should proceed is not so obvious. In these few pages, let me draw a few general conclusions from the analysis of the culture of aged poverty in the other America.

First, there is the possibility of prevention, noted before. Cut down on disease and inadequate medical care during youth and middle age, and you eliminate some of the most unnecessary misery of the elderly.

Second, medical care is obviously the single greatest item in the budget of aged poverty. If this financial pressure were taken off the elderly, their lives would immediately be brightened.

Third, it must be emphasized and emphasized again that the old people, of all the citizens of America, are the most victimized by bureaucratic routine. All their ills and disabilities ultimately express themselves in a feeling of social rejection and puzzlement. It would be possible to provide care for their bodies and still leave their spirits filled with bitterness. At every point in a policy to deal with the problems of aging, this special need must be taken into account. Medical programs must be designed with a maximum of personal care; special housing must be created that takes into account the infirmities of the aged poor; and so on.

How does one get this kind of individualized and human care? To begin with, by paying for it. If there were adequate funds, if the social workers were not overwhelmed by their case load, if the clinics were sufficiently manned and equipped, then it would be possible to escape from many of the evils of a bureaucratic regimen. Those who criticize the impersonality of the welfare state and call for a return to the virtues of individual charity have located a very real problem—and proposed an impossible solution. Individual charity and private pension plans account for only a fraction of the needs of these people. To introduce human and individual relations between the aging and the society requires, not the restriction of the welfare state, but the going beyond it.

And finally, perhaps the most important thing that must be done with regard to the aged is to change our operative philosophy about them. We have, as the Senate Committee well described it, a "storage bin" philosophy in America. We "maintain" the aged; we give them the gift of life, but we take away the possibility of dignity. Perhaps one of the most basic reasons why America has such problems with its elderly men and women is that America really doesn't care about them.

These are only a few broad suggestions for an approach to the problem of aged poverty in the United States. If these ideas, or better ones, are not taken up, if something drastic is not done, then one of the most dramatic areas of increase in poverty in the United States will be among those over sixty-five.

As of now, the situation is extreme. There are some 8,000,000 or more people living in the most miserable of conditions. They are the rural aged poor who were never covered by social security and who live in states with utterly inadequate welfare systems. They are the urban poor, some of them born to poverty, some of them experiencing the humiliating experience of recruitment to poverty. They are the lonely and rejected.

In one of his books, Justice William O. Douglas spoke of a dilemma one encounters in an underdeveloped society. A swamp produces disease. For a few dollars, a plane can dust the area with DDT, and people will live. But then, should one do so if one does not increase the means of life at the same time? This terrible choice seems remote, a situation that India must solve but that is not really relevant to prosperous, wealthy America. Yet, it is descriptive of our situation. We have wiped out swamps in this land, and made it possible for people to live, for millions to survive past sixty-five. Only, we have done nothing more for them. We have given them bare survival, but not the means of living honorable and satisfactory lives as valued members of our society.

Seven: The Twisted Spirit

> We shall probably discover that the poor are even less ready
> to part with their neuroses than the rich, because the hard
> life that awaits them when they recover has no attraction,
> and illness in them gives them more claim to the help of
> others.
>
> —SIGMUND FREUD

There are few people in the United States who accept Rousseau's
image of the "noble savage," of primitive, untutored man as being
more natural than, and superior to, his civilized descendants. Such
an idea could hardly survive in a society that has made technological progress one of its most central values. There are occasional
daydreams about "getting away from it all," of going to an idyllic
countryside, but these are usually passing fancies.

Yet, there is a really important remnant of Rousseau's myth. It
is the conviction that, as far as emotional disturbance and mental
disease go, the poor are noble savages and the rich are the prime
victims of tension and conflict.

There are the literature of the harried executive, the tales of
suburban neurosis, the theme of the danger of wealth and leisure.
It is not so much that anyone says that the poor are healthy in

spirit because they are deprived of material things. Rather, the poor are just forgotten, as usual. The novels and the popular sociology are written by the middle class about the middle class, and there is more than a little strain of self-pity. The result is an image in which personal maladjustment flourishes at the top of the society, the price the well-off pay for their power. As you go down the income scale, this theory implies, life becomes more tedious and humdrum, if less upset. (However, it should be noted that the white-collar strata have the chronicler of their quiet desperation in Paddy Chayevsky.)

The truth is almost exactly opposite to the myth. The poor are subject to more mental illness than anyone else in the society, and their disturbances tend to be more serious than those of any other class. This conclusion has emerged from a series of studies made over the past few decades. There is still considerable controversy and disagreement with regard to the reasons behind this situation. But the fact itself would seem to be beyond dispute.

Indeed, if there is any point in American society where one can see poverty as a culture, as a way of life, it is here. There is, in a sense, a personality of poverty, a type of human being produced by the grinding, wearing life of the slums. The other Americans feel differently than the rest of the nation. They tend to be hopeless and passive, yet prone to bursts of violence; they are lonely and isolated, often rigid and hostile. To be poor is not simply to be deprived of the material things of this world. It is to enter a fatal, futile universe, an America within America with a twisted spirit.

I

Perhaps the most classic (but still controversial) study of this subject is the book *Social Class and Mental Illness* by August B. Hollingshead and F. C. Redlich. Published in 1958, it summarizes a careful research project in New Haven, Connecticut. It is an academic, scholarly work, yet its statistics are the description of an abyss.

Hollingshead and Redlich divided New Haven into five social

classes. At the top (Class I) were the rich, usually aristocrats of family as well as of money. Next came the executives and professionals more newly arrived to prestige and power. Then, the middle class, and beneath them, the workers with decent paying jobs. Class V, the bottom class, was made up of the poor. About half of its members were semiskilled, about half unskilled. The men had less than six years of education, the women less than eight.

As it turned out, this five-level breakdown was more revealing than the usual three-class image of American society (upper, middle, and lower). For it showed a sharp break between Class V at the bottom and Class IV just above it. In a dramatic psychological sense, the skilled unionized worker lived much, much closer to the middle class than he did to the world of the poor. Between Class IV and Class V, Hollingshead and Redlich found a chasm. This represents the gulf between working America, which may be up against it from time to time but which has a certain sense of security and dignity, and the other America of the poor.

Perhaps the most shocking and decisive statistic that Hollingshead and Redlich found was the one that tabulated the rate of treated psychiatric illness per 100,000 people in New Haven. These are their results:

Classes I and II	556 per 100,000
Class III	538
Class IV	642
Class V	1,659

From the top of society down to the organized workers, there are differences, but relatively small ones. But suddenly, when one crosses the line from Class IV to Class V, there is a huge leap, with the poor showing a rate of treated psychiatric illness of almost three times the magnitude of any other class.

But the mental suffering of the poor in these figures is not simply expressed in gross numbers. It is a matter of quality as well. In Classes I and II, 65 per cent of the treated psychiatric illness is for neurotic problems, and only 35 per cent for the much graver disturbances of psychoses. But at the bottom, in Class V, 90 per cent of the treated illness is for psychosis, and only 10 per cent for neurosis. In short, not only the rate but also the intensity of mental illness is much greater for the poor.

One of the standard professional criticisms of Hollingshead and Redlich is that their figures are for treated illness (those who actually got to a doctor or clinic) and do not indicate the "true prevalence" of mental illness in the population. Whatever merits this argument has in relation to other parts of the study, it points up that these particular figures are an understatement of the problem. The higher up the class scale one is, the more likely that there will be recognition of mental illness as a problem and that help will be sought. At the bottom of society, referral to psychiatric treatment usually comes from the courts. Thus, if anything, there is even more mental illness among the poor than the figures of Hollingshead and Redlich indicate.

The one place where this criticism might have some validity is with regard to the intensity of emotional disturbance. Only 10 per cent of the poor who received treatment are neurotics, yet the poor neurotic is the least likely person in the society to show up for treatment. He can function, if only in an impaired and maimed way. If there were something done about this situation, it is quite possible that one would find more neurosis in the other America at the same time as one discovered more mental illness generally.

However, it is not necessary to juggle with statistics and explanations in order to corroborate the main drift of the New Haven figures. During the fifties the Cornell University Department of Psychiatry undertook an ambitious study of "Midtown," a residential area in New York City. The research dealt with a population of 170,000 from every social class, 99 per cent of them white. (By leaving out the Negroes, there probably was a tendency to underestimate the problem of poverty generally, and the particular disabilities of a discriminated minority in particular.) The goal of the study was to discover "true prevalence," and there was interviewing in depth.

The Cornell scholars developed a measure of "mental health risk." They used a model of three classes, and consequently their figures are not so dramatic as those tabulated in New Haven. Yet they bear out the essential point: the lowest class had a mental health risk almost 40 per cent greater than the highest class. Once again the world of poverty was given definition as a spiritual and emotional reality.

The huge brute fact of emotional illness in the other America is fairly well substantiated. The reasons behind the fact are the subject of considerable controversy. There is no neat and simple summary that can be given at the present time, yet some of the analyses are provocative for an understanding of the culture of poverty even if they must be taken tentatively.

One of the most interesting speculations came from the Cornell study of "Midtown" in New York City. The researchers developed a series of "stress factors" that might be related to an individual's mental health risk. In childhood, these were poor mental health on the part of the parents, poor physical health for the parents, economic deprivation, broken homes, a negative attitude on the part of the child toward his parents, a quarrelsome home, and sharp disagreements with parents during adolescence. In adult life, the stress factors were poor health, work worries, money worries, a lack of neighbors and friends, marital worries, and parental worries.

The Cornell team then tested to see if there was any relationship between these factors and mental health. They discovered a marked correlation. The person who had been subjected to thirteen of these stress factors was three times more likely to be mentally disturbed than the person who had felt none of them. Indeed, the researchers were led to conclude that the sheer number of stress factors was more important than the quality of stresses. Those who had experienced any three factors were of a higher mental risk than those who had experienced two.

If the Cornell conclusions are validated in further research, they will constitute an important revision of some widely held ideas about mental health. The Freudian theory has emphasized the earliest years and the decisive trauma in the development of mental illness (for example, the death of a parent). This new theory would suggest a more cumulative conception of mental illness: as stress piles upon stress over a period of time, there is a greater tendency toward disturbance. It would be an important supplement to the Freudian ideas.

But if this theory is right, there is a fairly obvious reason for the emotional torment of the other America. The stress factors listed by the Cornell study are the very stuff of the life of the poor: physical illness, broken homes, worries about work and money, and all the rest. The slum, with its vibrant, dense life hammers away at the individual. And because of the sheer, grinding, dirty experience of being poor, the personality, the spirit, is impaired. It is as if human beings dilapidate along with the tenements in which they live.

However, some scholars have attempted to soften the grimness of this picture with a theory about "drift." The poor, they argue, have a high percentage of disturbed people, not because of the conditions of life in the urban and rural slums, but because this is the group that gets all the outcasts of society from the rest of the classes. If this thesis were true, then one would expect to find failures from the higher classes as a significant group in the culture of the poor.

Hollingshead and Redlich tested this theory in New Haven and did not find any confirmation for it. The mentally impaired poor had been, for the most part, born poor. Their sickness was a product of poverty, instead of their poverty being a product of sickness. Similarly, in the Midtown study, no evidence was turned up to indicate that the disturbed poor were the rejects from other classes. There are some exceptions to this rule: alcoholics, as noted before, often tend to fall from a high position into the bitterest poverty. Still, current research points to a direct relationship between the experience of poverty and emotional disturbance.

And yet, an ironic point turned up in the Midtown research. It was discovered that a certain kind of neurosis was useful to a minority of poor people. The obsessive-compulsive neurotic often got ahead: his very sickness was a means of advancement out of the other America and into the great world. And yet, this might only prepare for a later crisis. On the lower and middle rungs of business society, hard work, attention to detail, and the like are enough to guarantee individual progress. But if such a person moves across the line, and is placed in a position where he must make decisions, there is the very real possibility of breakdown.

II

Someone in trouble, someone in sorrow, a fight between neighbors, a coffin carried from a house, were things that coloured their lives and shook down fiery blossoms where they walked.

—SEAN O'CASEY

The feelings, the emotions, the attitudes of the poor are different. But different from what? In this question there is an important problem of dealing with the chaotic in the world of poverty.

The definition makers, the social scientists, and the moralists come from the middle class. Their values do not include "a fight between neighbors" as a "fiery blossom." Yet that is the fact in the other America. (O'Casey was talking about Ireland; he might as well have been describing any slum in the United States.) Before going on and exploring the emotional torment of the poor, it would be well to understand this point.

Take the gangs. They are violent, and by middle-class standards they are antisocial and disturbed. But within a slum, violence and disturbance are often norms, everyday facts of life. From the inside of the other America, joining a "bopping" gang may well not seem like deviant behavior. It could be a necessity for dealing with a hostile world. (Once, in a slum school in St. Louis, a teacher stopped a fight between two little girls. "Nice girls don't fight," she told them. "Yeah," one of them replied, "you should have seen my old lady at the tavern last night.")

Indeed, one of the most depressing pieces of research I have ever read touches on this point. H. Warren Dunham carefully studied forty catatonic schizophrenics in Chicago in the early forties. He found that none of them had belonged to gangs or had engaged in the kind of activity the middle class regards as abnormal. They had, as a matter of fact, tried to live up to the standards of the larger society, rather than conforming to the values of the slum. "The catatonic young man can be described as a good boy and one who has all the desirable traits which all the social agencies would like to inculcate in the young men of the community."

The middle class does not understand the narrowness of its judgments. And worse, it acts upon them as if they were universal and accepted by everyone. In New Haven, Hollingshead and Redlich found two girls with an almost identical problem. Both of them were extremely promiscuous, so much so that they eventually had a run-in with the police. When the girl from Class I was arrested, she was provided with bail at once, newspaper stories were quashed, and she was taken care of through private psychotherapy. The girl from Class V was sentenced to reform school. She was paroled in two years, but was soon arrested again and sent to the state reformatory.

James Baldwin made a brilliant and perceptive application of this point to the problem of the Negro in a speech I heard not long ago. The white, he said, cannot imagine what it is like to be Negro: the danger, the lack of horizon, the necessity of always being on guard and watching. For that matter, Baldwin went on, the Negro problem is really the white problem. It is not the Negro who sets dark skin and kinky hair aside as something fearful, but the white. And the resolution of the racial agony in America requires a deep introspection on the part of the whites. They must discover themselves even more than the Negro.

This is true of all the juvenile delinquents, all the disturbed people, in the other America. One can put it baldly: their sickness is often a means of relating to a diseased environment. Until this is understood, the emotionally disturbed poor person will probably go on hurting himself until he becomes a police case. When he is finally given treatment, it will be at public expense, and it will be inferior to that given the rich. (In New Haven, according to Hollingshead and Redlich, the poor are five times more likely to get organic therapy—including shock treatment—rather than protracted, individual professional care.)

For that matter, some of the researchers in the field believe that sheer ignorance is one of the main causes of the high rate of disturbance among the poor. In the slum, conduct that would shock a middle-class neighborhood and lead to treatment is often considered normal. Even if someone is constantly and violently drunk, or beats his wife brutally, people will say of such a person, "Well, he's a little odd." Higher up on the class scale an individual with such a problem would probably realize that something was wrong (or his family would). He will have the knowledge and the money to get help.

One of the researchers in the field who puts great stress on the "basic universals" of the Freudian pattern (mother figure, father figure, siblings) looks upon this factor of ignorance as crucial. He is Dr. Lawrence Kubie. For Dr. Kubie, the fundamental determinants of mental health and illness are the same in every social class. But culture and income and education account for whether the individual will handle his problem; whether he understands himself as sick; whether he seeks help, and so on. This theory leaves the basic assumptions of traditional psychoanalysis intact, but, like any attempt to deal with the poor, it recognizes that something is different.

For the rich, then, and perhaps even for the better-paid worker, breakdowns, neurosis, and psychosis appear as illness and are increasingly treated as such. But the poor do not simply suffer these disturbances; they suffer them blindly. To them it does not appear that they are mentally sick; to them it appears that they are trapped in a fate.

III

Much of this can be made specific if one looks at the grim winter of 1960–1961. This was a time of unemployment, of lagging production, of general economic downturn. The statistics of the Gross National Product in this period were familiar to every newspaper reader in the nation. But behind them was a correlation between social tragedy and emotional disturbance.

During this time the National Federation of Settlements and Neighborhood Centers collected data from its agencies across the United States. Some of them were reporting on the inhabitants of the other America; others were describing the impact of a recession on organized workers who had made a good wage before the bottom dropped out of the economy. But in every case there is a sense of the way in which a social fact has its impact upon the delicate structure of a human personality, upon marriage and hope itself:

Rochester, New York: We are especially concerned about the effect [of the recession] on family life. Unemployment often leads to marital discord and desertions of families by the father, increased welfare dependency, increased crime, especially robberies, burglaries and muggings, and alcoholism among both teens and adults. . . . The "A" family—father, mother, and six children. The father separated but provided $35 per week support until recently unemployed. Mother received Aid to Dependent Children, applied for additional assistance and was informed that oldest boy, senior in high school, not eligible because of age. Assistance arranged but mother passes stresses and strains on to son who feels he should quit school and get a job. (Not a realistic possibility.) Settlement must support son to stay in school without guilt feelings, help mother not to take anxieties out on son. Boy does well scholastically, is outstanding athlete and has excellent chances to go to college, which he wanted to do until current economic crisis occurred. But now questions this.

Chicago, Illinois: There has been a 30% increase in unemployment since September, 1960. . . .
This is creating criminal elements not before known to the

community. Some are seeking some form of public assistance, thus overloading the rolls when found eligible. Loss of dignity because they are no longer able to support their family.

A 33-year-old man known to our agency was found hanged in his apartment just seven hours ago. He was apparently despondent over not being able to find a job, and unemployment compensation had been exhausted. His wife and four children had left him and had returned to Mississippi where they had immigrated from seven years ago. The family had been several months arrears in rent, and there was not proper food and clothing for the family during the harsh Chicago winter months.

Schenectady, New York: Among children and youth, resistance to paying fees, lack of pocket money for candy and pop, attendance at few movies. Concern about cost for social dances, general appearance, talk about enlisting in military service.

Young adults, lessening of aggressiveness in job-hunting pursuits, little conversation about the future, much conversation about getting out of town, greater lethargy about belonging, and doing more pocketing—"Ghettoizing" provincialism, small cliques who band together with beer, cards, and TV.

Cleveland, Ohio: Garnishments, overbuying on credit, increased dependency, crime.

Lorain, Ohio: "Rising tide of appeals to private and public agencies. Family frustrations, sharp upcurve in children's illness and mental illness among the adults. Families are afraid to call the doctor because of lack of money to pay him and for medicine. One child almost died of pneumonia and family was charged with neglect. Fathers feel obliged to abandon families so that they will receive help more quickly.

Chicago, Illinois: The situation is serious here, probably as serious as in any other part of Chicago. The problem is complicated by the type of people in this area. They are, for the most part, unskilled laborers with little education, a language handicap and limited work experience. This means that they can do one type of work. When that job is not available they are unlikely to be transferred to another job or promoted.

Worried men and women, neglected health needs such as

glasses, medical care and medicine, evictions, desertion of wage earner, creditors repossessing furniture and cars because payment cannot be met, and inadequate diets.

The group work staff reports that children have no money for bus fares; the girls in sewing class have no money for sewing material; children less warmly dressed; and the need of haircuts . . .

Detroit, Michigan: Junior club members have been unable to pay the fifty cents annual membership fee. At Christmas children mentioned that they did not expect to receive any toys or new clothes. Adults sit home and when visited by settlement staff look helpless, depressed and not interested in participating in neighborhood life. "What's the use?" they ask. We have observed increased drunkenness among men and women to pass the time. Some neighbors are drinking Hadacol, a patent medicine.

In family camp last July, leaders observed that children who came to the program without breakfast ate and drank the milk with great relish. The mothers of the hungry children tried to cover up the reason for not serving breakfast at home. One mother with a large family told of going home to prepare a main meal of bread and spaghetti without meat. Another time this mother brought a poor-looking cake with peculiar icing for her contribution to the refreshments of a family life meeting. Her white and Negro neighbors who specialized in cake decorating rejected the cake, and the staff members were the only ones who ate it at the meeting.

Chicago, Illinois: With unemployment and the fear of it come an increase in tensions within the home, a tendency toward more rebellion and deviant behavior on the part of pre-teens and teens, etc. Practically every family situation is a multi-problem one.

Seattle, Washington: Personal depression and loss of personal value. One man in a housing project told us: "I have been out of work for nine months. I feel like half a man."

Some of these people, it is clear, are the inhabitants of the other America. But some of them are workers who are being pushed down, and the social chaos which these reports convey is another aspect of the attack upon the living standard of the middle third who gained through the rise of trade unionism. Moreover, these observations chronicle only the effects of a recession. But then these conditions are permanent in the culture of poverty; they persist in good times as well as in bad. The broken marriages, the drunkenness, the crime that comes to a neighborhood which once had known prosperity is a regular, daily aspect of life in the other America.

In this context, one might well take the word "depression" in a double sense, as applying to the human spirit as well as to the national economy. The people who are put down like this, who feel their social existence as if it were a futile fate imposed on them from above and without—these are the ones who swell the statistics of the mental health researchers in New Haven and Midtown, New York.

IV

Out of all this, the research more and more suggests, there emerges the personality of poverty, the "typical citizen" of the other America.

This is how the Midtown researchers described the "low social economic status individual": they are "rigid, suspicious and have a fatalistic outlook on life. They do not plan ahead, a characteristic associated with their fatalism. They are prone to depression, have feelings of futility, lack of belongingness, friendliness, and a lack of trust in others." Translated into the statistics of the Midtown study, this means that the bottom of the society is three times more emotionally depressed than the top (36.2 per cent for the low, 11.1 per cent for the high).

A small point: America has a self-image of itself as a nation of joiners and doers. There are social clubs, charities, community drives, and the like. Churches have always played an important social role, often marking off the status of individuals. And yet this entire structure is a phenomenon of the middle class. Some time ago, a study in Franklin, Indiana, reported that the percentage of people in the bottom class who were without affiliations of any kind was eight times as great as the percentage in the high-income class.

Paradoxically, one of the factors that intensifies the social isolation of the poor is that America thinks of itself as a nation without social classes. As a result, there are few social or civic organizations that are separated on the basis of income and class. The "working-class culture" that sociologists have described in a country like England does not exist here, or at least it is much less of a reality. The poor person who might want to join an organization is afraid. Because he or she will have less education, less money, less competence to articulate ideas than anyone else in the group, they stay away.

Thus, studies of civilian-defense organizations during World War II showed that almost all the members were white-collar people. Indeed, though one might think that the poor would have more friends because they are packed densely together, there are studies that indicate that they are deprived in this regard, too. In one report, 47 per cent of the lower-class women said that they had no friend or no intimate friend.

Such a life is lonely; it is also insecure. In New Haven, Hollings-head and Redlich could find only 19 per cent of the people in the bottom class who thought that their jobs were safe. The Yale group described 45 per cent of the poor as "inured," and found that their motto was "We take what the tide brings in."

This fatalism is not, however, confined to personal experience alone, to expectations about job and family. It literally permeates every aspect of an individual's life; it is a way of seeing reality. In a poll the Gallup organization did for *Look* magazine in 1959 (a projection of what people anticipated in the sixties), the relationship between social class and political pessimism was striking. The bottom group was much more likely to think that World War III was coming, that a recession was around the corner, that they would not take a vacation in the coming year. As one went up the income scale, the opinion of the world tended to brighten.

This pessimism is involved in a basic attitude of the poor: the fact that they do not postpone satisfactions, that they do not save. When pleasure is available, they tend to take it immediately. The smug theorist of the middle class would probably deplore this as showing a lack of traditional American virtues. Actually, it is the logical and natural pattern of behavior for one living in a part of American life without a future. It is, sad to say, a piece of realism, not of vice.

Related to this pattern of immediate gratification is a tendency on the part of the poor to "act out," to be less inhibited, and sometimes violent. There are some superficial observers who give this aspect of slum life a Rousseauistic twist. They find it a proof of the vitality, of the naturalness of the poor who are not constrained by the conventions of polite society. It would be hard to imagine a more wrongheaded impression. In the first place, this violence is the creature of that most artificial environment the slum. It is a product of human density and misery. And far from being an aspect of personality that is symptomatic of health, it is one more way in which the poor are driven to hurt themselves.

If one turns to the family life of the other America, there is an almost summary case of the dislocation and strains at the bottom of society.

In New Haven, for instance, Hollingshead and Redlich found that in Class V (the poor) some 41 per cent of the children under seventeen lived in homes that had been disrupted by death, desertion, separation, or divorce. This, of course, has profound consequences for the personalities of the young people involved. (This would be an instance in which the traditional Freudian account of mental illness would be relevant to the other America. An unstable family structure, with a father or mother figure absent, would predict devastating personal consequences.)

Then, the types of family structure the Yale researchers found among the poor are important. Some 44 per cent of the children lived in "nuclear families," which unite father, mother, and children. But 23 per cent grew up in a "generation stem family," where different generations are thrown together, usually with a broken marriage or two. Under such circumstances there is the possibility of endless domestic conflict between the different generations (and this is exacerbated when the old people are immigrants with a foreign code). Another 18 per cent came from broken homes where one or the other parent was absent. And 11 per cent had experienced the death of a parent.

Another aspect of this family pattern is sexual. In New Haven the researchers found that it was fairly common for young girls in the slums to be pregnant before they were married. I saw a similar pattern in St. Louis. There, children had a sort of sophisticated ignorance about sexual matters at an early age. Jammed together in miserable housing, they knew the facts of sex from firsthand observation (though often what they saw was a brutalized and drunken form of sex). In this sense, they were much more sophisticated than the children in middle-class neighborhoods.

But the poor are never that really well informed. As noted before, along with a cynical version of the facts of life there went an enormous amount of misinformation. For instance, young girls were given systematic miseducation on the menstrual period. They were often frightened and guilt ridden about sex at the same time that they were sophisticated.

And finally, the family of the poor lives cheek and jowl with other families of the poor. The sounds of all the quarreling and fights of every other family are always present if there happens to be a moment of peace in one household. The radio and the television choices of the rest of the block are regularly in evidence. Life is lived in common, but not in community.

So it is that the adolescents roam the streets. For the young, there is no reason to stay around the house. The street is a moment of relief, relaxation, and excitement. The family, which should be a bulwark against the sheer physical misery of the poor, is overwhelmed by the environment.

In this context, some of the rhetorical pieties of this society take on an unwitting irony. For example, here is Mayor Wagner of New York discussing the role of the promiscuous, addicted, violent girls in the gang wars of his city: "Of course, he continued, the ultimate prevention of delinquency must begin in the home. Nothing the

Government of the community can do, he said, will substitute for the reassertion of parental control."

The only trouble with this familiar formula is that delinquency begins in the home and that these girls are, in all probability, fleeing a domestic shambles. To wait around until parental authority reasserts itself under the present conditions is to wait forever. The Government and the community must first make it possible for there to be a "home" in the deepest sense of the word. But that, of course, means massive action against the culture of poverty in the other America.

V

Poverty is expensive to maintain.

The tensions, the chaos, the dislocations described in this chapter arc a major item in the budget of every municipality. In some cities a quarter of the annual funds are devoted to taking care of the special fire, police, and health problems created by the slums. The cost of keeping these people at the bottom year in and year out (rather than making an investment in real change once for all) is considerable.

Another aspect of the high cost of poverty was computed a few years ago by Ernest M. Gruenberg and Seymour S. Ballin. They estimated that there were 9,000,000 people in the United States "suffering from a wide range of diagnosible disorders." (The disorders referred to were emotional and mental.) Of these, 1,500,000 were hospital cases (but only half that number were in hospitals at a given time). These figures did not include the 1,500,000 who were mentally retarded.

In these statistics, one out of every sixteen persons in the United States was living an impaired life because of emotional disturbances. Gruenberg and Ballin suggest that mental illness of this magnitude causes the loss of a billion dollars in wages every year. And they compute the Government expenditures in dealing with the problem at a little over a billion dollars. (This does not count the money spent by private agencies.) Thus, the immediate cost of these illnesses is over two billion dollars.

A major component of this enormous loss is provided by the other America. And, as noted before, their torment is a form of realism.

The emotional turmoil of the poor is, as Freud intimates in the quotation prefacing this chapter, a form of protection against the turmoil of the society, a way of getting some attention and care in an uncaring world. Given this kind of "defense," it requires an enormous effort for these people to cross over into the great society.

Indeed, emotional upset is one of the main forms of the vicious circle of impoverishment. The structure of the society is hostile to these people: they do not have the right education or the right jobs, or perhaps there are no jobs to be had at all. Because of this, in a realistic adaptation to a socially perverse situation, the poor tend to become pessimistic and depressed; they seek immediate gratification instead of saving; they act out.

Once this mood, this unarticulated philosophy becomes a fact, society can change, the recession can end, and yet there is no motive for movement. The depression has become internalized. The middle class looks upon this process and sees "lazy" people who "just don't want to get ahead." People who are much too sensitive to demand of cripples that they run races ask of the poor that they get up and act just like everyone else in the society.

The poor are not like everyone else. They are a different kind of people. They think and feel differently; they look upon a different America than the middle class looks upon. They, and not the quietly desperate clerk or the harried executive, are the main victims of this society's tension and conflict.

Eight: Old Slums, New Slums

In 1949 the Housing Act authorized the construction of 810,000 new units of low-cost housing over a four-year period. Twelve years later, in 1961, the AFL-CIO proposed that the new housing law should provide for 400,000 units—in order to complete the total projected in 1949. The Kennedy Administration asked for 100,000 new units.

This has been one of the greatest single domestic scandals of postwar America. The statistics have all been nicely calculated; everyone knows the dimension of the problem; and articles appear regularly, predicting the next catastrophe that will come from inaction. But nothing is done to attack the basic problem, and poor housing remains one of the most important facts about the other America. This is where the nation builds the environment of the culture of poverty.

So it was that the 1960 census (these are preliminary figures) reported that 15.6 million of the 58,000,000 occupied dwelling units in the United States were substandard. This represented 27 per cent of the nation's total housing supply. Of these, some 3,000,000 were shacks, hovels, and tenements. Another 8.3 million units were "deteriorating," and 4.3 million units were structurally sound but lacking some or all of the essential plumbing facilities. In addition, these figures do not take account of "sound" housing that is terribly overcrowded.

As the AFL-CIO Civil Rights Department put it, "It seems, therefore, certain that 30 per cent of American families are living in substandard homes today." For those interested in historical echoes, that amounts to one third of a nation that is ill housed.

Perhaps a more dramatic statement of the problem was made by Charles L. Farris, the president of the National Association of Housing Officials: at the end of the fifties there were more Americans living in slums than on farms.

These figures apply only to the "old" slums, the obvious tenements and the broken-down houses. But the new public housing projects themselves have become a major problem. Many of them have become income ghettos, centers for juvenile gangs, modern poor farms where social disintegration is institutionalized. In addition, the destruction of old slum neighborhoods for public housing or Title I programs has resulted in mass evictions. The new public housing did not provide enough units for those who had been driven out to make way for improvement. The projects thus created new slums and intensified the pressures within the old slums, particularly for minority groups.

This grim inventory could be continued indefinitely, yet that would be to miss a major point about America's slums. The problem of housing is not simply a physical matter. In 1950, for instance, the Census defined "dilapidation" as occurring when "a dwelling unit is run down or neglected, or is of inadequate original construction so that it does not provide adequate shelter or protection against the elements or it endangers the safety of the occupants." Such a definition has a bureaucratic neatness to it, but it misses the very essence of what a slum is.

A slum is not merely an area of decrepit buildings. It is a social fact. There are neighborhoods in which housing is run-down, yet the people do not exhibit the hopelessness of the other Americans. Usually, these places have a vital community life around a national culture or a religion. In New York City, Chinatown is an obvious example. Where the slum becomes truly pernicious is when it becomes the environment of the culture of poverty, a spiritual and personal reality for its inhabitants as well as an area of dilapidation. This is when the slum becomes the breeding ground of crime, of vice, the creator of people who are lost to themselves and to society.

Thus, there are in the United States old slums where the buildings are miserable and decayed; and there are new slums in which the culture of poverty has been imported into modern housing projects. Both are parts of the other America.

I

First, take the obvious slum of tenements and hovels. The most important fact about these places in the sixties is that they are the environment of pessimism and of hopelessness.

Indeed, there is a sense in which the "old" slums are new. There once was a slum in American society that was a melting pot, a way station, a goad to talent. It was the result of the massive European immigration in the late nineteenth and early twentieth centuries. That flood of human vitality came to an end after World War I when the nation established quota systems, but the tradition of the ethnic groups survived for a generation. Symbolically, the tenements in which these newcomers lived had been built for them and had not been trickled down after the middle class found them inadequate. The neighborhoods were dense and the housing was inadequate, yet the people were not defeated by their environment. There was community; there was aspiration.

In most cities in the United States, it is still possible to take a bus or subway into this part of the American past. The Kerry Patch, the Ghetto, Little Italy, and other ethnic slums remain. Yet, like archaeological remnants of some dead culture, they are being buried under the new metropolis. Yet, even today, there is still a unique feeling of life in the remains of the old ethnic slums. The crowding gives rise to a lusty richness of existence. The children swarm on the streets throughout the day and into the early evening, but they rarely form themselves into violent gangs. If the neighborhood is strident, it is vital, too; if it is dotted with the signs of the Old Country, it is a way station to the new land as well.

I remember in the early fifties when I moved into a Jewish slum on the Lower East Side of New York. The first day in my new apartment, I went into a store on my block. After I had paid for my purchase, the man behind the counter said, "You live in 740, don't you?" The community was self-enclosed; it knew everyone, and could figure out the street number of a stranger within twenty-four hours. On Saturday, the streets were deserted for the Sabbath; on Sunday there was an air of festival and excitement.

From one point of view, these ghettoes were narrow, and there is no sense in romanticizing them, for they were also centers of poverty and physical misery. Yet George Orwell was right in saying that a good society would preserve one of these neighborhoods, not so much to show how bad life had been in the past, but rather to let people know how good it had been in spite of everything. Or, the insight can be put into the formal language of sociology. As Oscar Handlin wrote in *The Newcomers,* "The ethnic community supplied its members with norms and values and with the direction of an elite leadership." Tenements did not prevail against people.

Now the incredible American adventure of the ethnic slum is coming to an end. There are those from the old experience who remain behind—in New York, the Irish and Germans of the south Bronx, the Jews of Williamsburg, the Italians of the South Village. Some of them are elderly people who cannot wrench themselves from their past. Some are the failures who never succeeded in breaching the economic and social walls of the ghetto. So it is that a social worker in Brooklyn will tell you that some of the people evicted from tenements will move out to Long Island and buy a house. Or the priest in the church in the Melrose section of the Bronx will talk of the Irish and German poor who must come to the parish for help so that their children can get the right clothes for their first Holy Communion.

But those who stay behind face a harder task than the previous generation. They are separated from the culture of aspiration: the best have long since gone. Their children will have most of the disadvantages of the ghetto and few of the advantages, for they will grow up surrounded by those who failed and those who could never make the transition to the new land.

Where the ethnic slum once stood, in the "old" slum neighborhood, there is a new type of slum. Its citizens are the internal migrants, the Negroes, the poor whites from the farms, the Puerto Ricans. They join the failures from the old ethnic culture and form an entirely different kind of neighborhood. For many of them, the crucial problem is color, and this makes the ghetto walls higher than they have ever been. All of them arrive at a time of housing shortage (when the public housing program was first proposed in the thirties, around a quarter of the slum units were vacant), and thus it is harder to escape even when income rises. But, above all, these people do not participate in the culture of aspiration that was the vitality of the ethnic slum.

Most of the examples in this section are from New York, which is hardly a typical American city. It is more of a melting pot; it has more multiple dwellings (the euphemism for tenement); and there are other important differences. Yet the New York transition is being repeated in various ways across the nation. In Chicago, an important element is the Negro; in St. Louis, the white sharecropper; in Los Angeles, the Mexican-American. But in each case the internal migrant joins with the traditionalists and failures from the ethnic slum.

When you leave the subway at the Marcy Street stop in Williamsburg, the first thing you notice is a Spanish record playing, Spanish titles on the movie marquee, Spanish shops along the street. But then, next to these signs of the Puerto Rican migrants, there are the shops with Hebrew lettering in the window. And down the street there is the center for the remnants of an old German community. There is "integration" here—some of the tenements house Negroes, Puerto Ricans, and whites—but it is the integration of poverty, of rootless transients, of disintegration.

As a young priest at Holy Trinity sees his parish, it is made up of people on relief and of workers with low-paying jobs, many of them in the garment industry. There are three or four children to a family (the most typical family in the American culture of poverty has seven or more members), but those who stayed behind in the German community have not produced much of a neighborhood social life. There are few clubs, and the church is the center of what community life there is. The people, the priest continues, are very worried because a Title I project is moving into the area and will uproot them.

Down the street, at a community center, a social worker has a different perspective. For him the large fact is that 6,000 people have moved out in the recent past. The poor among them have gone to other slums, the better off to the suburbs. (In every slum in New York there is a group of people who have fairly decent incomes but who stay behind out of attachment to a neighborhood, a school, a church.) Since 1955 there has been a steady influx of Negroes and Puerto Ricans, and all this movement has produced an environment of social disintegration and with it violent gangs like the Phantom Lords and the Hell Burners. There is a low-cost housing project near by, but the natural leaders have been evicted because their income rose too quickly for the legal maximum.

Perhaps the most spectacular and visible effect of this transition is in juvenile delinquency. In his study of the New York gangs, Harrison Salisbury quoted a police estimate that there were 8,000 young people actively engaged in violent antisocial conduct, and another 100,000 who lived on the verge of this underworld, shuttling between it and the rest of society. Significantly, the gangs Salisbury described were often integrated, for this interracialism is regularly a basic component of these neighborhoods of transience.

Thus, the new form of the old slum. If the ethnic slum had been a narrow world of a single religion, language, and culture, it was also a goad toward the outside world. This new type of slum groups together failures, rootless people, those born in the wrong time, those at the wrong industry, and the minorities. It is "integrated" in many cases, but in a way that mocks the idea of equality: the poorest and most miserable are isolated together without consideration of race, creed, or color. They are practically forbidden any real relationship with the rest of society.

These neighborhoods have, of course, a solid economic base of poverty. In pointing to the cultural and psychological elements in the life of the new slum dweller, this cannot be forgotten for a moment.

In New York City, for instance, there are some 300,000 "hard core" Public Assistance cases. These are the mentally ill, the aged, the sick, and their children. In good times and in bad, they are ever present, inhabiting the slums and housing projects. In a recession like that of 1958, their number is immediately increased by a hundred thousand or so people who live on the verge of economic helplessness. But this group is only the beginning, for, according to the New York State Interdepartmental Committee on Low Incomes, they represent less than one-fourth of those actually qualified for Public Assistance. In other words, there is a basic group of 1,200,000 who lack the "basic necessities" (food, shelter, minimal medical care) and who qualify for Public Assistance.

In the late fifties, 26 per cent of the Public Assistance families in New York City lived in furnished rooms. Most of them will never work. There is another group living right next to them: the sweatshop operatives. In 1959 I. D. Robbins, president of the City Club of New York, testified before the State Commission on Governmental Operations that around 300,000 heads of families in New York City were making in the neighborhood of a dollar an hour (just a little better than $2,000 a year—if they received a year's work). He estimated that perhaps a fourth of the city budget —welfare, hospital, correction, fire, health, and school items—was attributable to "the enormous number of poor people living here."

In New York City, as one would expect, the minorities form an important part of the slum population. The Public Assistance recipients in the fifties included 31.3 per cent whites, 40.0 per cent Negroes, and 28.7 per cent Puerto Ricans. New York, with an estimated two million Negroes and Puerto Ricans in the metropolitan area, would show minority participation in the slum culture more dramatically than most cities. Yet, the Northern migration of Negroes is affecting almost every city outside the South (and the poor white farmers, probably not too important a group in New York, are a major factor in many Midwestern and border-state cities).

Income is one index of the slum dweller; health is another. According to the New York City Health Department, there was a direct correlation in 1959 between slums and infant mortality rates. In the "worst district" that the Health Department found, central Harlem, the infant mortality rate was three times that of the best district and had increased by more than 5 per cent since 1958.

The incomes are low; the housing is dilapidated; the health is bad. But now, it is important to trace the factors that intensify the pessimism and hopelessness that differentiate the new form of the slum from the old ethnic neighborhoods.

There is a wall around these slums that did not exist before: the suburbs. The President's Civil Rights Commission in 1959 reported that the suburban zoning laws keep out low-income housing and force the poor to remain in the decaying, central area of the cities. The very development of the metropolitan areas thus has the tendency to lock the door on the poor.

This becomes even more of a factor when one realizes how important color is in the new form of the old slums. There has never been a disability in American society to equal racial prejudice. It is the most effective single instrument for keeping people down that has ever been found. In this context, the decline of aspiration is partly a function of a sophisticated analysis of society: there *is* less opportunity than there was in the days of the huge ethnic slums. The people understand this even if they do not articulate it precisely.

Then, the ethnic slum usually centered upon a stable family life. The pattern of the slums of the sixties is "serial monogamy" where a woman lives with one man for a considerable period of time, bears his children, and then moves on to another man. In a National

Educational Association study, Walter B. Miller estimated that between a quarter and a half of the urban families in the United States are "female based." This holds most strongly in these slums.

For that matter, Miller and his colleague, William C. Kavaraceus, speak of a lower-class culture in the United States that embraces between 40 per cent and 60 per cent of the people. Not all of them are poor; not all of them are slum dwellers. But they share a common alienation from the middle-class norms of the society.

To be sure, the older ethnic slums produced their share of violence and gangsterism. Yet their family patterns, their value systems, their very access to the outside world provided a strong counterforce to the degradation of environment. In the new form of the slum, these checks are not so strong, and the culture of poverty becomes all the more powerful for that fact.

Lastly, the inhabitants of the slums of the sixties are regularly the victims of a bureaucratically enforced rootlessness. (This is still one more case of the "upside-down" welfare state, helping those least who need aid most.) The housing programs, and particularly the Urban Renewal activities of the mid- and late fifties, set off a migration within the cities. In 1959, for instance, the Mill Creek area of St. Louis was cleared as part of an urban renewal effort. In the place of a Negro slum there arose a middle-income housing development. Typically, the majority of those evicted were forced to find housing within the existing, and contracted, Negro ghetto. (In St. Louis 50 per cent of the families displaced disappeared from sight of the authorities altogether; of those whose movements are known, only 14 per cent found their way into low-cost projects.)

This constant movement makes it impossible for a community to develop in these slums. In 1958 a study in New York carried the poignant cry of an old resident in one of these transitional areas: "Nobody, not even an angel, can avoid trouble here! Too many people with no investment and no pride in the neighborhood! Too many just passing through! I feel sorriest for the kids—they've never known what a decent neighborhood is like!"

II

The current American answer to the problem of the slum is the low-cost housing project. The theory behind this approach contains at least the beginnings of an attack upon the culture of poverty: a public commitment to create a new environment for human beings.

But the practice has lagged far behind the intention. The concerned citizen, as noted earlier, sees that tenement eyesores have been torn down, and he is satisfied. He does not understand that the number of units that have been built do not equal the number that have been destroyed in clearing the project sites. In New York in 1954, for instance, there was one unit for every 7.1 eligible new families; in 1956, one for every 10.4 eligible new families. And these figures are roughly typical of the nation as a whole.

In some areas people who have priority for getting low-cost housing do not take advantage of it. Some refuse to go in because of their reputation for violence or because of their interracial character. Some are on the fly and fear any contact with the public authorities—and not necessarily because of crime; perhaps because of marriage irregularities, for instance. Still another group, according to Tom Wolfe of New York's Hudson Guild, simply do not know about the opportunity. Long-time citizens of the other America, they assume that there is no real hope, that no one is going to help them, and they vanish. That is one reason why over half of the people displaced by projects in the United States are listed on the records as "address unknown."

So, first of all, there is not enough public housing to go around. But there are some hundreds of thousands of people who have gone into projects recently, and their experience is perhaps even more significant than that of those who were simply displaced.

Probably the most dramatic and well-publicized failure of the housing project has been in the tendency toward violence, and juvenile crime in particular, in the low-cost projects. Harrison Salisbury's brilliant study of New York gangs, *The Shook-Up Generation,* centered on housing projects. Here is a vivid description of the way in which the culture of poverty persists within the new buildings:

Theirs [the gangs'] is a world of young people harshly buffeted by grim realities—poverty, hunger, physical hardship, danger, displacement, diseases and deprivation. Beset by force and violence they escape into paranoid visions of grandeur, daydreams of demonic power, ecstasies of sadism, endless fantasies with a gun.

In December, 1959, a Grand Jury investigation in St. Louis found a similar pattern in the projects of that city. "Generally speaking," the jury wrote of the housing developments, "the rates of crimes against the person—murder, rape, robbery and aggravated assault—is approximately two and a half times higher than the citywide average." And "based on testimony we have received, outside teenage hoodlums have used the project buildings for gambling, drinking and all kinds of minor crimes for which there has been, in the eyes of the tenants, little or no effective prosecution in the City Courts."

All of these facts are true and important in their own right, yet they have too much of a tabloid simplicity. There are projects without violent gangs (one of them will be discussed shortly). But even here, social disintegration continues, and this is perhaps the more important, more subtle thing to understand about America's response to the slum.

The projects, whether they have a juvenile problem or not, tend to be huge, impersonal, bureaucratic environments. This is often most disorienting to people transplanted from a slum community. Writing of a Lower East Side development in New York City, a young sociologist, Michael Miller, describes the way in which the people respond to their experience with administrative routine. The management is distant, and it represents powerful disciplinary authority. There are many rules, constant checking on violations, and all of the formalities of the bureaucratic world. For a Puerto Rican family, Miller points out, the first encounter with the eviction notice (sent out automatically when the rent is not paid by a certain day) is a perplexing, even a frightening, matter. They do not know that this is just a first step, that they are far from evicted, and that they still have rights. They come from a much more informal culture, and the whole affair seems strange to them. (Many observers have pointed out that the "rent girl," a sort of combination social worker and bill collector, was once a major, positive link between the people and the management.)

The result of all this is a considerable amount of confusion and fear on the part of the project dweller. How is he to cope with this distant, powerful authority? How is he to find an identity in the huge concrete building? It is an enormous jump from the teeming slum street to this modern administered existence. Indeed, some of the project dwellers are literally terrified at first by their new advantages. In St. Louis a social worker tells of encountering families who become constipated because of their perplexity in the presence of modern plumbing.

Poverty has a nose; the middle class does not. One of the most characteristic things about a tenement slum is that it smells: of cooking, of closely packed human beings, of bad plumbing. But in some projects, where the people have good sanitary facilities for the first time, the halls and elevators still become noisome with the odor of urine and feces. This is a most unmistakable sign of the survival of the old culture of poverty in the new hygienic environment.

Miller describes three "styles of life" that are the responses of the people in the Lower East Side project. One group adopts a strategy of complete withdrawal from whatever community the project affords. They isolate themselves in their own apartments, or else they maintain ties to some ethnic group of the old neighborhood on the outside. As a result, they are utterly alienated precisely when they are in their homes. At best, they must travel for friendship and social life; at worst, they become faceless.

Another group finds ethnic or religious identification inside the project. Miller describes the "bench culture" in front of the Lower East Side project: on the south side, the Jewish benches; across from them, the Puerto Ricans; and across the play area, the Negroes. Naturally enough, this situation causes hostilities and makes it extremely difficult for any effective kind of community to develop in the project as a whole, or for the Tenants' Association to become a meaningful instrument for dealing with management. Within the income ghetto, there emerge the subghettos, and the worst aspects of the old and new slums are merged and institutionalized.

A third group, Miller notes, works with the Tenants' Association. It is small, composed of the people within the project who are most adjusted to the world in which they live. By a predictable irony of bureaucratic practice, they have been the prime targets for eviction, for their incomes rise more rapidly than that of the rest of the project, and they are in constant danger of exceeding the maximum established by law. These activists can find a fairly rich life for themselves, yet, as a couple who are involved in tenant work in another project sadly pointed out, they often end up talking to one another, forming a sort of élite community. They do not have the resources to prevail against the environment.

Thus, the gang violence is but a symptom of a deeper process within the housing projects: the failure to develop a project community or (which is much more important) a community integrating the project and the surrounding neighborhood. Only one factor in the culture of poverty is changed by these high-rise buildings. Housing is no longer dilapidated. But the long schooling in the slums has built up a resistance to better times; the other elements of poverty remain; and the bureaucratic aspects of the new life promote alienation and rootlessness. In short, the other America survives in high style.

Most of these examples have been taken from projects with serious problems. But there is a development on the west side of Manhattan that has often been cited as an instance of what can be done. It is worth looking at for a moment.

Perhaps the most obvious advantage of this project is the existence of the Hudson Guild, an old, established community center that has had some success (and some controversial problems) in building a bridge between the newcomers and the older neighborhood. The Guild is opposed to the concept of the "project community" because it regards it as a form of segregation. So it has conceived of its work as covering the entire neighborhood. It has also employed closed-circuit television in an attempt to provide the project itself with an exciting means of communication. This experiment was not successful: according to the Guild, because of poor programing; according to some of the project people, because the system interfered with the reception of the regular commercial channels.

The surrounding neighborhood is itself more mixed than most of the slum areas that ring housing projects. A few blocks away is a large middle-class apartment house. The Irish and Italian workers have remained in considerable numbers, living in the "old-law" tenements that, under rent control, cost only $45 or $50 a month. In some cases old property has been rehabilitated, and this has brought a new stratum of middle-class people into the neighborhood. In the near future there will be a Garment Workers' Union Cooperative, and this will broaden the base of the community even more.

All in all, these factors add up to a considerable advantage for the project dwellers. The housing development itself is fairly well integrated (45 per cent of the residents are Puerto Rican, 25 per cent Negro, and 30 per cent white). Tenants with whom I talked could not recall seeing anything like the ethnic "bench culture" that Miller found on the Lower East Side. And there are no violent gangs that base themselves on the project in the surrounding neighborhood. There was one incident some time ago, but its exceptional character was demonstrated by the shock it inspired in Chelsea.

And yet it would seem that all this has not been enough to destroy the impact of poverty, the crushing inheritance of the past. A nursery in the Guild has difficulty in attracting people from the project, yet it can draw upon middle-class children who are sent from blocks away to take advantage of the facilities. This phenomenon, so common in the culture of poverty, is another case in point of the old problem: that it takes a certain level of aspiration before one can take advantage of opportunities that are clearly offered.

Or there is the story, told by some active members of the Tenants' Association, of a family with a substantial income. They have money, a low-rent apartment, and all the opportunities offered by groups like the Hudson Guild. But the attitudes toward education, the atmosphere of the home, the whole sorry pattern of old habits are stronger than the new reality. The children are indifferent in school, frightened of authority, marking time until they can take their assigned place in a low-income world.

Much of this can be summarized in the report of a single incident. One project family took their children and some of their playmates to the beach—hardly a difficult or expensive task for a New Yorker. When they came back, there were excitement and surprise at their adventure. People who had lived within a subway ride of the ocean for most of their lives had never seen it, and neither had their children. The trip to the beach required more than an afternoon and a subway token; it involved a transition in their values, one that they had not yet made.

After the family told me this story, I remembered a part of the novel *The Cool World*. A young Negro prostitute who has taken up with a gang longs to see the Pacific Ocean. When her boy friend tells her there is an ocean at New York's doorstep, called the Atlantic, she refuses to believe him at first. When I read this, I thought it was extreme. Now I know that it is one more description of the utter depth of the culture of poverty. It is something that simply cannot be done away with by a high-rise housing project.

In short, most public housing, even at its best, fails to solve the problem of the slum and, above all, the problem of slum psychology. In some cases the gains appear minimal, for one must balance the physical improvement (and, hopefully, the consequent improvement in health) against the new forms of alienation and, at the extreme, of violence. But, perhaps most crucial, the housing policy of

America has sought the integration of the poor with the poor—
which is to say, the segregation of the other Americans from the
society at large.

III

For some people the failures of public housing are cited as an
argument against national involvement in this problem. This is a
disastrous and wrongheaded deduction.

With all that has been said about the inadequacies of the housing projects, it is clear that only one agency in America is capable
of eradicating both the slum and slum psychology from this land:
the Federal Government. Time and time again, private builders
have demonstrated that they are utterly incapable of doing anything. If the Federal Government deserts the field, that would be
tantamount to a decision to enlarge the slums of America. A new
determination and imagination are needed, not a retreat.

The cost of an all-out attack upon the slums is measurable. In
1955 Joseph P. McMurray, then State Housing Commissioner of
New York (and now chairman of the Federal Home Loan Bank),
testified before the House Subcommittee on Housing. He estimated
that it would take $125,000,000,000 of public and private invest-
ment to end slums within twenty-five years. This, he said, would
require a combined program five times larger than the current Government commitment. Clearly, this is an expensive business; clearly
it is not beyond the bounds of possibility.

In 1961, Leon Keyserling, former chairman of the President's
Council of Economic Advisers, calculated that a serious attack
upon the problem would require about two million units a year for
the next four years. Of these, 1.2 million would be privately financed
housing for upper-middle-income families; about 500,000 would
be provided for lower-middle-income families (with some kind of
Government subsidies); and about 300,000 homes a year would
be brought into the reach of low-income families, including the
aging, through joint Federal and local contributions.

Predictably, the plans put forward by Washington as the sixties began fell far short of these appraisals. The Kennedy Administration proposed funds for 100,000 new low-income public-housing units (this would mean that the United States would still be short of the goals projected in 1949 for a four-year period!), and subsidies that would provide for about 75,000 middle-income housing units.

Second, under the present setup, it is the poor who are victimized by urban renewal. In 1959 Charles Abrams told a Senate Committee that the public housing program had become "tattered, perverted and shrunk . . . little more than an adjunct of the publicly subsidized private urban renewal program. This urban renewal program too, while it does help the cities to get rid of slums, has developed into a device for displacing the poor from their footholds to make way for higher rental dwellings which those displaced cannot afford. Thus, the lowest-income family remains the forgotten family, though it is still the most home-needy in the American family circle."

If these problems of financing are not solved, if America does not have the will to eradicate the slum in its midst, then no amount of imagination will deal with the situation. But if the will were there, if the money were appropriated, then there is a crying need for new directions in public housing.

Public housing must be conceived of as something more than improved physical shelter with heat and plumbing. It must be seen as an important organism for the creation of community life in the cities. First and foremost, public housing should avoid segregating the poor off in some corner of the metropolis. That is the "modern poor-farm mentality," as one critic described it. The projects and subsidized homes should be located as parts of neighborhoods, so that income groups, races, and cultures will mingle.

Many housing experts have already laid down some fairly obvious principles for accomplishing these ends. (The vision is not lacking; only the will.) For example, Charles L. Farris of St. Louis has proposed specific steps: low-cost and middle-income units should be interspersed, and there should be an attempt to integrate public housing with existing and vital neighborhoods. There should be a limit on building size (Farris suggests eight families) so as to avoid the creation of an impersonal, bureaucratic environment. And the private individual housing that still exists should become the focus of a campaign for rehabilitation.

Private ownership is one of the great myths of American life—for more than half the people do not, and cannot, own their homes. In 1959 Charles Abrams estimated that an annual income of over $6,000 was required before an American family could seriously think of buying a home. In 1957, for instance, less than 6 per cent of the families who purchased new homes under the FHA had incomes under $4,200. In other words, the upper half of the population benefited from this program to the extent of 94 per cent of the housing, while those who most desperately needed it shared 6 per cent of the total.

It would be magnificent if America were to make home ownership a goal of national policy. As it is today, the poor are completely excluded from this possibility, and even the great middle third of the income pyramid have considerable difficulties.

Where projects are undertaken (and it must be emphasized that the reference is not to huge high-rise ghettos, but to a new kind of public housing) there must be an adequate budget for social work. You cannot take people out of an old-fashioned slum, where reality has been giving them a grim, distorted education for years, place them in a project, and expect them to exhibit all kinds of gentle, middle-class virtues. This transition is a crucial moment. If the people are left to themselves, then the chances are that they will import the culture of poverty into the public housing. If they are helped, if there is real effort to forge neighborhood communities, this need not happen.

Many of the public-housing administrators are sincere and imaginative public servants, but they have been frustrated at every turn by the inadequacy of funds and by the fact that the nation has yet to make a real commitment to build a human environment.

And the cost? The point has already been made, but it deserves repeating: we already pay an inordinately high price for poverty in the United States. Misery generates social chaos, and it takes money just to police it, just to keep it from becoming so explosive that it will disturb the tranquillity of the better off. In cold cash-and-carry terms, there would be a long-range pay-off if slums were abolished in the United States. In human terms, such an action would mean that millions of people would be returned to the society and enabled to make their personal contribution.

At this writing, one must sadly report that it does not seem likely that there will be an adequate crusade to end the misery of the millions of Americans who live in substandard housing. The figures have all been tabulated; the reports are in; and the direction of human advance is clear. But, as the sixties open, there is not yet the political will to get at the root of the problem.

So the new form of the old slums will continue; the inadequacies and tragedies of our past public housing policy will remain with us; and that tenacious organism, the culture of poverty, will settle down comfortably in our urban rot.

Nine: The Two Nations

The United States in the sixties contains an affluent society within its borders. Millions and tens of millions enjoy the highest standard of life the world has ever known. This blessing is mixed. It is built upon a peculiarly distorted economy, one that often proliferates pseudo-needs rather than satisfying human needs. For some, it has resulted in a sense of spiritual emptiness, of alienation. Yet a man would be a fool to prefer hunger to satiety, and the material gains at least open up the possibility of a rich and full existence.

At the same time, the United States contains an underdeveloped nation, a culture of poverty. Its inhabitants do not suffer the extreme privation of the peasants of Asia or the tribesmen of Africa, yet the mechanism of the misery is similar. They are beyond history, beyond progress, sunk in a paralyzing, maiming routine.

The new nations, however, have one advantage: poverty is so general and so extreme that it is the passion of the entire society to obliterate it. Every resource, every policy, is measured by its effect on the lowest and most impoverished. There is a gigantic mobilization of the spirit of the society: aspiration becomes a national purpose that penetrates to every village and motivates a historic transformation.

But this country seems to be caught in a paradox. Because its poverty is not so deadly, because so many are enjoying a decent standard of life, there are indifference and blindness to the plight of the poor. There are even those who deny that the culture of poverty exists. It is as if Disraeli's famous remark about the two nations of the rich and the poor had come true in a fantastic fashion. At precisely that moment in history where for the first time a people have the material ability to end poverty, they lack the will to do so. They cannot see; they cannot act. The consciences of the well-off are the victims of affluence; the lives of the poor are the victims of a physical and spiritual misery.

The problem, then, is to a great extent one of vision. The nation of the well-off must be able to see through the wall of affluence and recognize the alien citizens on the other side. And there must be vision in the sense of purpose, of aspiration: if the word does not grate upon the ears of a gentile America, there must be a passion to end poverty, for nothing less than that will do.

In this summary chapter, I hope I can supply at least some of the material for such a vision. Let us try to understand the other America as a whole, to see its perspective for the future if it is left alone, to realize the responsibility and the potential for ending this nation in our midst.

But, when all is said and done, the decisive moment occurs after all the sociology and the description is in. There is really no such thing as "the material for a vision." After one reads the facts, either there are anger and shame, or there are not. And, as usual, the fate of the poor hangs upon the decision of the better-off. If this anger and shame are not forthcoming, someone can write a book about the other America a generation from now and it will be the same, or worse.

I

Perhaps the most important analytic point to have emerged in this description of the other America is the fact that poverty in America forms a culture, a way of life and feeling, that it makes a whole. It is crucial to generalize this idea, for it profoundly affects how one moves to destroy poverty.

The most obvious aspect of this interrelatedness is in the way in which the various subcultures of the other America feed into one another. This is clearest with the aged. There the poverty of the declining years is, for some millions of human beings, a function of the poverty of the earlier years. If there were adequate medical care for everyone in the United States, there would be less misery for old people. It is as simple as that. Or there is the relation between the poor farmers and the unskilled workers. When a man is driven off the land because of the impoverishment worked by technological progress, he leaves one part of the culture of poverty and joins another. If something were done about the low-income farmer, that would immediately tell in the statistics of urban unemployment and the economic underworld. The same is true of the Negroes. Any gain for America's minorities will immediately be translated into an advance for all the unskilled workers. One cannot raise the bottom of a society without benefiting everyone above.

Indeed, there is a curious advantage in the wholeness of poverty. Since the other America forms a distinct system within the United States, effective action at any one decisive point will have a "multiplier" effect; it will ramify through the entire culture of misery and ultimately through the entire society.

Then, poverty is a culture in the sense that the mechanism of impoverishment is fundamentally the same in every part of the system. The vicious circle is a basic pattern. It takes different forms for the unskilled workers, for the aged, for the Negroes, for the agricultural workers, but in each case the principle is the same. There are people in the affluent society who are poor because they are poor; and who stay poor because they are poor.

To realize this is to see that there are some tens of millions of Americans who are beyond the welfare state. Some of them are simply not covered by social legislation: they are omitted from Social Security and from minimum wage. Others are covered, but since they are so poor they do not know how to take advantage of the opportunities, or else their coverage is so inadequate as not to make a difference.

The welfare state was designed during that great burst of social creativity that took place in the 1930's. As previously noted its structure corresponds to the needs of those who played the most important role in building it: the middle third, the organized workers, the forces of urban liberalism, and so on. At the worst, there is "socialism for the rich and free enterprise for the poor," as when the huge corporation farms are the main beneficiaries of the farm program while the poor farmers get practically nothing; or when public funds are directed to aid in the construction of luxury housing while the slums are left to themselves (or become more dense as space is created for the well-off).

So there is the fundamental paradox of the welfare state: that it is not built for the desperate, but for those who are already capable of helping themselves. As long as the illusion persists that the poor are merrily freeloading on the public dole, so long will the other America continue unthreatened. The truth, it must be understood, is the exact opposite. The poor get less out of the welfare state than any group in America.

This is, of course, related to the most distinguishing mark of the other America: its common sense of hopelessness. For even when there are programs designed to help the other Americans, the poor are held back by their own pessimism.

On one level this fact has been described in this book as a matter of "aspiration." Like the Asian peasant, the impoverished American tends to see life as a fate, an endless cycle from which there is no deliverance. Lacking hope (and he is realistic to feel this way in many cases), that famous solution to all problems—let us educate the poor—becomes less and less meaningful. A person has to feel that education will do something for him if he is to gain from it. Placing a magnificent school with a fine faculty in the middle of a slum is, I suppose, better than having a run-down building staffed by incompetents. But it will not really make a difference so long as the environment of the tenement, the family, and the street counsels the children to leave as soon as they can and to disregard schooling.

On another level, the emotions of the other America are even more profoundly disturbed. Here it is not lack of aspiration and of hope; it is a matter of personal chaos. The drunkenness, the unstable marriages, the violence of the other America are not simply facts about individuals. They are the description of an entire group in the society who react this way because of the conditions under which they live.

In short, being poor is not one aspect of a person's life in this country; it is his life. Taken as a whole, poverty is a culture. Taken on the family level, it has the same quality. These are people who lack education and skill, who have bad health, poor housing, low levels of aspiration and high levels of mental distress. They are, in the language of sociology, "multiproblem" families. Each disability is the more intense because it exists within a web of disabilities. And if one problem is solved, and the others are left constant, there is little gain.

One might translate these facts into the moralistic language so dear to those who would condemn the poor for their faults. The other Americans are those who live at a level of life beneath moral choice, who are so submerged in their poverty that one cannot begin to talk about free choice. The point is not to make them wards of the state. Rather, society must help them before they can help themselves.

II

There is another view about the culture of poverty in America: that by the end of the seventies it will have been halved.

It is important to deal in some detail with this theory. To begin with, it is not offered by reactionaries. The real die-hards in the United States do not even know the poor exist. As soon as someone begins to talk on the subject, that stamps him as a humanitarian. And this is indeed the case with those who look to a relatively automatic improvement in the lot of the other America during the next twenty years or so.

The second reason why this view deserves careful consideration is that it rests, to a considerable extent, upon the projection of inevitable and automatic change. Its proponents are for social legislation and for speeding up and deepening this process. But their very arguments could be used to justify a comfortable, complacent inaction.

So, does poverty have a future in the United States?

One of the most reasonable and sincere statements of the theme that poverty is coming to an end in America is made by Robert Lampman in the Joint Committee Study Paper "The Low-Income Population and Economic Growth." Lampman estimates that around 20 per cent of the nation, some 32,000,000 people, are poor. (My disagreements with his count are stated in the Appendix.) And he writes, "By 1977–87 we would expect about 10 percent of the population to have low income status as compared to about 20 percent now."

The main point in Lampman's relatively optimistic argument is that poverty will decline naturally with a continuing rate of economic growth. As the sixties begin, however, this assumption is not a simple one. In the postwar period, growth increased until about the mid-fifties. Then a falling off occurred. In each of the postwar recessions, the recovery left a larger reservoir of "normal" prosperity unemployment. Also, long-term unemployment became more and more of a factor among the jobless. There were more people out of work, and they stayed out of work longer.

In the first period of the Kennedy Administration, various economists presented figures as to what kind of Government action was necessary so as really to attack the problem of depressed areas and low-income occupations. There were differences, of course, but the significant fact is that the legislation finally proposed was usually only a percentage of the need as described by the Administration itself. There is no point now in becoming an economic prophet.

Suffice it to say that serious and responsible economists feel that the response of the society has been inadequate.

This has led to a paradoxical situation, one that became quite obvious when economic recovery from the recession began in the spring of 1961. The business indicators were all pointing upward: production and productivity were on the increase. Yet the human indexes of recession showed a tenacity despite the industrial gain. Unemployment remained at high levels. An extreme form of the "class unemployment" described earlier seemed to be built into the economy.

At any rate, one can say that if this problem is not solved the other America will not only persist; it will grow. Thus, the first point of the optimistic thesis strikes me as somewhat ambiguous, for it too quickly assumes that the society will make the needed response.

But even if one makes the assumption that there will be steady economic growth, that will not necessarily lead to the automatic elimination of poverty in the United States. J. K. Galbraith, it will be remembered, has argued that the "new" poverty demonstrates a certain immunity to progress. In making his projection of the abolition of half of the culture of poverty within the next generation, Lampman deals with this point, and it is important to follow his argument.

Lampman rejects the idea that insular (or depressed-areas) poverty will really drag the poor down in the long run. As an example of this point, he cites the fact that the number of rural farm families with incomes of under $2,000 fell during the 1947–1957 period from 3.3 million to 2.4 million because of a movement off the farm.

This point illustrates the problem of dealing with simple statistics. A movement from the farm to the city, that is, from rural poverty to urban poverty, will show an upward movement in money income. This is true, among other reasons, because the money income of the urban poor is higher than that of the country poor. But this same change does not necessarily mean that a human being has actually improved his status, that he has escaped from the culture of poverty. As was noted in the chapter on the agricultural poor, these people who are literally driven off the land are utterly unprepared for city life. They come to the metropolis in a time of rising skill requirements and relatively high levels of unemployment. They will often enter the economic underworld. Statistically, they can be recorded as a gain, because they have more money. Socially, they have simply transferred from one part of the culture of poverty to another.

At the same time, it should be noted that although there has been this tremendous exodus of the rural poor, the proportion of impoverished farms in America's agriculture has remained roughly the same.

Then Lampman deals with Galbraith's theory of "case poverty," of those who have certain disabilities that keep them down in the culture of poverty. Here it should be noted again that Galbraith himself is somewhat optimistic about case poverty. He tends to regard the bad health of the poor, physical as well as mental, as being facts about them that are individual and personal. If this book is right, particularly in the discussion of the twisted spirit within the culture of poverty, that is not the case. The personal ills of the poor are a social consequence, not a bit of biography about them. They will continue as long as the environment of poverty persists.

But Lampman's optimism goes beyond that of Galbraith. He believes that disabilities of case poverty ("mental deficiency, bad health, inability to adapt to the discipline of modern economic life, excessive procreation, alcohol, insufficient education") are "moderated over time." And he takes as his main case in point education. "For example, average educational attainment levels will rise in future years simply because younger people presently have better education than older people. Hence, as the current generation of old people pass from the scene, the percent of persons with low educational attainment will fall."

This is true, yet it is misleading if it is not placed in the context of the changes in the society as a whole. It is much more possible today to be poor with a couple of years of high school than it was a generation ago. As I have pointed out earlier, the skill level of the economy has been changing, and educational deficiency, if anything, becomes an even greater burden as a result. In this case, saying that people will have more education is not saying that they will escape the culture of poverty. It could have a much more ironic meaning: that America will have the most literate poor the world has ever known.

Lampman himself concedes that the aged are "immune" to economic growth. If this is the case, and in the absence of ranging and comprehensive social programs, the increase in the number and percentage of the poor within the next generation will actually increase the size of the other America. Lampman also concedes that families with female heads are immune to a general prosperity, and this is another point of resistance for the culture of poverty.

Finally, Lampman is much more optimistic about "nonwhite" progress than the discussion in this book would justify. I will not repeat the argument that has already been given. Let me simply state the point baldly: the present rate of economic progress among the minorities is agonizingly slow, and one cannot look for dramatic gains from this direction.

Thus, I would agree with Galbraith that poverty in the sixties has qualities that give it a hardiness in the face of affluence heretofore unknown. As documented and described in this book, there are many special factors keeping the unskilled workers, the minorities, the agricultural poor, and the aged in the culture of poverty. If there is to be a way out, it will come from human action, from political change, not from automatic processes.

But finally, let us suppose that Lampman is correct on every point. In that case a generation of economic growth coupled with some social legislation would find America in 1987 with "only" 10 per cent of the nation impoverished. If, on the other hand, a vast and comprehensive program attacking the culture of poverty could speed up this whole development, and perhaps even abolish poverty within a generation, what is the reason for holding back? This suffering is such an abomination in a society where it is needless that anything that can be done should be done.

In all this, I do not want to depict Robert Lampman as an enemy of the poor. In all seriousness, the very fact that he writes about the subject does him credit: he has social eyes, which is more than one can say for quite a few people in the society. And second, Lampman puts forward "A Program to Hasten the Reduction of Poverty" because of his genuine concern for the poor. My argument with him is not over motive or dedication. It is only that I believe that his theory makes the reduction of poverty too easy a thing, that he has not properly appreciated how deeply and strongly entrenched the other America is.

In any case, and from any point of view, the moral obligation is plain: there must be a crusade against this poverty in our midst.

III

If this research makes it clear that a basic attack upon poverty is necessary, it also suggests the kind of program the nation needs.

First and foremost, any attempt to abolish poverty in the United States must seek to destroy the pessimism and fatalism that flourish in the other America. In part, this can be done by offering real opportunities to these people, by changing the social reality that gives rise to their sense of hopelessness. But beyond that (these fears of the poor have a life of their own and are not simply rooted in analyses of employment chances), there should be a spirit, an élan, that communicates itself to the entire society.

If the nation comes into the other America grudgingly, with the mentality of an administrator, and says, "All right, we'll help you people," then there will be gains, but they will be kept to the minimum; a dollar spent will return a dollar. But if there is an attitude that society is gaining by eradicating poverty, if there is a positive attempt to bring these millions of the poor to the point where they can make their contribution to the United States, that will make a huge difference. The spirit of a campaign against poverty does not cost a single cent. It is a matter of vision, of sensitivity.

Let me give an example to make this point palpable. During the Montgomery bus boycott, there was only one aim in the Negro community of that city: to integrate the buses. There were no speeches on crime or juvenile delinquency. And yet it is reported that the crime rate among Negroes in Montgomery declined. Thousands of people had been given a sense of purpose, of their own worth and dignity. On their own, and without any special urging, they began to change their personal lives; they became a different people. If the same élan could invade the other America, there would be similar results.

Second, this book is based upon the proposition that poverty forms a culture, an interdependent system. In case after case, it has been documented that one cannot deal with the various components of poverty in isolation, changing this or that condition but leaving the basic structure intact. Consequently, a campaign against the misery of the poor should be comprehensive. It should think, not in terms of this or that aspect of poverty, but along the lines of establishing new communities, of substituting a human environment for the inhuman one that now exists.

Here, housing is probably the basic point of departure. If there were the funds and imagination for a campaign to end slums in the United States, most of the other steps needed to deal with poverty could be integrated with it. The vision should be the one described in the previous chapter: the political, economic, and social integration of the poor with the rest of the society. The second nation in our midst, the other America, must be brought into the Union.

In order to do this, there is a need for planning. It is literally incredible that this nation knows so much about poverty, that it has made so many inventories of misery, and that it has done so little. The material for a comprehensive program is already available. It exists in congressional reports and the statistics of Government agencies. What is needed is that the society make use of its knowledge in a rational and systematic way. As this book is being written, there are proposals for a Department of Urban Affairs in the Cabinet (and it will probably be a reality by the time these words are published). Such an agency could be the coordinating center for a crusade against the other America. In any case, if there is not planning, any attempt to deal with the problem of poverty will fail, at least in part.

Then there are some relatively simple things that could be done, involving the expansion of existing institutions and programs. Every American should be brought under the coverage of social security, and the payments should be enough to support a dignified old age. The principle already exists. Now it must be extended to those who need help the most. The same is true with minimum wage. The spectacle of excluding the most desperate from coverage must come to an end. If it did, there would be a giant step toward the elimination of poverty itself.

In every subculture of the other America, sickness and disease are the most important agencies of continuing misery. The New York *Times* publishes a list of the "neediest cases" each Christmas. In 1960 the descriptions of personal tragedy that ran along with this appeal involved in the majority of cases the want of those who had been struck down by illness. If there were adequate medical care, this charity would be unnecessary.

Today the debate on medical care centers on the aged. And indeed, these are the people who are in the most desperate straits. Yet it would be an error of the first magnitude to think that society's responsibility begins with those sixty-five years of age. As has been pointed out several times, the ills of the elderly are often the inheritance of the earlier years. A comprehensive medical program, guaranteeing decent care to every American, would actually reduce the cost of caring for the aged. That, of course, is only the hardheaded argument for such an approach. More importantly, such a program would make possible a human kind of existence for everyone in the society.

And finally, it must be remembered that none of these objectives can be accomplished if racial prejudice is to continue in the United States. Negroes and other minorities constitute only 25 per cent of the poor, yet their degradation is an important element in maintaining the entire culture of poverty. As long as there is a reservoir of cheap Negro labor, there is a means of keeping the poor whites down. In this sense, civil-rights legislation is an absolutely essential component in any campaign to end poverty in the United States.

In short, the welfare provisions of American society that now help the upper two-thirds must be extended to the poor. This can be done if the other Americans are motivated to take advantage of the opportunities before them, if they are invited into the society. It can be done if there is a comprehensive program that attacks the culture of poverty at every one of its strong points.

But who will carry out this campaign?

There is only one institution in the society capable of acting to abolish poverty. That is the Federal Government. In saying this, I do not rejoice, for centralization can lead to an impersonal and bureaucratic program, one that will be lacking in the very human quality so essential in an approach to the poor. In saying this, I am only recording the facts of political and social life in the United States.

The cities are not now capable of dealing with poverty, and each day they become even less capable. As the middle class flees the central urban area, as various industries decentralize, the tax base of the American metropolis shrinks. At the same time, the social and economic problems with which the city must deal are on the rise. Thus, there is not a major city in the United States that is today capable of attacking poverty on its own. On the contrary, the high cost of poverty is dragging the cities down.

The state governments in this country have a political peculiarity that renders them incapable of dealing with the problem of poverty. They are, for the most part, dominated by conservative rural elements. In every state with a big industrial population, the gerrymander has given the forces of rural conservatism two or three votes per person. So it is that the state legislatures usually take more money out of the problem areas than they put back into them. So it is that state governments are notoriously weighted in the direction of caution, pinchpenny economics, and indifference to the plight of the urban millions.

The various private agencies of the society simply do not have the funds to deal with the other America. And even the "fringe benefits" negotiated by unions do not really get to the heart of the problem. In the first place, they extend to organized workers in a strong bargaining position, not to the poor. And second, they are inadequate even to the needs of those who are covered.

It is a noble sentiment to argue that private moral responsibility expressing itself through charitable contributions should be the main instrument of attacking poverty. The only problem is that such an approach does not work.

So, by process of elimination, there is no place to look except toward the Federal Government. And indeed, even if there were alternate choices, Washington would have to play an important role, if only because of the need for a comprehensive program and for national planning. But in any case there is no argument, for there is only one realistic possibility: only the Federal Government has the power to abolish poverty.

In saying this, it is not necessary to advocate complete central control of such a campaign. Far from it. Washington is essential in a double sense: as a source of the considerable funds needed to mount a campaign against the other America, and as a place for coordination, for planning, and the establishment of national standards. The actual implementation of a program to abolish poverty can be carried out through myriad institutions, and the closer they are to the specific local area, the better the results. There are, as has been pointed out already, housing administrators, welfare workers, and city planners with dedication and vision. They are working on the local level, and their main frustration is the lack of funds. They could be trusted actually to carry through on a national program. What they lack now is money and the support of the American people.

There is no point in attempting to blueprint or detail the mechanisms and institutions of a war on poverty in the United States. There is information enough for action. All that is lacking is political will.

Thus the difficult, hardheaded question about poverty that one must answer is this: Where is the political will coming from? The other America is systematically underrepresented in the Government of the United States. It cannot really speak for itself. The poor, even in politics, must always be the object of charity (with the major exception of the Negroes, who, in recent times, have made tremendous strides forward in organization).

As a result of this situation, there is no realistic hope for the abolition of poverty in the United States until there is a vast social movement, a new period of political creativity. In times of slow change or of stalemate, it is always the poor who are expendable in the halls of Congress. In 1961, for instance, the laundry workers were dropped out of the minimum wage as part of a deal with the conservatives. Precisely because they are so poor and cruelly exploited, no one had to fear their political wrath. They, and others from the culture of poverty, will achieve the protection of the welfare state when there is a movement in this land so dynamic and irresistible that it need not make concessions.

For that matter, it is much easier to catalogue the enemies of the poor than it is to recite their friends.

All the forces of conservatism in this society are ranged against the needs of the other America. The ideologues are opposed to helping the poor because this can be accomplished only through an expansion of the welfare state. The small businessmen have an immediate self-interest in maintaining the economic underworld. The powerful agencies of the corporate farms want a continuation of an agricultural program that aids the rich and does nothing for the poor.

And now the South is becoming increasingly against the poor. In the days of the New Deal, the Southern Democrats tended to vote for various kinds of social legislation. One of the most outspoken champions of public housing, Burnet Maybank, was a senator from South Carolina. For one thing, there is a Southern tradition of being against Wall Street and big business; it is part of the farmers' hostility to the railroads and the Babylons of the big city. For another, the New Deal legislation did not constitute a challenge to the system of racial segregation in the South.

But in the postwar period, this situation began to change. As industrialization came to the South, there was a growing political opposition to laws like minimum wage, to unions, and to other aspects of social change. The leaders of this area saw their depressed condition as an advantage. They could lure business with the promise of cheap, unorganized labor. They were interested in exploiting their backwardness.

The result was the strengthening of the coalition of Southern Democrats and conservative Northern Republicans. The Northern conservatives went along with opposition to Civil Rights legislation. The Southerners threw their votes into the struggle against social advance. It was this powerful coalition that exacted such a price in the first period of the Kennedy Administration. Many of the proposals that would have benefited the poor were omitted from bills in the first place, and other concessions were made in the course of the legislative battle. Thus poverty in the United States is supported by forces with great political and economic power.

On the other side, the friends of the poor are to be found in the American labor movement and among the middle-class liberals. The unions in the postwar period lost much of the élan that had characterized them in the thirties. Yet on questions of social legislation they remained the most powerful mass force committed to change in general, and to bettering the lot of the poor in particular. On issues like housing, medical care, minimum wage, and social security, the labor movement provided the strongest voice stating the cause of the poor.

Yet labor and the liberals were caught in the irrationalities of the American party system, and this was an enormous disadvantage to the other America. The unionists and their liberal allies are united in the Democratic party with the Southern conservatives. A Democratic victory was usually achieved by appealing to those who were concerned for social change. But at the same time it brought the forces of conservatism powerful positions on the standing committees of the Congress.

Indeed, part of the invisibility of poverty in American life is a result of this party structure. Since each major party contained differences within itself greater than the differences between it and the other party, politics in the fifties and early sixties tended to have an issueless character. And where issues were not discussed, the poor did not have a chance. They could benefit only if elections were designed to bring new information to the people, to wake up the nation, to challenge, and to call to action.

In all probability there will not be a real attack on the culture of poverty so long as this situation persists. For the other America cannot be abolished through concessions and compromises that are almost inevitably made at the expense of the poor. The spirit, the vision that are required if the nation is to penetrate the wall of pessimism and despair that surrounds the impoverished millions cannot be produced under such circumstances.

What is needed if poverty is to be abolished is a return of political debate, a restructuring of the party system so that there can be clear choices, a new mood of social idealism.

These, then, are the strangest poor in the history of mankind.

They exist within the most powerful and rich society the world has ever known. Their misery has continued while the majority of the nation talked of itself as being "affluent" and worried about neuroses in the suburbs. In this way tens of millions of human beings became invisible. They dropped out of sight and out of mind; they were without their own political voice.

Yet this need not be. The means are at hand to fulfill the age-old dream: poverty can now be abolished. How long shall we ignore this underdeveloped nation in our midst? How long shall we look the other way while our fellow human beings suffer? How long?

Appendix: Definitions

When I first began research on the culture of poverty in the United States, I was writing a piece for *Commentary* magazine. The article was in galley proof when I got a call from one of the editors there. Someone, he said, had just run across an analysis in *Fortune* that gave a much more optimistic picture of the income pattern in the United States. How could this be, given the fact that I was arguing that there were 50,000,000 or more poor people in this land?

I read the article. *Fortune* was using the same basic research that I was quoting. The difference was in point of view. The *Fortune* writer focused on the development of the middle third in American society—the organized worker in well-paying industry, those who benefited from rising levels of education, and so on—and there was indeed a heartening rise in standard of living for these people. Yet, in the *Fortune* analysis the bottom group was there. It was simply that these people were not commented upon.

The *Fortune* writer had been looking for improvement in American society, and he had located a very real area of advance. In this book, let it be said candidly, I have been looking for retrogression and stagnation. Those in American society who have been moving up in the world have enough celebrants and chroniclers; they are the stuff of proud boasts and claims. But those who have been omitted from progress have been, over long stretches of time, forgotten.

If my interpretation is bleak and grim, and even if it overstates the case slightly, that is intentional. My moral point of departure is a sense of outrage, a feeling that the obvious and existing problem of the poor is so shocking that it would be better to describe it in dark tones rather than to minimize it. No one will be hurt if the situation is seen from the most pessimistic point of view, but optimism can lead to complacency and the persistence of the other America.

This is not to say that the statistics in this book have been invented or misrepresented. They come from Government sources and they have been confirmed in most cases by my own experiences in walking the streets of the slums and talking to the people, or visiting the broiling-hot fields of the California migrants. Yet there is an understandable and legitimate area in which interpretation and point of view give rise to different conclusions.

In Robert Lampman's Senate study, for instance, the author notes that the estimate of low-income people in the United States could "reasonably range" between 16 per cent and 36 per cent of the population. Stated as percentages, the differences involved in these definitions might not seem to be too huge. But if one translates these figures into numbers of human beings, the discrepancy is huge and obvious: the high figure includes 36,000,000 more people than the low one.

Moreover, the choice of figure will determine one's picture of the kind of people who make up the culture of poverty. The lower the cut-off line by which one establishes poverty, the fewer large families will be included, and the aged will be a higher percentage. This obviously is of great importance, for at least one consequence of a study of poverty should be to point America toward those groups that must be given special help.

In this Appendix I have presented the statistical assumptions and basic interpretations that underlie the rest of the book. In such a discussion it is inevitable that one gets mixed up with dry, graceless, technical matters. That should not conceal the crucial fact that these numbers represent people and that any tendency toward understatement is an intellectual way of acquiescing in suffering.

I have been guided by two principles: to be as honest and objective as possible about the figures; to speak emotionally in the name of the common humanity of those who dwell in the culture of poverty. If some statistician should find an error in technical approach, if he could say, there are 10,000,000 less poor, that would not really be important. Give or take 10,000,000, the American poor are one of the greatest scandals of a society that has the ability to provide a decent life for every man, woman, and child.

I

In the nineteenth century, conservatives in England used to argue against reform on the grounds that the British worker of the time had a longer life expectancy than a medieval nobleman.

This is to say that a definition of poverty is, to a considerable extent, a historically conditioned matter. Indeed, if one wanted to play with figures, it would be possible to prove that there are no poor people in the United States, or at least only a few whose plight is as desperate as that of masses in Hong Kong. There is starvation in American society, but it is not a pervasive social problem as it is in some of the newly independent nations. There are still Americans who literally die in the streets, but their numbers are comparatively small.

This abstract approach toward poverty in which one compares different centuries or societies has very real consequences. For the nineteenth century British conservative, it was a way of ignoring the plight of workers who were living under the most inhuman conditions. The twentieth century conservative would be shocked and appalled in an advanced society if there were widespread conditions like those of the English cities a hundred years ago. Our standards of decency, of what a truly human life requires, change, and they should.

There are two main aspects of this change. First, there are new definitions of what man can achieve, of what a human standard of life should be. In recent times this has been particularly true since technology has consistently broadened man's potential: it has made a longer, healthier, better life possible. Thus, in terms of what is technically possible, we have higher aspirations. Those who suffer levels of life well below those that are possible, even though they live better than medieval knights or Asian peasants, are poor.

Related to this technological advance is the social definition of poverty. The American poor are not poor in Hong Kong or in the sixteenth century; they are poor here and now, in the United States. They are dispossessed in terms of what the rest of the nation enjoys, in terms of what the society could provide if it had the will. They live on the fringe, the margin. They watch the movies and read the magazines of affluent America, and these tell them that they are internal exiles.

To some, this description of the feelings of the poor might seem to be out of place in discussing a definition of poverty. Yet if this book indicates anything about the other America, it is that this sense of exclusion is the source of a pessimism, a defeatism that intensifies the exclusion. To have one bowl of rice in a society where all other people have half a bowl may well be a sign of achievement and intelligence; it may spur a person to act and to fulfill his human potential. To have five bowls of rice in a society where the majority have a decent, balanced diet is a tragedy.

This point can be put another way in defining poverty. One of the consequences of our new technology is that we have created new needs. There are more people who live longer. Therefore they need more. In short, if there is technological advance without social advance, there is, almost automatically, an increase in human misery, in impoverishment.

And finally, in defining poverty one must also compute the social cost of progress. One of the reasons that the income figures show fewer people today with low incomes than twenty years ago is that more wives are working now, and family income has risen as a result. In 1940, 15 per cent of wives were in the labor force;

in 1957 the figure was 30 per cent. This means that there was more money and, presumably, less poverty.

Yet a tremendous growth in the number of working wives is an expensive way to increase income. It will be paid for in terms of the impoverishment of home life, of children who receive less care, love, and supervision. This one fact, for instance, might well play a significant role in the problems of the young in America. It could mean that the next generation, or a part of it, will have to pay the bill for the extra money that was gained. It could mean that we have made an improvement in income statistics at the cost of hurting thousands and hundreds of thousands of children. If a person has more money but achieves this through mortgaging the future, who is to say that he or she is no longer poor?

It is difficult to take all these imponderables together and to fashion them into a simple definition of poverty in the United States. Yet this analysis should make clear some of the assumptions that underlie the assertions in this book:

Poverty should be defined in terms of those who are denied the minimal levels of health, housing, food, and education that our present stage of scientific knowledge specifies as necessary for life as it is now lived in the United States.

Poverty should be defined psychologically in terms of those whose place in the society is such that they are internal exiles who, almost inevitably, develop attitudes of defeat and pessimism and who are therefore excluded from taking advantage of new opportunities.

Poverty should be defined absolutely, in terms of what man and society could be. As long as America is less than its potential, the nation as a whole is impoverished by that fact. As long as there is the other America, we are, all of us, poorer because of it.

II

Probably the simplest way to get an idea of how many poor people there are in the United States is to use the income figures supplied by various Government agencies.

Without question, this approach misses many subtle distinctions. It does not, for example, allow for individual variation: How skilled a cook is a certain wife? What are the foods of a particular ethnic group and how much do they cost? Using this method, the very important issue of the increase in working wives is slighted. But, though it misses the quality of life in the other America, the income test does provide a rough index of poverty in the United States.

In the late forties the low-income studies of special congressional committees fixed a poverty line at $2,000 money income for an urban family of four. If this were brought up to date (that is, if it were simply corrected for inflationary changes that have taken place in the intervening years) it would be around $2,500 a year. However, at the time this figure was set various authorities argued that the definition put the minimum income much too low. And by merely revising it so that it expresses 1961 prices, this test tacitly assumes that there should be no progress over the course of a decade. In short, it leaves out the fact that this was a time when other groups in the society advanced.

Recently, Robert Lampman's study used the $2,500 cut-off as establishing the low-income line for an urban family of four. Lampman then assumed that other family sizes would be in direct proportion to this figure; an urban individual would be low-income if he received $1,157; a six-person family would meet the definition if its annual money take was $3,236, and so on. On this basis, Lampman came to the conclusion that 19 per cent of the American population, 32,000,000 people, were in the low-income classification.

In the same period, the AFL-CIO used a slightly higher definition of what constituted low income. It found that 36,000,000 Americans were living in households of two persons or more with 1958 incomes of less than $3,000. Another 5,500,000 individuals were living on incomes of under $1,500 (which is less than $29 a week before taxes). Thus the AFL-CIO statisticians would argue that there were 41,500,000 Americans—24 per cent of the population—who had demonstrably substandard incomes.

Since the Lampman and AFL-CIO estimates, the Bureau of Labor Statistics has issued a report that would indicate that both of these studies had a tendency toward understating the problem. Throughout his work Lampman assumed that the "adequate" budget for a four-person urban family in Bureau of Labor Statistics terms would be just over $4,000 a year. The AFL-CIO had the same figure pegged at $4,800 a year.

However, both of these calculations were based on an approach to "adequacy" developed by the Government in the late forties (and adjusted, without changing the basic concepts, for price increases over the intervening years). More recently, the Bureau of Labor Statistics has produced a new budget for an urban family of four. It varies from $5,370 in Houston to $6,567 in Chicago, with Washington, D.C., close to an average at $6,147. According to the Government, these figures define a budget that is above "minimum maintenance" and well below "luxury." It is seen as "modest but adequate," although it is "below the average enjoyed by American families."

This budget is an important attempt at specifying income needs, and it is worth going into a little detail about it before attempting a definition of poverty. The family of four in these Government figures assumes an employed thirty-eight-year-old husband, a wife who is not employed outside the home, a girl of eight and a boy of thirteen. The family lives in a rented dwelling in a large city or its suburbs. The budget is based on prices in the fall of 1959.

Here are some typical examples of the budget items as they were computed in Washington, D.C. (the city closest to the average): the total allotment for food was $1,684, with $1,447 spent on meals at home and $181 on dining out; rent was calculated at $1,226; the wife had $160 to spend on clothing during the year. Clearly, this is not a budget for the gracious living depicted by the American magazines. It is not, in contemporary terms, poverty or anything like it. But such a family would face a serious crisis in the event of a protracted illness or long-term unemployment for the family head.

Another important factor in the Bureau of Labor Statistics budget is the way in which it computes the cost for maintaining families that are smaller or larger than the typical case of four. The two-person budget, for instance, is a little better than 60 per cent of the budget for the family of four.

On this basis, if one were to take approximately half of this budget as the standard for low income or poverty (making all the adjustments for smaller families, for low-income individuals, for lower costs, and for food grown in farm areas), if the cut-off were established somewhere between $3,000 and $3,500 for an urban family of four, then the culture of poverty would be roughly defined in the United States as composed of around 50,000,000 people. (Using Lampman's figures, and taking $4,000 as the cut-off, which is the top level he considers to be a "reasonable" estimate of low-income, it would be over 60,000,000.)

There is no point in getting involved in an endless methodological controversy over the precise point at which a family becomes impoverished. Lampman's estimate of 32,000,000 poor people can be taken as a minimal definition; the AFL-CIO figure of 41,000,000 would be an extremely reasonable definition; and, in view of the revisions made by the Bureau of Labor Statistics, the total of 50,000,000 poor Americans would reflect our latest statement of living standards.

In short, somewhere between 20 and 25 per cent of the American people are poor. They have inadequate housing, medicine, food, and opportunity. From my point of view, they number between 40,000,000 and 50,000,000 human beings.

However, it is important not to be overly cautious. It is quite possible that these figures will require upward revision. In the Department of Commerce statistics, one of the most striking factors is the way in which the number of low-income people vary according to a recession or prosperity situation. In 1947, for instance, Commerce estimated that 34 per cent of the family units had under $3,000 money income as expressed in 1961 dollars. In 1949, a recession year, this moved up to 36 per cent of the families with incomes under $3,000 in 1961 dollars. In 1950, a year of renewed prosperity, the number dropped to 33 per cent of the total. This pattern continued throughout the fifties.

Thus, when using these percentages and numbers, one must understand that they express the conditions of a given time and place. In this case, they describe a time of mild recession and renewed prosperity. (The current, 1961, figures refer to the late fifties.) The direction that the statistics of poverty will take in the future depends in part upon general economic conditions in the United States. The other Americans do not automatically share in the gains of good times, for they tend to be progress-immune; but they do automatically share in the losses of bad times. Millions of people live just above the poverty line. Stagnation, recession, or even continuing high levels of unemployment during prosperity would require an upward revision of all the figures in this chapter.

So far, most of this analysis has been based on an attempt to discover a minimum measure for life at the bottom of American society and to determine how many people live beneath this line. If one moves on to a related question— How has the general-distribution pattern of income been changing in the United States?—the results are even more shocking. The following table is an extremely revealing illustration of what has been happening. (It is taken from an AFL-CIO publication; it was derived from Department of Commerce figures.)

How Total Family Income Was Shared Before Taxes 1935–36, 1944, and 1958

Families by fifths	1935–36 (Per cent)	1944 (Per cent)	1958 (Per cent)	Average income per family 1958
Lowest	4.1%	4.9%	4.7%	$1,460
2nd	9.2	10.9	11.1	3,480
3rd	14.1	16.2	16.3	5,110
4th	20.9	22.2	22.4	7,020
Highest	51.7	45.8	45.5	14,250

How do we interpret these percentages? In 1958 the lowest fifth of families in the United States had 4.7 per cent of total personal income; and the highest fifth, those families with top income, had 45.5 per cent. But even more important than this incredible comparison is the direction that American income distribution took in this period. Between 1935–1936 and 1944, the poor (for the lowest fifth, and more, dwell in the culture of poverty) increased their share of personal income from 4.1 per cent to 4.9 per cent. There was a slow, tortoise-like trend toward bettering the relative position of the neediest citizens of the United States. But in the postwar period, this trend was reversed. In 1958 the poor had less of a share of personal income than they had in 1944.

Indeed, this chart is one of the statistical keys to the invisibility of poverty in the United States. The third, fourth, and highest groupings are those that contain the college-educated, the politically more active, the writers and editors, and so on. In the middle level there has been steady progress, and the general experience is one of optimism and advance. At the very top there has been a decline, but it must be put into context. Between 1944 and 1958, the average real-income rise of the neediest fifth in America was $80; while the top 5 per cent (with average 1958 incomes of $25,280) rose by $1,900. In short, even though the percentages at the very top indicate a mild decline (and, as will be seen, it is questionable whether this is the reality), the experience has hardly been a traumatic one.

If these figures are shocking, a further qualification must be made that intensifies their affect. Almost all these income statistics are based on Government reports that systematically understate the wealth of the rich. There is no malice in stating this fact. It is simply the result of the ability of top-income families and individuals to conceal income for the purpose of avoiding income taxes. This can be done through the utilization of lavish expense accounts (which are part of a standard of living but not of income figures), through stock transactions that are not included in the Commerce computations, and so on.

It might come as a surprise to some to learn that taxes generally work against the poor. According to a 1960 study of the Tax Foundation, 28.3 per cent of family income under $2,000 is paid out to Federal, state, and local governments, while families earning five to seven times as much surrender only 24 per cent of their income to the public authorities. (One of the reasons for this is the widespread use of property and excise taxes on the state and municipal levels. These, falling "evenly" upon all, take a much greater percentage from the poor.)

Thus, put most modestly and without correcting for the systematic misreporting that goes on at high-income levels, the poor have a worse relative position in American society today than they did a decade and a half ago. As technology has boomed, their share in prosperity has decreased; their participation in recession and misery has increased.

III

The identity of the major groups in the other America has been made fairly clear in the preceding chapters. The main subcultures of poverty are those of the aged, the minorities, the agricultural workers, and the industrial rejects.

What are the proportions of these people in the world of the poor?

Our current myth has two main ways of rationalizing away the importance of poverty in American society. On the one hand, people speak of "pockets" of poverty, an argument that has already been dealt with. On the other hand, there is a most strange theory. The poor, it says, are rural and nonwhite. This is unfortunate, to be sure, but it means that poverty is something on the fringes of the nation, that it is associated with areas of backwardness, and that it will inevitably be obliterated by advancing technology. (In Australia, I am told, it was once the custom to develop income and standard-of-living statistics by omitting the aborigines. The Negroes and the rural poor often get the same kind of treatment in this country.)

The facts, however, run counter to the notion that poverty in America is primarily nonwhite and rural.

In Robert Lampman's study there is a modest estimate of the total low-income population: 32,000,000 people. One of the consequences of Lampman's definition, as he himself notes, is that it excludes a considerable number of large family units that lie just the other side of his cut-off line. Granted his low estimate in defining poverty, and this one distortion resulting from it, Lampman's work is useful in determining the proportion of the various groups in the culture of poverty.

In Lampman's impoverished population of 32,000,000, 8,000,-000 were sixty-five years or older; 6,400,000 were nonwhite; 8,000,000 in consumer units headed by women; 21,000,000 were in units headed by a person with an eighth-grade education or less. Clearly, these figures overlap, for one of the most important single facts about the culture of poverty is that it tends to cluster misery.

Lampman found that 70 per cent of the low-income population had one or more of the characteristics that tend to push a person down. (In the general population, the figure is 50 per cent with one or more of these disabilities.) Consequently, it is common to find a person who is the victim of a whole chain of disadvantages: a Negro, facing job discrimination, with inferior educational training, and living in a family unit headed by a woman, would be a not untypical figure in the racial ghetto.

One of the disabling characteristics noted by Lampman is age. But here a certain refining of terms is necessary. Statistically, "age" is now thought of as beginning in America at sixty-five. Yet, as the chapter on displaced workers and depressed areas makes clear, the actual cut-off in these situations is much younger. The economic definition of age in industry is somewhere between forty and fifty; that is, if a worker between forty and fifty is laid off, his chances of finding a new job at the old level of pay are less whatever his skill may be; and if he is an unskilled or semiskilled worker (or if his skill has been destroyed by technology), the probabilities are against his ever finding a comparable job.

This is an example of the way in which biological facts are made relative to social standards. For along with the fact of discrimination against the blue-collar worker forty years or older goes the terrible psychological experience of rejection and defeat. If, as seems to be the case, this problem intensifies in the immediate period ahead, it may well be necessary to readjust the very definition of what constitutes aging in America.

At the other end of the age scale, Lampman draws a most important conclusion: children are a more significant percentage of the culture of poverty than old people. In his low-income population of 32,000,000, there are 8,000,000 individuals over sixty-five —and 11,000,000 under eighteen. The young are thus one-third of the total. (And once again, it must be emphasized that I regard Lampman's definition as representing a rock-bottom estimate.)

This fact has enormous significance. Among the aged, as was noted in a previous chapter, there are a good many people who become poor after working lives that had a decent standard of living. That is one particular kind of tragedy, one the nation has manufactured by increasing life without providing for its decent maintenance. But with the children of the poor, there is another grim process at work: it is likely that they will become the parents of the next generation of the culture of poverty.

As Lampman remarks, "A considerable number of younger persons are starting life in a condition of 'inherited poverty.' " At the present time, as I have argued elsewhere in this book, this fact may be of greater significance than ever before in the history of the nation. The character of poverty has changed, and it has become more deadly for the young. It is no longer associated with immigrant groups with high aspirations; it is now identified with those whose social existence makes it more and more difficult to break out into the larger society. At the same time, the educational requirements of the economy are increasing.

These millions of poor children are the ones who are going to the most inferior schools. Even when they have educational opportunities, they come from families who have a low opinion of education and who encourage the earliest possible legal leave-taking from school.

The nation is therefore beginning the sixties with a most dangerous problem: an enormous concentration of young people who, if they do not receive immediate help, may well be the source of a kind of hereditary poverty new to American society. If this analysis is correct, then the vicious circle of the culture of poverty is, if anything, becoming more intense, more crippling, and problematic because it is increasingly associating itself with the accident of birth.

In any case, poverty in the United States is not a nonwhite phenomenon, nor is it confined to the rural areas. The nonwhites constitute about 25 per cent of the other America (that is, to be sure, double their percentage in the nation as a whole); the rural poor are even less of the total (and there is overlap, because poor Negroes in the countryside are an important grouping). The theory that somehow finds comfort in the idea of "marginal" poverty does not stand up against the facts.

In an earlier chapter, the special health tragedies of the aged were documented. Yet it is important to understand that illness is a general disability of everyone in the culture of poverty, young or old. I first noticed this during the Asian-flu problem in New York in the fifties. The newspapers noted that the epidemic hit on a social-class basis, that is, areas like Harlem and the Lower East Side, where people were packed together under unhygienic circumstances, had a much higher incidence of the disease than better-off neighborhoods.

Here are just a few of the statistics from the United States National Health Survey on the way in which the poor are physically victimized in America:

In the age group between five and fourteen, children in families with incomes of $4,000 and over had a rate of dental visits three times that for children in families with a lower income.

The rate for Americans who lose their teeth is directly proportional to family income; the less money a family has, the more likely that there will be a total loss of teeth.

In all age groups, the number of people who suffer limitations of activity or mobility are directly related to income; between the ages of forty-five and sixty-four the families with incomes under $2,000 have six times more limitation of mobility than those with incomes of $7,000 or better.

The consequence of this is that the poor suffer more loss of work than any other group in the society: "Families having incomes under $2,000 experienced 32.4 restricted-activity days per person per year. The corresponding figure for families with incomes between $2,000 and $3,999 was 20.5 restricted-activity days per person, and for families with incomes of $4,000 and over, about 16.5 days of restricted activity."

The last quotation is from a National Health Survey study of conditions between July, 1957, and June, 1958. After citing these facts, the analysis continues, "A possible explanation for this relationship is that persons in lower-income families are more subject to restricting illness because of less utilization of medical care, poorer diet, and other factors."

The facts of health insurance do not give any cause for feeling that this situation will change for the better in the immediate future. The National Health Survey studied a period from July to December, 1959. At this time, the group with incomes under $1,999 constituted 15 per cent of the population, yet they accounted for only 7.4 per cent of hospital insurance, 6.6 per cent of surgical insurance, and 7.0 per cent of doctor-visit insurance. By way of contrast, the group with an income between $4,000 and $6,999 makes up 35.6 per cent of the population, but it possesses 42.1 per cent of the hospital insurance, 43.1 per cent of the surgical insurance, and 40.6 per cent of the doctor-visit insurance.

Finally, another important aspect of the culture of poverty is geographical. According to the Department of Commerce figures, the Northeast and the West had 16 per cent of the families with incomes under $3,000 in 1959; the North Central area had a figure of 21 per cent; and the South had the highest concentration with 34 per cent. The great progress, between 1953 and 1959, was made in the West (the number of families with incomes under $3,000 fell from 23 per cent to 16 per cent), and the area with the least advance was the North Central, where the number of impoverished families declined by only 1 per cent over a six-year period.

In reading these figures (or any statistics dealing with families), it must be remembered that "unattached individuals" who are poor have a much higher percentage who live in cities and who are unconnected with farm life. This would make the relative position of the South just a little less of a scandal than it is when viewed from the criterion of family poverty. (According to AFL-CIO estimates, there are 5,500,000 "single person families" with income under $1,500. This excludes the aged institutional population, which is over 250,000.)

In conclusion, one can draw a summary statistical picture of the other America.

The poor in America constitute about 25 per cent of the total population. They number somewhere between 40,000,000 and 50,000,000, depending on the criterion of low income that is adopted.

The majority of the poor in America are white, although the nonwhite minorities suffer from the most intense and concentrated impoverishment of any single group.

A declining number and percentage of the poor are involved in farm work, and although rural poverty is one of the most important components of the culture of poverty, it does not form its mass base.

In addition to the nonwhite minorities, the groups at a particular disadvantage are: the aged, the migrant workers, the industrial rejects, children, families with a female head, people of low education. These various characteristics of the culture of poverty tend to cluster together. (The large families have had the least gain of all family groups in recent years, and hence more children among the poor.)

The people who are in this plight are at an enormous physical disadvantage, suffering more from chronic diseases and having less possibility of treatment.

The citizens of the culture of poverty also suffer from more mental and emotional problems than any group in American society.

These figures do not confirm any of the complacent theories that poverty is now in "pockets," that it is nonwhite and rural, and so on. Rather, they indicate a massive problem, and one that is serious precisely because it concerns people who are immunized from progress and who view technological advance upside-down.

I would conclude this chapter as I began it. These are the figures, and there is legitimate reason for sincere men to argue over the details, to claim that a particular interpretation is too high or too low. At this point I would beg the reader to forget the numbers game. Whatever the precise calibrations, it is obvious that these statistics represent an enormous, an unconscionable amount of human suffering in this land. They should be read with a sense of outrage.

For until these facts shame us, until they stir us to action, the other America will continue to exist, a monstrous example of needless suffering in the most advanced society in the world.

Afterword

Editor's note: The following two essays by Michael Harrington appeared in previous editions of The Other America. *They provide an historical perspective on this country's shameful lack of resolve to wage war on poverty during the past two decades.*

Poverty in the Seventies

In the Seventies the poor may become invisible again. And even if that tragedy does not occur, there will still be tens of millions living in the other America when the country celebrates its two hundredth anniversary in 1976.

This prediction should be improbable. Lyndon B. Johnson declared an "unconditional war" on poverty in 1964, Congress agreed, and for the next four years the White House recited awesome statistics on the billions that were being spent on social purposes. And the Sixties were a time of marches and militancy, of students and churches committing themselves to abolish want, and of documentary presentations of the nation's domestic shame by all the mass media. Indeed the impression of frenetic Government activity was so widespread that Richard Nixon campaigned in 1968 with a promise to slow down the pace of innovation. So how, then, argue that poverty will persist in the Seventies and perhaps once again drop out of the society's conscience and consciousness?

As usual, the Government has carefully assembled the figures to debunk the former President's optimism and the current President's quietism. In every crucial area—food, housing, education and other social responsibilities—the United States provides its worst-off citizens only a percentage of what they desperately need. And since half of the poor are young people destined to enter a sophisticated economy at enormous disadvantage, unless countermeasures are taken the children of this generation's impoverished will become the parents of an even larger generation of the other America.

This is not to say there has been no progress. The boom generated by public policy in the Sixties did finally reduce the unemployment rates and there were people who made real, but precarious, gains as a result. And Medicare for the aged was the one program where there was something like a quantum jump in social investment, even though inflation vitiated part of its effect.

Still the very same groups which were poor when this book was written in 1961 and published in 1962 are poor today: the blacks, the Spanish-speaking, the unemployed and the underemployed, the citizens of depressed regions, the aging. And I should add one minority that I quite wrongly omitted from my original analysis: the American Indian, probably the poorest of all.

Yet even though the society has failed to redeem the pledges of the Sixties it has taken to celebrating paper triumphs over poverty. Thus in August of 1969 the Department of Commerce announced the happy news that the number of poverty-stricken had dropped from 39,000,000 to 25,000,000 in a matter of nine years. The only problem, as will be seen, is that the numbers prettied up the reality. This was a sign that, in the Seventies, America might be going back to the established procedures of the Eisenhower years, deluding itself with happy reports on the state of the nation. It was another ominous portent that one of Richard Nixon's top domestic advisers, Arthur Burns, said in the summer of 1969 that poverty is only an "intellectual concept" defined by "artificial statistics." That is precisely the kind of callous thinking that made the poor invisible in the first place. And it can happen again.

So in order to understand the cruel prospects for poverty in the Seventies, it is necessary to go behind the current optimism with its juggling of the social books. That is much more easily done now than in the early Sixties since this society, in one of its typical ironies, has spared no expense in recording its injustices. The problem is to examine the official figures critically and to glimpse the human faces and the tragic tendencies that are hidden in them. Only then can we know how much still needs to be done.

In an economy drowning in data, many people think that statistics are a neutral, scientific reflection of the objective world. Actually, the numbers depend on debatable and very political assumptions, which is how poverty can persist while some agencies of Government are preparing to celebrate its abolition.

When Lyndon Johnson declared his social war in the State of the Union message of 1964, there was very little research to draw on. Much of it had been done by Robert Lampman, a dedicated scholar who had seen through the myth of universal prosperity in the Fifties. Using his work, the Council of Economic Advisers said in 1964 that poverty was a family income of less than $3,000 a year. That was a rough measure since it didn't take into account family size or geographic location, yet it was extremely useful in identifying the particular groups that were particularly afflicted.

In the next few years the criteria were made much more sophisticated. In a brilliant attempt to define poverty objectively, the Social Security Administration took the Department of Agriculture's Economy Food Plan as a base figure. This was about 80 percent of the Low Cost Plan that many welfare agencies had used to figure budgets; it was a temporary, emergency diet. In January 1964 the Economy Plan provided $4.60 per person a week, or 22 cents a meal, and the "line" was $3,100. In 1967 it was $4.90 a week, and a four-person family was said to be poor if its income was below $3,335 a year. And in 1969, when the Department of Commerce was announcing its cheerful news, the poverty line was increased all the way up to $3,553 a year.

These definitions were drawn up by concerned public servants, some of them with a deep personal commitment to abolish the outrage they were defining. But even when, in 1968, the poverty line was adjusted for increases in the cost of living on the Consumer Price Index, it was still much too low. For one thing, organized groups in the society, like the unions, and the professionals and technicians of the middle class, always strive to increase their annual income by more than the price of inflation. For it is assumed that one's absolute standard of living should increase every year. But the statisticians, by only correcting the poverty definition for rise of prices, are essentially saying that the poor should never progress as a group. And secondly, the inflationary increases of the late Sixties were most dramatic in the area of medical services and effectively canceled out all the increase in Medicare and forced some people out of Medicaid.

And before there is too much jubilation about the paper triumphs in the war on poverty, it would be well to look at the report of the President's Commission on Income Maintenance Programs in 1969. It told the country that a Department of Labor study argued that the official definition should be increased by more than half (from $2.43 per person a day to $4.05). But even more revealing was the Commission's statement that, between 1965 and 1966, while 36% of the families were escaping poverty, 34% were falling into it. That emphasized how risky life was for those who had managed to scramble above the line; it meant that even in the middle of a boom and a "war" on poverty millions were being forced into the other America.

There was also another optimistic assumption in the official definition. The Economy Food Plan was taken as the base figure and it was assumed that all other needs would cost two times the grocery bill. As Herman Miller of the Bureau of the Census has pointed out, this relationship between diet and income was identified in 1955. So to keep up with changes in the economy and society since then, one should compute the other items at three times the price of food, not two. By using the assumptions of the Eisenhower Fifties, Miller concluded, the Government abolished the poverty of twelve million Americans who were still poor.

If it seems extreme to suggest that honest, and even concerned, experts could thus overlook the anguish of twelve million of their fellow citizens, consider the famous Census undercount in 1960. Almost six million Americans, mainly black adults living in Northern cities, were not even enumerated. Their lives were so marginal—no permanent address, no mail, no phone number, no regular job—that they did not even achieve the dignity of being a statistic. Here again the extent of misery was underestimated in drastic fashion but in this case the error has been publicly proclaimed.

When officialdom thus becomes too sanguine it is not simply the poor who suffer. To be sure they inhabit a subculture of special indignities in which institutions such as the police, the family and the schools behave differently than in the rest of the society. But they are also a part of the larger society and, when they are ignored, so are many, many millions who are not poor. Paradoxically, the white worker who was tempted to support George Wallace in 1968 because he was tired of the Government doing "too much" for the blacks and the poor will himself be hurt if the programs are cut back.

For there were in 1967 some twelve million citizens whom the Council of Economic Advisers called the "near poor" (with incomes between $3,335 and $4,345 for families of four). If these numbers were underestimated in the same way as the definition of poverty itself, then there are sixteen million Americans who are one illness, one accident, one recession away from being poor again. If, as now seems so possible, America in the Seventies reduces its social efforts, this group will lose almost as much as the poor.

But there is another, and even larger, segment of the population whose destiny is, without their knowing it, related to that of the other Americans. In late 1966, which is light-years distant from the Seventies in terms of inflation, the Bureau of Labor Statistics figured that it would take $9,191 for a "moderate standard of living" for an urban family of four—you could buy a two-year-old used car and a new suit every four years. And a majority of the American people had less than that. They had to scrape for housing, food and education. And just as raising the minimum wage for the lowest paid workers tends to help raise the take of those who are organized and much better off, so turning our backs on the poor poor creates a political and social atmosphere in which the needs of the majority can be overlooked.

So the poor in the Seventies will be more numerous than the official figures admit. But perhaps the simplest way to get a summary view of the dangerous trends is to examine one generation of broken promises in the area of housing and to see that the Seventies will most likely be one more decade of failure.

The Government promised every citizen a decent dwelling in 1949. Under the leadership of a conservative Republican, Senator Robert A. Taft, the Congress agreed that the private housing market was not serving the needs of the poor. They therefore pledged to build 810,000 units of low-cost housing by 1955. In 1970, one generation later, that target has not yet been achieved. But then the problem was not just what the Government did not do but what it did instead. For while Washington was providing cheap money and princely tax deductions for more than ten million affluent home builders in suburbia, it was actually taking housing away from the poor. As the President's Commission on Urban Problems, chaired by Senator Paul Douglas, reported in January 1969, "Government action through urban renewal, highway programs, demolition on public housing sites, code enforcement and other programs has destroyed more housing for the poor than Government at all levels has built for them."

Thus it was that in 1968 a law was passed solemnly pledging the United States to do in the Seventies what it had solemnly pledged to do in the Fifties. But within a year it became clear that it was unlikely that the nation would redeem this second, shamefaced promise. To build twenty-six million new housing units in ten years, six million of them low-cost, would require speeding up the production of dwellings for the poor to twenty times the present rate. And as George Romney, the Secretary of Housing and Urban Development, admitted in 1969, it is quite possible that we will fall ten million units behind the official goal.

What this means for the Seventies is the further decay of the central cities of America, an increase in the already massive level of housing poverty which afflicts a third of the people—and the emergence of ghost towns in the middle of metropolis.

For the plight of the cities is becoming so grievous that even slums are not as profitable as they used to be. As a result, the Real Estate Research Corporation told the *Wall Street Journal* in 1969 that between ten and fifteen thousand buildings are being abandoned in the course of the year. In St. Louis, Missouri, for instance, there is a neighborhood I knew well as a child, for my grandfather lived there. It had big three-story homes and spacious lawns and backyards, and it was peopled by the white middle class. Returning to that familiar street twenty-five years later was like visiting a war zone. The houses were falling apart and some of them were boarded up and abandoned. That street was literally dying.

Many Americans would ride down that block and think that it proves that poor people don't care about property and will ruin a decent home if one is foolish enough to give them one. That is the exact opposite of the truth. That street, and the thousands like it in the big cities of America, is the result of one generation of broken promises, of massive economic trends like job relocation and inflation, which worked to isolate and imprison the poor, both black and white, in the ramshackle hand-me-down houses of the white middle class which had taken advantage of Federal subsidies and gone to suburbia.

On July 4, 1976, when the nation celebrates its two hundredth birthday, there will probably be more ghost towns in the cities.

But the statistics do not communicate the emotional quality of the Sixties when hopes were raised up so high and then dashed down. Perhaps a few personal experiences will.

In January 1964 Lyndon Johnson announced a war on poverty which John Kennedy had initiated within the Government but did not have the opportunity to proclaim publicly. In February, Sargent Shriver was named to head the effort. I went to Washington to have lunch with Shriver and stayed for two weeks as part of a task force which worked feverishly for sixteen or eighteen hours a day trying to define the basic concepts of the project.

The important thing was not just that the President was going to commit money to the war on poverty. More than that, the enormous moral and political power which the White House can summon was channeled into this undertaking. There was a sense of excitement, of social passion, in the capital. Friends of mine in the Government phoned to say that they would work at reduced pay and rank if only they could become a part of this crusade. At the end of those hectic fourteen days, Frank Mankiewicz, Paul Jacobs and I drafted a memorandum for Shriver saying that bold innovations going beyond the New Deal were demanded if the job was going to be done. Shriver incorporated part of our analysis in his first presentation at the White House and, he told us, Mr. Johnson was not phased by the radical definition of the issue.

A few weeks later there was a rally at the Berkeley campus of the University of California. A large audience of students was enthusiastic when I talked of the Johnson program. These were the same young men and women who, within a matter of two or three years, were to become bitterly opposed to the President and who, in 1968, would help to drive him out of politics. And one of the reasons for their militant disenchantment would be, precisely, that they had trusted in the promises made in 1964.

In 1964 during the Presidential campaign the Teamsters Union in Los Angeles held a strike meeting. The leadership, knowing that strike and contract ratification votes always pull out a very large crowd, took the unusual step of scheduling an educational session before the business session. I told a jammed hall of white workers that it was in their economic interest to make common cause with the blacks and the poor in order to create a real full-employment economy. And there was loud, vocal support for that position.

Then the Community Action provisions of the Economic Opportunity Act had a positive effect. There was, as Daniel Patrick Moynihan has argued, a great deal of confusion over the meaning of "maximum feasible participation" of the poor in the war on poverty; mayors looked for more patronage and wanted the poor to be "deserving"; sociologists and psychologists saw an opportunity to test theories. But even though the Government began to retreat from the notion of democratic participation almost as soon as it was announced, the activists of the other America seized the moment.

In March of 1965 there was a demonstration in Oxnard, California. There was a mariachi band in the lead and a man on a horse and the procession wound its way through the Mexican-American section of town. This was an early manifestation of the movement which Cesar Chavez organized among the migrant farm workers—Philippine and Anglo as well as Mexican-American. With solid support from the established unions and help from students and religious people, Chavez for the first time in a generation had raised up the hopes of the men and women who harvest the grapes of wrath.

The farm workers in Oxnard were a new insurgency. That same month there was another demonstration in Montgomery, Alabama, which marked the culmination of a much older struggle. As the marchers from Selma came to Montgomery with Martin Luther King, Jr., at their head, they were joined by tens of thousands who had come from every section of the country. As we moved toward the capital, we passed through black slums. The people sitting on the rickety porches were dazed by the massive show of solidarity. Some fell into the line of march; others stared in disbelief; some wept. The Negroes, with the trade unionists, priests, ministers, rabbis, nuns, liberal and radical politicals who were their allies, were in effect winning the Voting Rights Act of 1965.

We stood in front of the capitol and everywhere Confederate flags were flying. And so the crowd defiantly sang "The Star-Spangled Banner," and the national anthem suddenly became a hymn of militant hope that the nation could become one. And had the forces represented there in Montgomery remained united, they would have represented a majority of the electorate. But they did not. For at this very moment of triumph, President Johnson was preparing the escalation of the war in Vietnam. The anti-poverty programs continued and the rhetoric remained bold. But the moral and political energy of Washington, as well as tens of billions of dollars, were not channeled into the right war at home but into the wrong war in Southeast Asia.

The black poor became bitter and disillusioned, and the most militant among them turned against the whole system. A minority of the idealistic students were driven into an impotent, but shrill, intransigence; the majority joined the Robert Kennedy and Eugene McCarthy movements in 1968 and helped to force the President out of the race. The unionists maintained their commitment to fight poverty—they contribute more political strength to the legislative effort than any other group—but they also supported Johnson's war policy. So as Vietnam came increasingly to dominate all of American lives, the allies who had stood together that March afternoon in Montgomery turned upon one another.

And finally, there were the funerals of 1968.

Martin Luther King, Jr., died in the midst of a Poor People's Campaign which sought an economic bill of rights for all Americans. The day before he was buried, the groups that had assembled in Montgomery—the blacks, the unionists, the liberals and radicals from the middle class, the churches—came together in Memphis. For when King was murdered he was working with striking sanitation men who were fighting for union recognition. Now in the name of the dead leader, we marched through an almost completely deserted downtown. The people of Memphis had stayed home that day and the only sound in the center of the city was the eerie tread of feet. At the side streets there were contingents of Federalized guardsmen who were there to protect our constitutional rights.

For ironically, the death of the greatest American spokesman of nonviolence had occasioned riots and tension throughout the land. That was how bitter the struggle had become.

And then in June of 1968 Robert Kennedy was killed. To the people of the other America, it seemed that fate was depriving them of the leaders who understood them and fought for them. I had supported Kennedy because I believed that he was uniquely able to talk to both white trade unionists and the poor, both black and white. One meeting in California during the primary was symbolic of that hope to me: I spoke along with Cesar Chavez and John Lewis, the chairman of the Student Nonviolent Coordinating Committee in its early, nonviolent days. But in June an assassin put an end to that dream of a movement which would reach out to the blacks, the Spanish-speaking, the unionists, the middle-class idealists.

That funeral train seemed to me to carry the finest hopes of the decade along with the body of the dead Senator. It passed through the other America because the affluent never live in sight of the tracks but the poor do. And those tens of thousands standing there—sometimes singing, sometimes saluting, sometimes simply present, silent—were mourning their own aspirations along with the man who had spoken for them. For in the 1960s, the greatest opportunity for social change since the New Deal was sacrificed to the tragedy in Vietnam. And the Seventies will inherit a legacy of disillusionment and the memory of these tragic deaths.

So after all the broken promises and false starts Richard Nixon was elected President and told the people that the Federal Government had tried to do too much and that he would therefore decentralize social programs and set more modest goals. There was a half-truth and a dangerous falsehood in his analysis, and that bodes ill for the poor in the Seventies.

Under Lyndon Johnson the Administration had indeed talked as if it were undertaking, and accomplishing, prodigies. One of the reasons why a disturbing number of white workers turned toward George Wallace in 1968 (even though, outside the South, they eventually voted for Hubert Humphrey) was that they were under the impression that Washington had done so much for the poor, and particularly the Negroes among them. They confused the bold rhetoric with action and did not understand that life in the ghettos had changed very little. Insofar as Nixon taxes Johnson for having talked too loudly, he is right. But the rest of his thesis— that the Government was too activist, efforts must be cut back and turned over to the states—is very much wrong.

In order to destroy this myth of the favored, pampered poor one need only consider a few of the official figures. In 1968 the National Commission on Civil Disorders—the "Riot" Commission —reported that in Detroit, New Haven and Newark, the cities where the violence was the most destructive in 1967, the median percentage of those eligible who were actually covered by any one of the major social programs was 33 percent. In other words, in the United States a majority of the poor are not on welfare at all. And, the Commission showed, the national average for welfare payments is "a little more than one half of need"—and in some cases one fourth of need. In January 1969 a special Cabinet committee reported to Lyndon Johnson that the existing domestic programs were already underfunded by $6 billion and that a moderate expansion of civilian efforts along lines already suggested by various commissions and study groups would cost another $40 billion by 1972.

So the statistics are clear enough: the Government by its own standards is falling billions of dollars behind modest estimates of what should be done. Among the minority of the poor lucky enough to get any money there are millions who must exist on a half or a fourth of their urgent needs. Moreover these people are often victimized by what the nonpoor think of them. To many citizens, people who receive welfare are thought of as a burden upon the hard-working common man. But, as Richard Titmus has pointed out, what is really happening is that many of the poor are being undercompensated for humiliations which the Government and the economy, or both, have visited upon them.

The most dramatic case in point is the rural poor who were driven into the cities in recent years. Billions of dollars in Federal subsidies were paid to rich individuals and corporate farmers—including hundreds of thousands to Senator James O. Eastland, the impartial plantation owner who sits on the Senate Agricultural Committee and helps determine his own rewards. These princely welfare payments to the wealthy allowed them to make a profit by reducing the land under cultivation and also provided them with funds for mechanization. So it was that productivity in the fields increased twice as fast as in the factories, and millions of the rural poor became economically superfluous.

Between 1950 and 1966 Federal monies thus helped to force 5.5 million black farm workers into the cities. They came from areas where education for Negroes was substandard and they were required to relate to a bewildering, complex urban environment and compete in a sophisticated labor market. They brought with them, as Harold Fleming has said, "the largest accumulation of social deficits ever visited upon an identifiable group. Now these people often seem to the average taxpayer to be a burden, yet the real source of the problem was the Federal policy to pay billions to the agricultural rich in such a way as to exile the poor from the land. In other words, most of the people on welfare rolls are victims of government action and technological progress. They receive only a fraction of the compensation they deserve, not in charity but in justice.

In short, it is not that Washington has done too much but that it has so often done too much of the wrong thing. And the central thesis of Mr. Nixon's 1969 welfare message—"A third of a century of centralizing power in Washington has produced a bureaucratic monstrosity, cumbersome, unresponsive, ineffective"—is just not an accurate description of what happened. Moreover, Mr. Nixon's major welfare proposal to establish a minimum income for families contradicts his own analysis, for it proposes to *Federalize* welfare benefits at a certain level. Mr. Nixon was quite rightly disturbed that Mississippi pays an average of $39.35 a month to support an entire family while New York has much higher standards. He therefore wants to use the Federal power to force Mississippi from abusing its states' rights in such an inhumane way, which is hardly decentralization.

So the President who will set the policy guidelines for at least the first period of the Seventies has a superficial, contradictory theory of poverty. And some of the problems he will confront will be even more serious than those faced by Lyndon Johnson.

One of the most disturbing facts about the poor is that roughly half of them are young. They will be flooding into the labor market so fast in 1975 that the Department of Labor expects that there will be 25 percent more 16–19-year-olds looking for a job than in 1965—and 50 percent more black youths. This will happen at a time when the blue-collar positions for which they will be competing will be opening up at a rate of about 15 percent a year. In other words, there is a very real possibility that many, even most, of the children of the poor will become the fathers and mothers of the poor. If that were to take place, then America would, for the first time in its history, have a hereditary underclass.

These dangerous trends did not explode in the Sixties, but two of the reasons were Vietnam and inflation. The nation's tragic commitment to the horror in Southeast Asia created 700,000 new "jobs" in the armed forces and a million new openings in defense industry. Since 80 percent of the draftees had high-school diplomas, the army did not actually take the poor in but removed some of their competition from the labor market. Then with inflation after 1965—which was triggered by a $10 billion "mistake" in Federal spending based upon optimistic assumptions about a victory in the war in 1966—the labor market tightened up even more.

But with peace in Vietnam, what are the acceptable substitutes for the employment generated by war and inflation? The policy answer to that question will not be found in a quietist Presidency but in radical new programs.

And yet every once in a while the President does recognize some of his difficulties rhetorically. In his Population Message to Congress in the summer of 1969, Nixon attacked a sweeping proposal of the National Committee on Urban Growth Policy for not being sufficiently daring. The Commission—which included Democratic regulars such as Hale Boggs and John Sparkman and even a Goldwater Republican, John Tower—had said that the nation must build ten new cities for one million citizens each and ten new towns for 100,000 inhabitants. After noting that there will be 100 million additional Americans by the year 2000, three quarters of them living in urbanized areas, the President said of the Commission's suggestion, "But the total number of people who would be accommodated if even those bold plans were implemented is *only* twenty million—a *mere* one fifth of the expected thirty-year increase." (Italics added.)

So Mr. Nixon is rightly saying that, unless there are radical innovations, the housing problem will become worse. Since his own Administration cut back on Model Cities spending and is doing even less than Mr. Johnson did, when Nixon insists upon how enormous the problem is, that is a way of saying that the failure of the 1949 Housing Act will endure half a century to the year 2000. In the 1968 campaign, the President would have dealt with the issue by suggesting that private enterprise would do the job for a profit. But the Committee he criticized for not going far enough found that private development of new towns and cities occurs only in "rare circumstances." For these ventures demand a tremendous investment in social capital, which free enterprise simply will not make.

In short, as the Seventies open there is every indication that housing poverty will become even more acute and that the children of the last decade's poor will, as parents in an economy without enough decent jobs, increase the size of the other America. Such tragedies are not, of course, fated; they will be the result of political choices. And even though the Nixon Administration has given every indication of not understanding the problem, it is still important to summarize briefly what must be done.

First of all there must be planning. There should be an Office of the Future attached to the Presidency and a Joint Congressional Committee on the Future which would receive, debate and adopt or modify annual reports from the White House (I spelled out this suggestion in *Toward a Democratic Left*).

This proposition might sound strange to American ears, yet there are signs that moderates, and even conservatives, are beginning to appreciate its logic. In his Population Message, President Nixon considered the prospect of 100 million additional citizens in a third of a century and asked, "Are our cities prepared for such an influx? The chaotic history of urban growth suggest they are not and that many problems will be severely aggravated by a dramatic increase in numbers." And a little later he got to the heart of the matter: "Perhaps the most dangerous element in the present situation is that so few people are examining these questions from the viewpoint of the whole society."

Precisely. Suburban home builders, automobile manufacturers and trucking companies all pick up their huge Federal subsidies without a thought of pollution, isolating the central-city slum or ravaging the countryside. And now—not simply if poverty is to be abolished, but if the quality of life in America is to be kept from deteriorating—we must adopt long-range priorities and consider the "side effects" of new technologies even more scrupulously than we do with new drugs. A year before his death, Dwight Eisenhower urged the building of new cities, racially and socially integrated and with new jobs. Mr. Nixon apparently agrees. But the enormously complex planning needed to accomplish such a task is not going to be done by the invisible hand of Adam Smith.

Secondly, there must be billions of dollars in social investments.

President Nixon, like President Johnson before him, hopes that all of these crises can be met by hiring private enterprise to do the job. Mr. Nixon's first version of this philosophy was called "black capitalism," and he ordered the concept extended to all the impoverished minorities when he took office. But the blunt economic facts of life are that costs in the slums are twice as high as in the suburbs, congestion much more serious, the labor market relatively untrained—i.e., all of the miseries which the nation has imposed upon the poor make their neighborhoods unprofitable for big business. Minority enterprises can, of course, make a contribution to their areas and should be helped generously, but for the vast majority they offer no real hope.

But then as the Sixties were ending there did seem to be one area when the cooperation of the public and private sector worked: employment. The National Association of Businessmen, with strong Federal help, is trying to put poverty-stricken and minority workers into good jobs and there has been a lot of publicity about the gains that have been made. However, a 1969 analysis by the *Wall Street Journal* was not so sanguine. The main reason for these hirings, Alan Otten wrote, was the tight labor market, and any increase in unemployment—which is inevitable given the Nixon strategy against inflation—would turn these people back out on the streets. Yet when the Automobile Workers Union proposed to the Ford Corporation that its older members be permitted to take a voluntary lay-off so that the new men could stay on, the company refused. The reason was simple enough: the supplementary unemployment compensation for a veteran is costlier than for a new worker. And in the winter of 1970 the layoffs in the auto industry began and hit precisely those men who had been recruited with such fanfare. The calculus of profit was stronger than social conscience.

Therefore new cities for 100 million new Americans and decent jobs for all will come only if there are large social investments. Early in the Seventies the Gross National Product of the United States will pass the $1 trillion mark. As an article in *Fortune* calculated this trend, there would be a fiscal "dividend"— the automatic increase in Government income without any rise in taxes which takes place when the GNP becomes larger—of $38 billion in 1974 and around $80 billion by 1980. The problem under these circumstances is not finding the resources but being intelligent enough to use them democratically and creatively. To do that the nation should adopt the Economic Bill of Rights advocated by Martin Luther King, Jr., in the last days of his life: every citizen has a right either to a decent job or to an adequate income.

In his 1969 welfare message, President Nixon made that sharp attack on the unevenness of the present, states'-rights welfare system. But in his positive proposals he urged Congress to delegate even more power to the very local administrations which had previously abused it, and he came out for a Federal minimum which would leave people well below the poverty line. In the Nixon program, Washington would provide the funds to bring family payments up to $1600 a year (and food stamps would add another $900), and the twenty states which now pay less than that would be required to contribute only half of their present welfare spending to the total.

Instead of thus institutionalizing a Federal minimum which is well below the poverty line, the United States should adopt the principle that all of its citizens are legally entitled to a decent income. Lyndon Johnson's outgoing Cabinet computed that one version of such a social investment—a negative income tax—would cost between $15 and $20 billion a year. Given the *Fortune* prediction of an $80 billion dividend by 1980, that amount is clearly within the country's means.

Such a program should have, of course, a work incentive. Instead of the typical American practice of taxing the earnings of the welfare recipient 100 percent (by reducing his benefits by the amount of his wages), the individual should be allowed to keep a decreasing portion of his income supplement as his pay goes up. But this also means that there must be a vast increase in the number of decent jobs. In New York City, where Aid for Dependent Children payments are around the level of menial jobs in the economy, there is no motive for mothers to look for work and they haven't. So a guaranteed income with a work incentive means a commitment to genuine full employment.

And that is where the notion of a guaranteed income ties in with the right to work. It was Franklin Roosevelt who first urged, in the campaign of 1944, that if the private economy does not provide jobs for the people, then the public economy must. If, after a generation of inexcusable hesitation, we finally adopt this proposal it would mean that the society could channel the enormous unused resource of the unemployed and the underemployed into constructing a new, livable environment. If the promises of the Housing Acts of 1949 and 1968 were carried out, there would be a labor shortage and the country would discover that it really needs the poor and the near poor. And the effect of such a program would not be inflationary because these workers would be producing valuable goods and services for their wages.

So the Seventies need planned, long-range social investments to provide a decent home for every citizen and to guarantee either a living income or a good job for all. But as the decade begins, the nation, including its Chief Executive, believes in myths which keep us from even defining the problem as it is. They think we tried too much when actually we did so little. And the official thinkers and statisticians are even winning paper victories over poverty and making the poor invisible.

Therefore there is reason for pessimism. But if these menacing trends are to be reversed, then America must understand one crucial proposition: that it is in the interest of the entire society to end the outrage of the other America.

The poor are the most sorely tried and dramatic victims of economic and social tendencies which threaten the entire nation. They suffer most grievously from unplanned, chaotic urbanization, but millions of the affluent are affected too. They are the first to experience technological progress as a curse which destroys the old muscle-power jobs that previous generations used as a means to fight their way out of poverty. Yet, as the current student radicalism makes clear, the nature of work is also becoming problematic for the most advantaged in the society. If, in other words, the cities sprawl and technology revolutionizes the land in a casual, thoughtless way, polluting the very fundamentals of human existence, like air and water, it is the poor who will be most cruelly used but the entire nation will experience a kind of decadence.

In morality and in justice every citizen should be committed to abolishing the other America, for it is intolerable that the richest nation in human history should allow such needless suffering. But more than that, if we solve the problem of the other America we will have learned how to solve the problems of all of America.

Poverty and the Eighties

January 1984 will mark the twentieth anniversary of the declaration of an "unconditional war" on poverty in the United States. When that anniversary arrives, it is likely that poverty in the United States will be at least as tenaciously established as it was when President Johnson declared that war. Indeed, it is not at all inconceivable that there will be *more* people living in the other America in the 1980s than in the 1960s. And it is certain that, under the very best of conditions, poverty will still be a major problem in this country.

Thus, this brief retrospect on what has happened during the past two decades—this book was originally published in 1962—is not simply an exercise in historical scholarship. It is, rather, an attempt to understand the past in order to be able to master the future. For the years since the war on poverty was announced have shown that the outrage of want, and even hunger, in the richest society in the world is rooted in our structure, our institutions, our normal way of doing things. And therefore, if the ideal announced by President Johnson in 1964 is ever to be fulfilled, and poverty banished from this nation, it will take more radical departures in economic and social policy than Johnson ever imagined.

Does this then mean that nothing has been accomplished in this area since the early Sixties? Not at all. There have been, as we will see, real gains, particularly in the period 1963–1969, and some of these, such as alleviation of the poverty of people over sixty-five years of age, persist until this very day, even though there is now danger of retrogression. Thus I do not want to argue that we failed completely, for that is not the case, but that we underestimated the challenge we had defined for ourselves. If we ever put this issue back on the urgent agenda of the nation—and I think we will, though not in the immediate future—it is critical that we understand this point, or else we doom ourselves, and above all the poor, to yet one more cycle of illusory hope and bitter disappointment.

This overview of the past two decades—this point of departure for the decade to come—will be developed in terms of three central themes. First, there will be an analysis of the interrelationships between poverty and the economy and political movements in the United States. Then, the definition of poverty will be examined carefully, particularly in the light of recent attempts to argue that we have *overestimated,* not underestimated, the problem. And finally, there will be a brief review of the programs of the past and an anticipation of the measures that, in the future, could actually eliminate poverty in the United States.

In discussing these issues it will be necessary to use statistics and other abstractions of economic and social analysis. This has to be done, not the least because there are many people who charge that those of us who speak passionately about the crime of poverty do so with much heart and little head. Indeed, it is even charged that by sentimentally persuading people that there is a massive other America, we divert resources from effective programs that could be mounted to deal with the small-scale problem of poverty in this country. In a sense, then, those of us who see the misery of the poor as one of the great challenges to our society must prove our case in a "professional," unemotional way.

But after all the statistics are in, the reader is advised to take a walk in any great city in the United States, or to drive around almost any rural area, and to open the eyes, not to the "data" but to the pinched and hopeless faces of men and women and children forced to live under intolerable conditions. That existential recognition is the beginning of a new war on poverty—and perhaps this time poverty will lose.

To begin with: poverty in the United States during the past twenty years has shown itself to be a dynamic phenomenon, not a static condition. The fate of the people living in the other America is largely determined by roller-coaster trends in the economy and in our political life.

The rediscovery of poverty that occurred in the 1960s took place during the longest period of prosperity in American history. Ironically, it was this relative affluence—and the word "relative" should be stressed, since a majority of Americans have always had, and still have, a problem making ends meet—that allowed us to see poor again. One reason was that it seemed that a war on poverty would not require anyone to make sacrifices. The cycle of economic boom and bust, the New Economics taught in the Kennedy-Johnson years, was finished. The Government had learned how to "fine tune" the economy simply by making rather small adjustments in fiscal policy (the U.S. budget) and monetary policy (the Federal Reserve system and the Treasury). To simplify, but not unfairly, in times of unemployment, Washington would incur a deficit and loosen up the money supply, which would create the buying power to get the economy moving again. This tactic seemed to have found empirical verification in the success of the Kennedy-Johnson tax cut. That decrease in taxes first reduced Federal revenues by transferring some of the Government's income to private consumers. But as those consumers spent the economy into prosperity, Washington actually increased its revenues; its percentage slice was smaller, but the pie from which it was cut was much larger.

Indeed, in a book published in 1969 on anti-poverty policy, Daniel Patrick Moynihan, who had worked on that program under Johnson, said that Washington faced "a situation utterly without parallel in modern government: administrations that must be constantly on the lookout for new ways to expend public funds in the public interest." The perpetually growing Gross National Product was going to generate more and more Federal revenue even though taxes had been cut. If Washington did not spend that money quickly, it would depress the economy by removing buying power from it. Therefore, in sharp contrast to the idea that Government must be frugal, successful economic management literally demanded investments in social justice. In the Johnson years, the President and some of the major leaders of American business, such as Henry Ford II, were convinced that this could best be done by a "partnership" between the corporations and the Federal Government. The private sector would make money building subsidized housing or providing subsidized education, training, and work for the poor; the Government would earn the gratitude of the entire nation; a Great Society would be built.

If by any chance inflation became a problem, it would be dealt with in the same fine-tuned way as unemployment. If too much money was chasing too few goods—the classic definition of inflation—then Government would reduce spending, run a surplus, and increase taxes. That idyll began to unravel because of the war in Vietnam. Lyndon Johnson was afraid to ask the people to finance that unpopular intervention by raising their taxes, and in any case, he always thought that one more burst of escalation would end the conflict. In 1967 the unemployment rate fell to 3.8 percent, the lowest since the end of World War II. Theoretically this was the time for Federal restraint, only Johnson ran a deficit of more than $12 billion that year, mainly because of Vietnam. So inflation rose.

The real shock, however, came two years later, in 1969, when Richard Nixon took over the White House. Acting according to standard liberal theory, Nixon decided to fight the Vietnam-induced inflation by provoking a recession. The unemployment rate went up—but prices did not come down. This was our first encounter with the dominant fact of economic life since: stagflation—simultaneous joblessness and high prices in violation of all these theories and policies for "fine-tuning." The poor became the prime victims of this unprecedented reality. During the Kennedy-Johnson years, poverty, as officially measured, went down every year. In 1970 the other America expanded for the first time in a decade because of the recession-inflation. That happened again in 1971, in 1974, and in 1975 because of yet another recession-inflation (the deepest since the Depression of the Thirties); and it is happening in 1980 as this Afterword is being written.

The most obvious victims of the stagflation roller-coaster are the working poor. There were 5.3 million families below the official poverty line in 1976. In almost half of those units—2.45 million—the head of the family worked during the year; in about one fifth of them, the head of the family worked full-time. Obviously these are people in low-paying jobs, often with large families. When a recession hits, they are either laid off, which puts them even further into poverty, or else their bargaining power for wages (which is weak in any case, since most of these workers are not organized in unions) declines. At the same time, a stratum of workers perched just above the poverty line is shoved into the other America for the same reasons.

But then, people wno are not in the labor market at all also suffer. These are the dependent poor who receive the bulk of their income from Government "transfer payments" (which is the official name for monies received *not* in return for work, popularly called "welfare"). Actually this group is much smaller than most people think—in the mid-Seventies only about 40 percent of the families of the poor were receiving public assistance—but it still includes about two million families, many of them quite large. Over the years there is abundant evidence that the income these people get from the Government varies according to the trends in the economy. When unemployment is high at the same time that wages for working people are losing their real buying power—which is what happened in the "bad" years of the Seventies and is still happening in the early Eighties—welfare payments are not raised. Politically and economically, the United States never lets such outlays get ahead of the market for menial, low-paying jobs. Indeed, in 1976 Charles Schultze, then at the Brookings Institution and later Chairman of the President's Council of Economic Advisors, warned Congress that if it legislated a right to a well-paid job in the public sector for everyone who could not find one in the private sector, it would undercut all the low-paying industries. This point is even more compelling to legislators and business people when it is a question of providing a welfare payment to people who are not even in the labor market.

Only one group among the poor did not suffer the miseries of stagflation as much as the others, although this might change in the future. Social security benefits are "indexed," i.e., periodically they are automatically raised in order to compensate for the increase in the cost of living. Moreover, in the Sixties and Seventies the benefits under social security were raised, and the result has been to reduce the number of the aging poor, as a percentage of all Americans over sixty-five, by about half. So the increased benefits and the indexing protected this stratum from indignities visited by the economy upon both the working poor and the welfare poor.

However, there is reason for a certain pessimism in this area. During the recession of 1974–1975, the monies normally received by Washington from the social security tax fell sharply as taxpayers were laid off from work. The social security system, it must be remembered, is not "funded," i.e., the money an individual pays in is not invested to provide for his or her eventual retirement. The social security taxes of the current generation in the labor force are used to pay the pensions of those in retirement; and when the former are old enough, their retirement will be financed by a still younger generation. So a recession reduces the money available for retirees, and a stagflation recession, with its accompanying high prices, increases the amount that must be paid out to them. As a result, the system faced a crisis in the mid-Seventies as revenues went down and obligations went up.

Under those circumstances, President Ford proposed a "cap" on social security indexing of 5 percent. That meant that if prices rose by more than 12 percent in a year, as they did in 1975, retirees would be compensated for only 5 percent of their lost buying power. Thus a President of the United States was proposing to lower the real standard of living of people over sixty-five years of age. In the debates over balancing the budget in 1980, this same idea was now floated from the center of the political spectrum. Thus, if the aging poor were somewhat exempted from the increase in poverty that afflicted other age groups during the bad years of the Seventies, there are disturbing reasons for believing that this exemption will come to an end if the economy continues to malfunction in the Eighties.

In assessing the fates of the various strata of the other America, I have used the convenient measures of income and buying power in order to fix their relative positions. But there is another, critically important, dimension of the problem, which was visible during the decade of the Seventies. Whenever unemployment mounts, and poverty with it, there is also an increase in social pathology: in alcoholism, drug addiction, family breakdown, and crime. I described this phenomenon in *The Other America* in 1962; it has, alas, continued in more or less the same way ever since. This is particularly disturbing when one looks at racial issues in the United States. Poverty is *not* primarily a phenomenon of race, i.e., blacks are one third of the poor, which is to say that two thirds are white. To be sure, that statistic has a racist content: black Americans are a bit more than 10 percent of the population as a whole and one third of the poverty population. But that still does not mean that one can equate poverty and race.

However, it is in one particular area that racist outcomes of the economy are most dramatic. Among young blacks and Hispanics in the slums, the unemployment rate of the Seventies often stood at 40 or 50 percent, that is, it was *higher* than the jobless percentage for the United States during the Great Depression of the Thirties. These young people are denied entry to the labor market at the point at which the first contact with the world of work is normally made. This is bad enough when it happens, but it is a dangerous portent of a future yet to come. For if there is a large and significant population of the youthful poor who are cast on the social scrap heap when they are in their teens, they are likely—almost certain—to provide a disproportionate percentage of the muggers and violent criminals of the Eighties. Society, in short, will pay a tragic price for its callousness. Not so incidentally, it costs more to keep a person in a prison than it does to send him or her to Harvard.

These economic and social trends do not, in and of themselves, create political trends. For instance, in 1969, when he took office, Richard Nixon clearly believed that he had a popular mandate to dismantle entirely whatever was left of the anti-poverty effort. But various programs of the Sixties had acquired a political clientele. There were, for instance, big-city mayors who had positive stakes in various job-training programs. Therefore, even though the mood shifted in the Seventies, it did not translate into an abrupt end to the programs of the Sixties. There was a political lag that had become institutionalized in a way that frustrated even the enormous power of the Presidency.

However, as the Seventies went on, that lag became less and less of a factor. So it is that one must count political and ideological trends, as well as economic developments, among the determinants of poverty in the United States. The first response to stagflation was a certain move to the Right in the nation. That, by the way, is in keeping with an established tradition. Bad times do not initially make people radical; rather, they become conservative as every individual tries to save him or herself, and there is a bewildered rejection of any kind of collective solution. The gains of the New Deal in the Thirties did not come in 1932 under Hoover, when the Depression was at its worst, or even in 1933 under Roosevelt, but in 1935 and 1936, when there was an upswing in the economy and Americans once again permitted themselves the luxury of hope.

Similarly, we have already noted that the rediscovery of poverty took place in a time of *relative* affluence and declining unemployment. Once again, it was not an automatic result of good times. It is almost certain, for instance, that the surge of social consciousness in the early Sixties would never have occurred were it not for Martin Luther King, Jr., and the movement he led. Starting with the Montgomery Bus Boycott of 1955, there was a huge, nonviolent movement in this country led by one of the most charismatic Americans who ever lived. King did not, in those early years, speak of the poverty of black America. Rather, he concentrated on juridical discrimination—above all, the denial of the right to vote and of access to public accommodations. Still, the obvious fact of the matter was that the blacks who followed Dr. King were from the poorest areas and social strata of the country. With a young and liberal President in the White House— another political variable—the *moral* and political pressure of the Civil Rights movement helped to move the Government in the direction of doing something about poverty.

Indeed, the fate of this book itself was clearly determined by those same factors. Had *The Other America* been published five years earlier or one year later, it would not have had the impact it had. But it came out precisely the moment when that young President was responding to both the black movement led by Dr. King and the discovery that the unemployment rate was more intractable than he had thought it would be. Kennedy had heard of the book and asked the Chairman of the Council of Economic Advisors if there were anything substantial in it. Told that there was, he read it, and, according to Arthur Schlesinger's history of the administration, it was a factor in making the President decide that poverty had to become an issue. The point is not to go into this footnote to history but to give yet one more example of the ways in which general political, as well as economic, conditions affect our perceptions of poverty.

In the Seventies and the early Eighties, political conditions were the opposite of the Sixties. The black movement was in some disarray and no one in it had even begun to replace Martin Luther King, Jr.; stagflation subverted the liberal wisdom of the Sixties, and the initial response was to look back to Herbert Hoover rather than go well beyond Lyndon Johnson and John F. Kennedy. To be sure, the situation was not that of a simple surge to the Right. In various surveys in the late Seventies, as Everett C. Ladd, a relatively conservative political scientist has pointed out, the people demonstrated themselves to be more conservative in general and quite liberal in particular. That is, people agreed with philosophic statements about the ineffectiveness and wastefulness of Federal intervention in the economy *and* simultaneously advocated more federal intervention to deal with unemployment, the environment, health care, and the like. There was, however, one significant exception: people were conservative in particular about "welfare," i.e., about doing something about poverty.

This tendency was reinforced by the fact that a number of analysts expected the poverty problem to be solved by demographics in the Eighties.

By 1985 the "postwar baby boom"—that vast increase in births initiated by the returning veterans in the late Forties and continuing into the early Sixties—will have ended within the labor market. At that point, the new yearly entrants to the work force will begin to decline in number, and there will be a smaller labor force. All other things being equal, this means that the unemployment problem will be easier to deal with, and therefore poverty, insofar as it relates to joblessness, will decline. But all things are never equal. For one thing, the "full employment-unemployment rate," which is our official definition of how well we are doing in this area, has been moving steadily upward over the past decade. John F. Kennedy said that full employment was reached when unemployment hit 3 percent; Lyndon Johnson raised that figure to 4 percent; Nixon-Ford and Jimmy Carter set it at around 5 percent; and in 1980, one of the top economists in the nation, Martin Feldstein, wrote in the *Wall Street Journal* that the number may be as high as 8 or 9 percent. When that rate is reached, inflation begins, and the Government starts to cut back on spending.

In other words, it is official doctrine that the American economy now requires roughly 5 million unemployed people (about 5 percent unemployment in a labor force of nearly 100 million) in order to function "normally" and it is being unofficially computed that the jobless must be 7 to 19 million if things are to proceed in an orderly fashion. By that stroke of statistical definition, an enormous amount of poverty is "justified" in good times. The Nixon recession of 1969–1971, which set off the first increase in the other America in a decade, did not see joblessness rise above 5.9 percent, i.e., the rate which is now considered approximately at, or even below, "full employment."

If then one believes, as I have argued at book length in *Decade of Decision: The Crisis of the American System,* that the Eighties are likely to see difficult economic weather and inadequate political responses, at least in the first years of the decade, then one comes to a gloomy assessment of the future of the poor. Under those circumstances, there could well be more poor people in 1984 than there were twenty years earlier, when Lyndon Johnson declared that "unconditional war" on poverty.

There are some serious and informed people who say that all of the figures I have used in making this case are grossly exaggerated—that there is actually less of a poverty problem than we think, not more.

In *The Other America,* I used a very rough measure of poverty, setting it at an annual income level of $3,000 in the late Fifties. After Johnson announced his program, the Federal Government undertook the creation of a systematic definition of the term, which was then used in legislation. The new, and more precise, concept was developed by Molly Orshansky at the Social Security Administration. Orshansky took the Department of Agriculture's economy food plan, the cheapest nutritionally sound food budget, and then, based on a 1955 study that showed that families spend one third of their income on food, multiplied the cost of that food plan by three. Thus a family that had less than three times the amount required for that minimal food outlay was considered to be poor. The cost, but not the nutritional composition of the economy food plan, was revised to take into account price increases, and the measure was adjusted for family size. There is not, therefore, one poverty "line" in the United States, but a series of poverty lines that vary by family size and, to a certain extent, by geographic location. (Farm families, which are presumed to grow some of their food, have a poverty "line" that is between 70 and 85 percent of the corresponding non-farm level.)

In the 1970s, when there was the shift toward the Right described earlier, the statisticians followed the politicians. I am not suggesting a plot, but simply arguing that in the Sixties a scholar received approbation for pointing out the poverty we had ignored, and in the Seventies praise came to those who discovered the poverty we had exaggerated. The critique of the poverty definition can be most clearly seen in Martin Anderson's *The Political Economy of Welfare Reform in the United States* (1978), which held that "the growth of jobs and income in the private economy, combined with an explosive increase in government spending for welfare and income transfer programs, has virtually eliminated poverty in the United States." Anderson is a conservative scholar, and his volume was appropriately published by the (Herbert) Hoover Institute. The Congressional Budget Office (CBO) made even a more serious attack on the poverty concept, since it is legislatively mandated to be non-partisan and was, at the time of the attack, under the direction of a liberal economist, Alice Rivlin.

The central theme of the CBO attack was that the Government had based its definition of poverty on *money* income alone. But that ignored the vast increase in "in kind" programs, in which people received free, or subsidized, goods or services, rather than money. The most important cases in point are health (Medicare for the aging, Medicaid for some of the poor) and food (Food Stamps). When the cash value of these "in kind" programs—valued by their cost to the Federal Government—was added to the money income of the poor, about one third of the poverty in the United States vanished. Some of the people who made this argument were liberals. By overstating poverty, they said, one convinced people that Government action in this sphere was ineffective and thus gave a rationalization for a decrease in expenditures, not an increase.

If the CBO had made its points about "in kind" income in the course of a balanced redefinition of poverty, much of what it said would be compelling. One could still question some of the assumptions—for instance, do the poor actually receive health care equal to the cost of Medicaid, or isn't it possible that some of that money is poorly and ineffectively spent or even ripped off? But the basic point would have a considerable validity. Then, however, one would also examine all of the possibilites of an *undercount,* as well as any overcounting. For instance, there is a huge population of "undocumented" workers in the United States (mainly Mexicans in the Southwest and people from the Caribbean in the Southeast and Northeast). They are not counted in any of our figures since they do not want to be identified by any agency of the Federal Government. The Census undercount of these people has been estimated as being as high as 10 million individuals. Most of these people are poor, but they are not in any of our definitions, and they do not receive, for the most part, any of the "in kind" benefits.

Molly Orshansky and others have argued that the original definition was too low for a number of technical reasons (not only is it necessary to upgrade the cost of the economy meal, but the character of the meal itself should be redefined). Not so incidentally, most Americans agree with Orshansky rather than with the CBO. When pollsters ask people how they would define poverty, the answer is surprisingly uniform: they locate the "line" at one half of median income. (Median income is the figure of the fiftieth percentile of the population, i.e., one half of the population have more and one half less than the median.) In 1977 the poverty "line" for an urban family of four was $6,191—but the "line" as the average American would define it, at one half median income (for families in this case), would have been at $8,613 in that year.

In *The Other America,* I used inadequate Government figures and more than a little intuition to argue that between 40 and 50 million people were poor. When the Government became more precise about the problem, it computed that in 1959—the year upon which most of my figures are based—the poverty population was about 39.5 million. In short, it concluded that my lower estimate had been approximately correct. By that same measure, Washington said that in 1976, about 25 million Americans were poor. The CBO found that this figure overestimated poverty by about 35 percent. But if one accepts my critique of the CBO, then there are more poor people than the Government estimates, not less. And if the previous analysis is right, there will be still more in the early Eighties because of economic and political trends. Where the government in 1976 found 13.5 percent of families poor, and the CBO said that the percentage was actually 8.3 percent, I think it was closer to 20 percent.

But does that mean, as some of the CBO's advocates say, that I am arguing that all of the Federal programs of the past failed? And if so, how does one formulate an approach to ending poverty in the future?

To begin with, some of the programs of the past were effective. In the Kennedy-Johnson years, eight years of steadily decreasing unemployment allowed a significant number of the working poor to escape from poverty. To be sure, the Seventies, under Nixon, Ford, and Carter, and now the Eighties, prove the converse: that rising unemployment pushes people down into the ranks of the working poor. But we know that progress is in fact possible in this area, a point to which I will return. Also, there were other programs that made a difference. The Food Stamps program is the most obvious case in point. Expenditures in this area increased steadily, providing an example of a truly *Federal* program that works. ("Welfare"—mainly Aid for Families of Dependent Children—and Medicaid are partly financed by Washington but designed by the states, which means that there are enormous variations in terms of eligibility and benefit levels; Food Stamps are distributed uniformly, according to Federal criteria.) Some of the job-training programs of the Sixties succeeded; others did not. The same is true with regard to expenditures for education. (These judgments are documented in *The Promise of Greatness*, by Sar Levitan and Robert Taggart, and by Henry Aaron in *Politics and the Professors: The Great Society in Perspective*.) And increases in social security benefits, as well as their being indexed, has had a dramatic impact upon the poverty of people over sixty-five years of age.

Therefore I am not saying that the programs of the Sixties all failed, but that the problems they challenged turned out to be more complex, more rooted in our institutions than had been imagined. If the euphoric hopes of the Kennedy-Johnson years had turned out to be right and the Gross National Product had increased steadily with stable prices, *then* it would have been relatively easy to end most poverty. (But not all: large families headed by a woman increased their poverty in good years as well as bad.) But those hopes were dashed, and the reason for that development is rooted in the structural tendencies of the American economy toward boom and bust. Therefore, if the poor are going to be rescued from their plight, it is clearly necessary that this country solve the problem of stagflation, which does not appear imminent in the early Eighties.

There is a related difficulty. On the day after the 1972 election, Richard Nixon granted a long interview to the *Washington Star*. In it he formulated his famous, and very influential, judgment that the Sixties "threw money at problems," i.e., that there was lavish spending for the poor which, on the whole, was not effective. As we have seen, some of the programs were effective: the simple expedient of increasing the incomes of the aging has rendered their lives somewhat less miserable. When people suffer from a marked deficiency of income, "throwing money" at that problem is an efficacious way of proceeding. But more important, there is a widespread exaggeration of the amount of money spent on the poor. Henry Aaron has shown that the innovations of the Sixties actually provided more money to the non-poor than the poor (Federal subsidies to college education are a dramatic illustration). And Charles Schultze has computed that there has been no increase in the portion of real output spent by the Federal Government between the presidencies of Eisenhower and Carter, i.e., over a quarter of a century.

The one group that did get significant increases from Washington in this period was the aging: two thirds of the new Federal expenditures in the Sixties went to social security and Medicare. But this is precisely the group that most people are sympathetic to, not the least because they will join it one day. Thus when one looks at the truly controversial programs—aid to minorities, to slum neighborhoods, and the like—they did not receive much at all. Charles Schultze has estimated their increment between 1965 and 1977 at $35 billion, or 1.7 percent of the Gross National Product. That is not a huge sum, and, in any case, the non-poor got much more. Part of the difficulty in this area has to do with Lyndon Johnson's expansive rhetoric. Johnson used to talk as if his administration were recreating the world every morning. It didn't, and people exaggerated the failures of those years because they exaggerated the outlays.

But, assuming that at some point in the Eighties the issue of poverty will once more be on the urgent political agenda, how can we eliminate the outrageous paradox of desperate human need in a relatively rich society? The answer to that question is implicit in the analysis I have made. First, and foremost, the absolute pre-condition to ending poverty is full employment—with full employment defined as jobs seeking workers, as in World War II, and not, as we now do, as an incredibly high level of tolerated joblessness. Full employment would allow us to eliminate the poverty of the working poor through the labor market (when unemployment was 1 percent during World War II, blacks and women made the greatest relative gains ever), and would provide the economic and political basis for attacking the poverty of those not in the labor market.

Secondly, we could eliminate all of the remaining money poverty of the aging by increasing social security benefits to the point where they would leave no one with an income deficit.

Thirdly, the most tenacious poverty in the land—that of the fatherless families in the slums and ghettoes—requires a commitment to planned development of viable neighborhoods for everyone in the society. That means that the current destruction of vast areas of the great cities of the Northeast and industrial Middle West has to be stopped. Here, too, full employment policy would be a key, e.g., by locating a Government-owned solar energy plant in the midst of a devastated community, or by creating new communities on both new and old land.

I will not go into further detail—I have done so in *Decade of Decision*—for my point is clear enough. On the one hand the unprecedented problems of a stagflationist economy make the eradication of poverty more difficult than in the relatively prosperous Sixties, when the economic indicators obligingly behaved the way the economic theories said they should. On the other hand, there are programs— above all, a planned full-employment economy—that could make it possible to put an end, once and for all, to the other America. But those effective programs require relatively radical new departures, policies that go as far beyond Franklin Roosevelt's and Lyndon Johnson's liberalism as their liberalism went beyond Hoover's conservatism. For the twenty years since the rediscovery of poverty have demonstrated that this outrage is much more structural, more institutional, than we dreamed. There is no way that the business-as-usual of the Seventies will end poverty in the Eighties.

I end this review, then, on an ambivalent note. There was progress; there could be more progress; the poor need not always be with us. But it will take political movements much more imaginative and militant than those in existence in 1980 to bring that progress about. Until that happens, the poor will be with us.